D1593988

Also by Saul K. Padover

THE REVOLUTIONARY EMPEROR: JOSEPH II
SECRET DIPLOMACY AND ESPIONAGE
(*with James Westfall Thompson*)
THE LIFE AND DEATH OF LOUIS XVI
JEFFERSON (a biography)
EXPERIMENT IN GERMANY
LA VIE POLITIQUE DES ÉTATS-UNIS
FRENCH INSTITUTIONS: VALUES AND POLITICS
THE GENIUS OF AMERICA
UNDERSTANDING FOREIGN POLICY
THE MEANING OF DEMOCRACY
THOMAS JEFFERSON AND THE FOUNDATIONS OF AMERICAN FREEDOM

∴

Edited by Saul K. Padover

SOURCES OF DEMOCRACY: VOICES OF FREEDOM, HOPE AND JUSTICE
THOMAS JEFFERSON ON DEMOCRACY
THE COMPLETE JEFFERSON
THOMAS JEFFERSON AND THE NATIONAL CAPITAL
A JEFFERSON PROFILE
THE WRITINGS OF THOMAS JEFFERSON
THE COMPLETE MADISON (also titled: THE FORGING OF AMERICAN FEDERALISM)
THE WASHINGTON PAPERS
THE MIND OF ALEXANDER HAMILTON
WILSON'S IDEALS
THE LIVING UNITED STATES CONSTITUTION
CONFESSIONS AND SELF-PORTRAITS
THE WORLD OF THE FOUNDING FATHERS
NEHRU ON WORLD HISTORY
TO SECURE THESE BLESSINGS

THE KARL MARX LIBRA

EDITED AND TRANSLATED BY

SAUL K. PADOVER
*Distinguished Service Professor of Political Science,
Graduate Faculty, New School for Social Research*

ALREADY PUBLISHED

On Revolution

On America and the Civil War

On the First International

On Freedom of the Press and Censorship

IN PREPARATION

On Religion: Christianity, Judaism, and Je

On Freedom
of the Press and Censorship

THE KARL MARX LIBRARY
VOLUME IV

On Freedom of the Press and Censorship

KARL MARX

TRANSLATED,

WITH AN INTRODUCTION

by Saul K. Padover

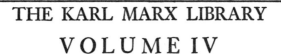

McGraw-Hill Book Company

NEW YORK   ST. LOUIS   SAN FRANCISCO

DÜSSELDORF   LONDON   MEXICO   PANAMA

SYDNEY   TORONTO

FIRST EDITION

1 2 3 4 5 6 7 8 9 BPBP 7 9 8 7 6 5 4

Library of Congress Cataloging in Publication Data
Marx, Karl, 1818–1883.
   The Karl Marx Library.
   Bibliography: v. 1, p.
   CONTENTS: v. 1. On revolution.—v. 2. On America and the Civil
War.—v. 3. On the First International. [etc.]
   1. Socialism—Collected works. I. Title.
HX276.M2773   1972   335.43'08   78–172260
ISBN 0–07–048077–X
ISBN 0–07–048085–0 (pbk.)

Contents

The Press, the Censors, and the First *Rheinische Zeitung*

The *Neue Rheinische Zeitung* and Its Suppression

Letters

Reports, Official Letters, and Documents by and about Marx

Contents

Introduction:
Young Marx as an Embattled
Journalist and Editor

THREE WEEKS before his twenty-third birthday, on April 15, 1841, Karl Marx was awarded the Ph.D. degree by Jena University for his erudite dissertation on classical Greek philosophy: "Difference between the Democritean and Epicurean Philosophy of Nature." He moved to Bonn, where his friend and mentor, the Hegelian philosopher Bruno Bauer, was on the theological faculty of the university, hoping to teach philosophy there. But Bauer himself was soon forbidden to teach by the clericalist Prussian Government, and Marx realized that there was no academic future for him in Germany. He had to find another occupation to support himself.

He chose journalism as the only feasible profession open to a writer and intellectual, especially an intellectual writer like himself. In mid-nineteenth-century Germany careers in established institutions were being increasingly closed to even the most gifted individuals if they had the hardihood to question the traditional foundations of Christianity, as thinkers like Bruno Bauer and Ludwig Feuerbach were doing, or to investigate the social system, which was the area that interested Marx and Engels and other Young Hegelians.[1] Germany, like the rest of monarchical-autocratic Europe, provided no institutionalized outlets for the energy, imagination, and aspirations of striving young idealists. This helps to explain why such a large number of Germans, many of them gifted, skilled, and enterprising, immigrated to the United States in the 1840s and 1850s (Marx, too, at one time had vague plans to immigrate—to Texas). If youthful Germans gave up their rebelliousness they could hope to find a haven in some safe edu-

---

1. The Young Hegelians were a group of intellectuals and theorists around the university in Berlin, where Hegel had taught. They called themselves the *Freien,* Free Ones.

cational, governmental, or ecclesiastical establishment. If they did not, and if they continued to feel alienated in religion and hostile in politics, they turned to revolutionary expression or activity, often both.

As a rebel and nonconformist, Marx had no occupational choice open to him other than writing. Given the volatile conditions of the period, with Germany and all of Continental Europe in a state of nationalist ferment and social unrest, and with governments almost without exception oppressive and censorship-ridden, journalism could not be a neutral pursuit. The journalist had the choice of either defending the status quo, in which case he was likely to be rewarded with money and other favors, or of attacking it, which was certain to expose him to harassment, legal prosecution, and, in the end, to exile. All of this was Marx's fate.

In his early years Marx wrote critically, polemically, and angrily. His passions were geared into his writings. His adoring young bride, Jenny, who had known him since their childhood in Trier, advised him to be moderate in order to be effective:

> Do not write too angrily and irritably. You know how much more effective your other writings have been. Write either factually and delicately or humorously and lightly. Please, dear heart, let the pen glide over the paper, and even if it drops and stumbles occasionally, and a sentence with it, your ideas stand like the grenadiers of the Old Guard, so honorable and firm, and like them they can say, *elle meurt mais elle ne se rend pas*.[2] What does it matter if the uniform hangs loosely and is not laced so tightly ... Loosen the harness, undo the cravat, and raise the shako—let the participles run free and place the words as they themselves would like. An army like yours must not march too rigidly. And your troops are after all going into battle[3]

Marx never ceased to be a combatant. As he put it in his succinct *Theses on Feuerbach* (1845): "The philosophers have only *interpreted* the world in various ways; the point, however, is to change it." Philosophy and jurisprudence, in which Marx had been thoroughly trained at the University of Berlin, and economics, which he was to master within a few years, were to serve as the fuel, and journalism as the vehicle of that change. Marx thus became not merely a journalist—he despised what he called "scribblers"—but a journalist *engagé*, committed to battle.

Everywhere on the Continent, with the sporadic exception of

2. The Old Guard "dies but does not surrender"—a famous phrase attributed to the Napoleonic general Pierre Cambronne (at Waterloo)—although he denied that he ever said it.

3. Letter from Jenny Marx to Karl Marx (in Paris), after June 20, 1844.

France, journalists and critical writers had to contend with the bane of the profession—censorship. In Germany there was no Bill of Rights or "First Amendment freedoms," and no consistent or clear-cut tradition of freedom of expression and communication. Freedom was what the government decided it was. Rulers "by the grace of God," as the Prussian (and other) kings claimed to be, asserted the right to decide what their subjects could safely read. The public censors were the instruments of that power, exercising it sometimes mildly and sometimes rigorously. A writer usually had to take his chances on the benevolence or malevolence, enlightenment or ignorance of government personified in some entrenched bureaucrat not subject to popular control. Behind the bureaucrat-censor stood the policeman, hovering over the writer's work.

At the time Marx was making his debut as a professional journalist freedom of expression was under increasingly severe restrictions in Prussia. On December 24, 1841, three leading Prussian cabinet members—the Minister of Culture, the Minister of Foreign Affairs, and the Minister of Interior (Police)—issued a combined censorship decree which, by equivocal elaboration of the comparatively mild censorship edict that had been in force since October 18, 1819, actually widened and extended its scope. The new decree aimed to suppress anything that was critical of the "fundamental principles of religion" and "offensive to morality and good will." It gave sweeping powers to the censors to decide not merely the actual content of any piece of writing but, what was more menacing, its *tendency*, that is, the presumed intent of the author—as determined by the censor.

Shortly after the new edict was issued, Marx boldly undertook an extended critique of it, comparing the old and new decrees to the disadvantage of the latter. "Remarks on the Latest Prussian Censorship Instruction"[4] was Marx's first major political essay. Its approach was "pre-Marxist," in that it did not base itself on economic or material causes but argued logically and humanistically. Compared to his later work, "Remarks" was prolix, diffuse, and overargumentative, but it contained some sharp insights and brilliant phrasing that anticipated the later, more mature Marx.

The underlying argument of the article was that censorship itself was so fundamentally faulty that no law or decree could remedy it. The output of the human mind was intrinsically of such a nature that it could not be curbed or tamed by bureaucratic decision. No censor, no outsider, was competent to dictate to a creative person either what he should express or how he should formulate his thoughts and findings. For even the form of a writer's expression, his style and

---

4. See page 89.

approach, was an integral part of his search for truth, and truth was
not a governmental commodity but was universal and belonged to
mankind. Only the writer himself, not some bureaucratic interloper
like a censor, could decide how he should convey truth. Censorship,
Marx pointed out, was both logically absurd and politically nihilistic.
It made, in effect, mere bureaucrats, untrained in philosophy, literature,
or science, the supreme arbiters over their intellectual superiors, the
writers and thinkers. If, Marx asked with rhetorical irony, the censors
have the scientific competence to judge scientific competence, why
are they not writers themselves? Censorship was nihilistic in that in
applying the vague and indefinable notion of *tendency* as a criterion,
it abolished all objective standards of truth and science. The consequence of such arbitrary power in the hands of censors was bound to
be tyrannical. "The writer," Marx argued,

> is subject to the most frightful terrorism, to jurisdiction based on
> suspicion. Tendentious laws, laws without objective norms, are laws
> of terrorism, such as those created by Robespierre because of a na-
> tional emergency and by Roman emperors because of corruption of
> the state. Laws that make as their chief criteria not *the action as
> such* but the *sentiment* of the acting person are nothing but *positive
> sanctions of lawlessness*. It would be better to act like the Czar of
> Russia, who had everybody's beard cut off by official Cossacks, than
> to make the idea of wearing a beard the criterion for cutting it off.

The arbitrary censorship was the product of a "dictatorial state"
based on force, not law. Prussia, in Marx's view, was a "police state"
showing an arrogant contempt for the people. "The public's sense
and good will," he wrote, "is not trusted with even the simplest thing;
but for the officials [the censors], even the impossible is to be possible."
    Was there a remedy for censorship? Yes: "The real, *radical cure of
the censorship* is its *abolition*. For it is a bad institution."
    An article attacking censorship could obviously not be published
in a country under censorship. Marx had written his piece for Arnold
Ruge's *Deutsche Jahrbücher*, a liberal journal published in Dresden,
Saxony. Ruge, a poet and a Young Hegelian who had spent five years
in prison for his activities on behalf of a free and united Germany, had
already lost one journal, the influential *Hallische Jahrbücher für
deutsche Wissenschaft und Kunst* [*Halle Yearbooks for German Science and Art*] to the censorship in Leipzig. Now, in Dresden, he was
again in trouble with the censors. Ruge moved his enterprise to Switzerland, where he was finally able to bring out Marx's article on
censorship, as well as one on religion,[5] in an anthology called *Anekdota*

---

5. "Luther as Arbiter Between Strauss and Feuerbach."

zur neuesten deutschen Philosophie und Publicistik [*Anecdota on the Latest German Philosophy and Journalism*] (Zurich and Winterthur, 1843). In one of his letters to Ruge, with whom he then maintained a lively and friendly correspondence (they were later to become enemies), Marx expressed his contempt for German officialdom, including censors and those responsible for the suppression of freedom, referring to some highly placed bureaucrats as "scoundrels," "roués," "dandies," "fops," and religious primitives: "This much I already knew when I was still young and pure," he wrote, "that the eggs that are laid in Berlin are not swans' eggs but goose eggs. Somewhat later came the insight that they are alligators' eggs."[6]

In May, 1842, Marx became a regular contributor to the *Rheinische Zeitung* in Cologne, capital of the Rhine Province. He began his career as a professional newspaperman with the publication, between May 5 and 19, of a number of articles, "Debates on Freedom of the Press and Publication,"[7] about a series of debates in the Rhenish Diet the year before. The articles were in effect a continuation of the polemics in "Remarks," but this time the emphasis was not on censorship as such but on how it affects freedom of the press; in the process of his argumentation Marx also dealt with the meaning of freedom and the role of newspapers. Arnold Ruge commented that these articles were "without doubt the best work on freedom of the press written until now."

Here Marx's method was to take up the arguments against a fully free press enunciated by the various speakers in the Rhenish Diet, and attempt to demolish them with a mixture of sarcasm, logic, and historical example.

To the "paradoxical" argument that censorship actually helped to improve the press, Marx replied, "The greatest orator of the French Revolution, Mirabeau ... trained himself in prison. Are prisons therefore the colleges of oratory?"

One speaker had argued that freedom was an ideal of perfection that could not be granted to society in the form of a free press because man was immature and imperfect. Marx replied with devastating logic: "What follows from this? That the reasoning of our speaker is imperfect, governments are imperfect, the Landtags are imperfect, freedom of the press is imperfect, every sphere of human activity is imperfect. If, therefore, one of these spheres should not exist because of its imperfection, then nobody has the right to exist, and man altogether has no right to exist."

Another speaker had attacked freedom of the press because it pro-

---

6. Marx to Ruge, March 20, 1842.
7. See page 3.

duced evil. Marx countered with the argument that if freedom was evil, why was it that government publications enjoyed absolute freedom? Besides, "Doesn't the censor exercise absolute freedom of the press every day, if not directly, then indirectly?"

Marx further elaborated this argument by pointing out that freedom had always existed, and the only question was whether it should be the privilege of a few or of the human spirit in general: "One asks whether the non-right of the one side should be the right of the other. One asks whether 'freedom of the mind' has a greater right than 'freedom against the mind.' "

Censorship of the press, Marx continued, is a bad police measure because it achieves the opposite of what it intends. It aims to prevent free expression as "something displeasing," but by allowing only select pieces of writing, it actually creates a mystery around the forbidden ones and consequently a widespread interest in them.

Freedom of the press, on the other hand, would rob writing of all mystery and provide a normal outlet for the ordinary, as well as extraordinary, activities of society. Marx then eulogized the role of a free press in idealistic, almost rhapsodic terms:

> The free press is the omnipresent open eye of the spirit of the people, the embodied confidence of a people in itself, the articulate bond that ties the individual to the state and the world, the incorporated culture which transfigures material struggles into intellectual struggles and idealizes its raw material shape. It is the ruthless confession of a people to itself, and it is well known that the power of confession is redeeming. The free press is the intellectual mirror in which a people sees itself, and self-viewing is the first condition of wisdom. It is the mind of the state that can be peddled in every cottage, cheaper than natural gas. It is universal, omnipresent, omniscient. It is the ideal world, which constantly gushes from the real one and streams back to it ever richer and animated anew.

He concluded his series with a quotation from Herodotus' *History* (Book 7). To the argument that a "mild censorship is better than a harsh freedom of the press," Marx replied by quoting what two Spartans said to the Persian Hydernes: "Hydernes, your advice to us has not been weighed equally on both sides. For the one you advise has already been tried; the other you have not tried. Specifically, you know what it is to be a vassal; but you have not yet tried freedom, to find out whether it is sweet or not. For if you had tried it, you would have advised us to fight for it not only with lances but also with axes."

Marx himself soon adopted the advice of the Spartans. At the first opportunity he turned the *Rheinische Zeitung* into a weapon for freedom.

The *Rheinische Zeitung*[8] was a young newspaper still striving to find itself and to develop a coherent editorial point of view. Launched with champagne on January 1, 1842, about five months before Marx joined its staff, it started as a middle-class stock company with a capitalization of 30,000 Taler, a substantial sum that was soon to be doubled by the sale of an additional 1,200 shares at 25 Taler each.

The new daily was the product of special conditions prevailing in Cologne, then the most progressive city in the Prussian kingdom. With a population of about 80,000 the Rhineland capital was the center of emerging industry and the home of energetic businessmen of enlightened, French-influenced views. The city's Catholic population in general and the business entrepreneurs in particular strongly opposed the Prussian Government in Berlin, the former on religious and the latter on economic grounds.

The Rhineland Catholics in general were ultramontanes with a historical antipathy for the Prussian Protestants who had ruled them from afar since France lost the province in 1815. The Cologne bankers and industrialists, some of whom were Jews and a number of whom associated with progressive intellectuals, viewed the central government with no less distaste than that of the population at large. To them Prussia was a feudal anachronism and Berlin an alien capital that governed them by force. Marx, a true Rhinelander, considered Prussians not much better than Russians. Western-minded, capitalistically oriented, and highly educated, the Rhineland leaders were the spokesmen for "modern" ideas in Germany. They favored unification of the splintered German states that would make a wider market possible; reform of the existing political institutions along democratic, parliamentary lines to enable them to participate in political power; and a constitution that would guarantee personal rights, including trial by jury, freedom of the press, and freedom of religion, the latter of particular importance to Cologne's cultured Jewish community.

The *Rheinische Zeitung* was founded as an instrument for attaining the aims of Cologne's progressive elements, and among its founders, directors, and shareholders were professional men, doctors and lawyers, as well as outstanding business leaders. The roster included Ludolf Camphausen, Cologne's leading industrialist and president of its Chamber of Commerce, and David Justus Hansemann, founder of the large Aachen Fire Insurance Company. Both these capitalists were later to play important roles—and to be sharply criticized by Marx—during the revolutionary upheavals in 1848, Camphausen as Prussian Prime Minister and Hansemann as Finance Minister. Also connected with the *Rheinische Zeitung* were Gustav von Mevissen, soon to become presi-

---

8. The full title of the paper was *Rheinische Zeitung für Politik, Handel und Gewerbe* (*Rhenish Gazette for Politics, Commerce and Trade*).

dent of the Rhine Railroad Association; Dagobert Oppenheim, brother of the owner of the big banking house Salomon Oppenheim and Company; Rudolf Schramm, son of a rich factory owner, later to be in conflict with Marx in London; and Georg Jung (who thought Marx "one of the sharpest brains" he had ever met), a wealthy Young Hegelian married to the daughter of a banker.

Ironically enough, the Prussian government licensed the *Rheinische Zeitung*—as Marx remarked, in Prussia "not even a dog can live without a police permit"—in the hope that it would serve as a counterweight to the *Kölnische Zeitung*, Cologne's old (founded in 1802) and influential Catholic newspaper. Cologne's Prussian governor, Karl Heinrich Eduard Friedrich von Gerlach, himself bought shares in the *Rheinische Zeitung*. He and his masters in Berlin were soon to be bitterly disappointed.

The *Rheinische Zeitung* was not averse to engaging in struggle with its well-established rival, but it was not prepared to become a tool of Prussian political interests. Inevitably, the *Rheinische* from the beginning faced a two-front war: rivalry with the *Kölnische* and battle with the censorship, which became increasingly severe. "Don't you believe," Marx wrote to Ruge, "that we in the Rhineland live in a political Eldorado. It takes the most steadfast tenacity for a paper like the *Rheinische* to fight its way through."[9]

The conflict with the *Kölnische Zeitung* was not merely a rivalry between two competing newspapers but also a matter of opposing ideas. The *Kölnische* represented the traditional conservative Catholic viewpoint about the "Christian state" and its presumably God-ordained institutions and values. It opposed the granting of "civil equality to Jews," which the *Rheinische Zeitung* was advocating, and criticized Marx's articles on freedom of the press. Marx attacked the *Kölnische*[10] and called its editor, who bore the Olympian name of (Karl Heinrich) Hermes an "ignorant," "insipid," "trivial" and mediocre prattler. The *Rheinische Zeitung*'s acting editor, Dagobert Oppenheim, acknowledging receipt of the piece on the *Kölnische Zeitung*, wrote him, "The article is splendid, but I fear that the beastly censorship will apply its knife again. You have no idea how relentlessly and unjustly we are being censored."

The struggle with the Prussian censorship was to be unceasing.

Until Marx's arrival on the scene as contributor, and later as editor, the *Rheinische Zeitung*, although gaining readers, had no firm leadership. Adolf Rutenberg, the editor who preceded Marx, was also a Young Hegelian Ph.D. He had been Marx's closest friend at the Uni-

---

9. July 9, 1842. See page 159.
10. *Rheinische Zeitung*, July 10, 12, 14, 1842. This three part article will appear in *Karl Marx on Religion*, Volume V of The Karl Marx Library. For the section dealing with press freedom see page 48 in this volume.

versity of Berlin. When Rutenberg left Berlin to work on the *Rhein-ische Zeitung* (before he became editor) he was preceded by an order from the watchful Prussian Minister of Interior, Gustav Adolf Rochus von Rochow, to the Cologne *Regierungs-Präsident* (Governor), Karl Heinrich Eduard Friedrich von Gerlach, that he should be "immedi-ately placed under Cologne police surveillance, as he has been in Berlin." Rutenberg turned out to be an ineffectual editor, and Marx soon ridiculed him to Ruge for his incompetence and his penchant for the frothy maunderings of Berlin's Young Hegelians, which Marx had by now outgrown. Nevertheless, the Prussian authorities considered him dangerous and soon demanded his removal. In Marx's opinion Rutenberg was "dangerous to nobody except the *Rheinische Zeitung* and himself," but under government pressure he had to go. On Octo-ber 15, 1842, Marx replaced Rutenberg as editor, and went to live in Cologne to direct the newspaper.

Marx set about to move the *Rheinische Zeitung* in a leftward, although not communist, direction. He was not at that point either a social radical or a communist. Rather, he was a critic of society, in-terested in rationality and justice. He had no coherent or systematic political philosophy, or, for that matter, any knowledge of economics. As he explained later in the preface to his *Critique of Political Econ-omy* (1859):

> My professional study was jurisprudence, which, however, I pur-sued only as a subordinate discipline alongside philosophy and his-tory. In the year 1842–43, as editor of the *Rheinische Zeitung*, I first came into embarrassment at having to discuss so-called material problems. The proceedings of the Rhenish Landtag on wood stealing and land parcelization . . . gave the first stimuli to my preoccupa-tion with economic questions.[11]

Marx not only knew little about economics but also about commu-nism, in which he was not particularly interested. In his first essay on the subject, published in the *Rheinische Zeitung* the day he took over as editor, he wrote, "The *Rheinische Zeitung*, which cannot concede the theoretical substance of communist ideas even in their present form, and can even less wish or consider possible their practical realization, will submit these ideas to a thorough criticism."[12]

In the fall of 1842, while busy as editor, Marx began a serious study of contemporary French utopian and socialist theories. He read in the

---

11. *"Debatten über das Holzdiebstahlgesetz"* ("Debates over the Wood-Stealing Law"), in *Rheinische Zeitung*, October 25, 1842.

12. *"Der Kommunismus und die Augsburger Allgemeine Zeitung"* ("Commu-nism and the Augsburg *Allgemeine Zeitung*"), October 16, 1842; see *Karl Marx on Revolution*, Volume I of The Karl Marx Library, pages 3–6.

French original Étienne Cabet's *Voyage en Icarie* (1842), Victor Considérant's *Destinée Sociale* (1834–38), Théodore Dézamy's *Calomnies et Politique de M. Cabet* (1842), Charles Fourier's *Théorie des Quatre Mouvements et des Destinées Générales* (2d ed., 1841), Pierre Leroux's *De L'Humanité* (1840), and Pierre Joseph Proudhon's *Qu'est-ce que la Propriété?* (1841). These writers did not then convert Marx to communism but they aroused his interest. Nor did they teach him the science of economics, about which the utopians knew as little as he. But Marx began to study economics—a discipline that helped lead him to communism—later in the year 1843, when he had left the *Rheinische Zeitung* and settled in Paris.

If Marx did not turn the *Rheinische Zeitung* into a radical newspaper, he nevertheless sharply changed its tone. Unlike other contemporary German papers, often satisfied with carrying official handouts and sanctimonious platitudes, the *Rheinische* refused, in Marx's words, to be "merely a mindless amalgam of dry reporting and base flattery." It became a contentious critic and a caustic polemicist, sometimes apparently enjoying contention for its own sake, and taking on other newspapers (even outside Cologne), bureaucrats, and government policies. Frederick Engels, not an impartial but a very acute critic, thought that under Marx the *Rheinische Zeitung* was the first "modern" German newspaper. It was certainly the liveliest and scrappiest, and this was soon to be its downfall.

The *Rheinische Zeitung* was being censored daily by a dull bureaucrat named Laurenz Dolleschall, who said he would not permit "making fun of divine things." He struck out much of what he did not understand and everything that appeared to him to be suspicious—for example, the section on marriage in Marx's article, "The Philosophical Manifesto of the Historical School of Law."[13] Marx liked to quote Dolleschall: "Now it's a matter of my bread and butter. Now I strike out everything."

Proof sheets had to be brought to the censor's home every evening, and since the *Rheinische Zeitung* was a morning paper, editor and writers had to stay up late at night to redo their copy after the red penciling. Once Marx played a trick on "the ruffian of a censor." The censor and his family were invited to the governor's ball, but Marx did not bring over the proofs that evening. The censor waited nervously until 10:00 P.M., sent his wife and daughters to the ball without him, and dispatched a servant to the *Rheinische* editorial office. He found it closed. The desperate censor then drove out to Marx's home. It was eleven o'clock by the time he got there. He rang the bell impatiently and after a long wait Marx put his head out the window of his third-

---

13. *Rheinische Zeitung*, August 9, 1842.

floor apartment. "Proof sheets!" yelled the censor. "Aren't any!" Marx yelled back. "But! ..." cried the censor. "The paper is not coming out tomorrow," Marx shouted, and shut the window. Understandably, the infuriated censor was subsequently even nastier.

On November 12, 1842, Berlin ordered Governor von Gerlach in Cologne to tell Joseph Engelbert Renard, publisher of the *Rheinische Zeitung*, to change the paper's hostile tone and to present the editor's name to the governor for approval. Marx drafted a reply for the publisher's signature claiming that the *Rheinische* was actually pro-Prussian, that it had defended important national policies, such as the idea of German unity and the Customs Union, and that under the Censorship Law of 1819 the governor was not empowered to approve editors. The *Rheinische*, the reply pointed out, was a newspaper whose characteristic was the expression of the "fearless speech of free men."[14]

The government was not mollified. Censorship continued "pitilessly" to mutilate the paper and political pressures were driving Marx to exhaustion. "We are," Marx wrote to Ruge, "burdened from morning to night with the most frightful censorship harassments, ministerial scribblings, gubernatorial complaints, Landtag accusations, stockholders' screamings, etc., etc."[15]

Despite all this, Marx continued his "fearless speech." He bravely attacked the government's suppression of the *Leipziger Allgemeine Zeitung*[16] and eloquently described the role of a free press as the indispensable organ of a people's needs and grievances:

> ... the administration and the administered both need a third element, which is political without being bureaucratic ... This complementary element, composed of a political head and a civic heart, is a *free press*. ... The "free press," as it is the product of public opinion, also produces public opinion ... Finally, the free press carries the people's misery to the foot of the throne, not in a bureaucratically approved form but in its own medium ...[17]

The Prussian bureaucracy did not find this kind of argument persuasive. But drastic action against the *Rheinische Zeitung* was finally stimulated from St. Petersburg rather than Berlin. On January 4, 1843, the *Rheinische* published an attack on czarist military despotism. The news of it enraged the despot himself. Czar Nicholas I blustered, berated Prussian Ambassador von Lieberman about the liberal German press, and wrote a protest to the Prussian King in Berlin. Since Russia

---

14. November 17, 1842; see page 179.
15. November 30, 1842; see page 160.
16. See page 53.
17. See "Defense of the Mosel Correspondent," page 69.

was Prussia's chief ally in foreign affairs, Frederick William IV was shaken by the Czar's threatening tone. On January 21, 1843, the King assembled a ministerial council which decided to kill the *Rheinische Zeitung* as of March 31. The royal order was immediately dispatched to Governor von Gerlach in Cologne:

> For some weeks now the *Rheinische Zeitung* has, if anything, surpassed itself in insolent language and pursued a tendency which openly aims to create antagonism to, as well as undermine, state and church, stir up discontent, to slander the government maliciously, especially to ridicule the censorship and censors in Prussia and Germany, and to insult friendly powers.

The order amounted to what Marx called a "death sentence" for the *Rheinische Zeitung*, with a nine-week reprieve to enable the stockholders to salvage what they could. From then until its expiration date the paper suffered from ever stricter censorship. Dolleschall, who tried to save his "bread-and-butter" job by claiming credit for having censored out no fewer than 140 articles, was replaced by another censor, named Wiethaus, whom Marx considered "an honorable man." The Ministry of Interior in Berlin sent a special censor to Cologne. He was Wilhelm Saint-Paul, a sophisticated bureaucrat with friends among Young Hegelians in Berlin, and he came to enjoy his philosophical sparrings with Marx. "We have had," Saint-Paul reported to Berlin in March, "several exhaustive conversations. The more Dr. Marx's views are based on deeper speculative error, as I tried to prove to him on his own terrain, the more convinced he is of their truth, as is true also of all his coworkers."

On February 12, 1843, there was an extraordinary meeting of the *Rheinische Zeitung*'s shareholders. Marx sensed their tendency to yield to the pressure and give up opposition to the government in order to save the paper. In defense of the *Rheinische* he had prepared a lengthy reply to the government's charges, pointing out that they were inaccurate and ambiguous, and arguing, somewhat disingenuously, that the paper was actually a patriotic supporter of Prussia, rather than an enemy.[18] The shareholders adopted Marx's reply and incorporated it in their memorandum to the authorities. It was, of course, wasted effort.

In its final days the *Rheinische Zeitung* operated under triple censorship. In addition to Saint-Paul and Wiethaus there was a routine censor under the direction of Governor von Gerlach, whom Marx called an "obediently passive *Dummkopf* [blockhead]." Before any issue could finally appear, it had to be submitted "to the police nose for

---

18. See "Marginal Notes on the Charges Made in the Ministerial Rescript," page 84.

smelling, and if it scents anything un-Christian, un-Prussian, the paper must not appear."

For some time now Marx had thought of resigning. He was weary of battling the censorship, which he knew to be a losing fight, and fed up with the general condition of unfreedom in Germany. As he told Ruge, "It is bad to perform menial services even for freedom, and to fight with needles instead of clubs. I became tired of hypocrisy, stupidity, raw authority, and our cringing, bowing, back turning, and word picking."[19]

Marx resigned. The *Rheinische Zeitung* carried the following curt announcement, datelined March 17, 1843: "The undersigned declares that, due to the *present censorship* conditions, he has resigned today from the editorship of the *Rheinische Zeitung*. Dr. Marx."

Saint-Paul immediately reported to Berlin that with the departure of the paper's "spiritus rector" (intellectual leader) a new wind was blowing in the editorial office, requiring little censorship. He recommended that the *Rheinische Zeitung*, once more under the editorship of the Cologne banker Dagobert Oppenheim—a "really moderate" and "insignificant man"—be permitted to continue. The government refused to reconsider its decision or even to accept a petition containing a few thousand signatures. On March 31, 1843, the *Rheinische Zeitung* went out in a blaze of poetry, so to speak. In a poem entitled "Farewell" (not by Marx) the last issue hailed its lost fight for freedom:

Boldly we let the flag of freedom wave,
and every mariner his duty did with a mien grave,
hence also in vain the spying on the crew:
The voyage was beautiful, and this we do not rue.
What the wrath of the Gods hath upon us wrought
does not scare us, nor that our mast got caught,
for Columbus, too, was at first looked upon with lips curled
but nevertheless he did finally see the New World.
You friends, whose applause was our light,
You opponents, who honored us with your fight,
We shall see each other again on a new ship,
When everything breaks down, courage remains without a rip.[20]

---

19. January 25, 1843; see page 163.
20. "*Wir liessen kühn der Freiheit Fahne wehen,/Und ernst tat jeder Schiffs-mann seine Pflicht/, War drum vergebens auch der Mannschaft Spähen:/ Die Fahrt war schön, und sie gereut uns nicht./ Was uns der Götter Zorn had nach-getrachtet,/ Es schreckt uns nicht, dass unser Mast gefallt,/ Denn auch Kolumbus ward zuerst verachtet,/ Und endlich sah er doch die neue Welt./ Ihr Freunde, deren Beifall uns geworden,/ Ihr Gegner, die ihr uns mit Kampf geehrt,/ Wir seh'n uns wieder einst an neuen Borden,/ Wenn alles bricht, der Mut bleibt unversehrt.*"

The quality of the poem was obviously not quite up to the standard of the sentiment that inspired it.

Toward the end of March, enjoying the feeling of liberation from a heavy burden, Marx took a short trip through Holland. What he saw there made him ashamed of his own country: "The littlest Dutchman is a citizen, compared to the biggest German." After his return home he married his childhood sweetheart, Jenny von Westphalen,[21] and made plans to leave Germany, where he felt suffocated. "In Germany," he wrote to Ruge, "everything is violently suppressed, a true anarchy of the spirit, a regime of *Dummheit* [stupidity] has broken in."[22] At the end of October he moved to Paris, where he and Ruge planned to publish a German-language journal, the *Deutsch-Französische Jahrbücher—German-French Yearbooks—*to serve as a literary link between Continental Europe's two major cultures. Its viewpoint, reflecting that of the editors, was to be prodemocratic and anticommunist. For at that point Marx was still a believer in "bourgeois" freedom and thought that the "highest ends" for a community of people were in a "democratic state." By the same token, he was opposed to any "ready-made" utopian system and was critical of communism, such as he knew it then, as a "dogmatic abstraction."[23]

The first—and last—issue of the *Deutsch-Französische Jahrbücher,* which carried two important articles by Marx,[24] came out at the end of February, 1844. Despite its name, it contained no articles by Frenchmen. Marx and Ruge quarreled, and the journal suspended publication late in March. Marx was now free-lancing and, as Ruge said, plunging "into an ocean of books."

The stay in Paris, where he lived for another year after the *Deutsch-Französische Jahrbücher* was published, was a turning point in Marx's life. He and his bride moved into a house[25] that was a kind of "communist community" inhabited by German radical intellectuals. Marx's circle of friends in Paris included the Russian revolutionist Michael Bakunin and the liberal landowner Pavel V. Annenkov, the German philosopher-socialist Moses Hess, and the poets Heinrich Heine and Georg Herwegh. The Germans were radical theorists, the best of whom had, like Marx, come out of the Hegelian school. The bemused Heine, no communist, called them "Doctors of Revolution," and added: "I fear the future belongs to them."

Paris itself was endlessly stimulating to young Marx. He called it

21. On June 19, 1843.
22. Marx to Ruge, March, 1843.
23. Marx to Ruge, September, 1843.
24. "Toward the Critique of Hegel's Philosophy of Law" (for an excerpt see *Karl Marx on Revolution,* pages 422–428) and "On the Jewish Question."
25. At 41 Rue Vaneau, Faubourg St. Germain.

the "old college of philosophy, *absit omen!* [may it be no evil omen!]
and the new capital of the new world."[26] The dazzling city was then
the center of European culture, the home of a galaxy of artists and
writers whose fame extended beyond France. Among the most re-
nowned were Honoré de Balzac, whom Marx read with admiration
and later paid tribute to in *Capital*;[27] Victor Hugo, whom he considered "brilliant" and often cited; and George Sand, whom Marx was to
quote with approval in *The Poverty of Philosophy* (1847).[28]

Paris was also a center of radical ferment, an effervescence still
bubbling from the great days of the Revolution of 1789, which continued to be a living tradition, both for the triumphant middle class—
the classic bourgeoisie in Marx's sense—now seemingly in solid control
of all levers of power under the reign of Louis Philippe, and for the
discontented workers, seething with radical idealism. In this, the greatest city on the Continent, with extremes of luxury and misery, class
divisions were open, sharp, palpable. Marx did not need to invent the
idea of the class struggle: he had only to look around him.

Paris provided Marx with the opportunity of getting to know real,
live proletarians, not only mere theorizers like Proudhon, whom he
met in July, 1844. Among the proletarians were many communists and
socialists. There were at that time in Paris some 10,000 German artisans and journeymen—"shoemaker" was then virtually synonymous
with "German"—with strong communist leanings. In the Faubourg
St. Antoine there were often violent street clashes between German
workers, who spoke no French, and Paris proletarians, who resented
them for undercutting their wages. Marx was introduced to the German artisans by August Hermann Ewerbeck, a refugee physician, who
was a member of the Communist League and head of the secret society
Bund der Gerechten (League of the Just). Marx attended their meetings and learned something about labor and "class conflict."

He also came in contact with French communist workers. A police
spy (Paris was then full of them) reported that in the summer of
1844 he often saw Marx attend secret meetings of French communist
societies in the Barrière du Trône, on the Rue de Vincennes. Marx
was enormously, perhaps romantically, impressed with the French artisans' intelligence, energy, and idealism. He observed that "nobility
shines out of the labor-hardened faces." He wrote to Ludwig Feuerbach, "You have to attend one of the meetings of the French *ouvriers*

---

26. Marx to Ruge, September, 1843.
27. In *Capital*, Volume III, Chapter 1, Section 1, Marx praises Balzac for being
"generally remarkable for his profound grasp of actual conditions." See also Volume I, Chapter 22, Section 7, footnote.
28. The quotation, from the novel *Jean Ziska*, reads: "Combat or death; san-
guinary struggle or nothingness. It is thus that the question is invincibly posed."

to realize the virginal freshness and nobility that is generated among these workingmen." Marx was ever after to have a special interest in the French proletariat, as can be seen in his later writings, especially *The Class Struggles in France, 1848–50* (1850) and *The Civil War in France* (1871).[29]

Marx did not join the secret French societies nor any of the German *Bunds* in Paris, but it is certain that by the summer of 1844 he had ceased to be a liberal idealist and had become a dedicated communist. His espousal of communism was crystallized that summer, when Frederick Engels stopped off in Paris on the way from Manchester to his native Barmen, Germany. He visited Marx, whom he had briefly met in Cologne during the *Rheinische Zeitung* days, and the two young men—Marx was twenty-six, Engels twenty-four—there and then struck up a lifelong friendship. They spent ten days discussing the whole range of philosophical, and social-economic problems, particularly as they related to European radicalism. They found themselves, to quote Engels, in "agreement on all theoretical fields," and they decided to collaborate in their future work. Their first collaboration was *The Holy Family*, written in Paris in September-November, 1844, and published in Frankfurt the following year. The book, subtitled *Against Bruno Bauer and Associates*, marked a radical break with Hegelians and Hegelianism and served as a bridge toward materialism. Marx said of it in later years that it "aimed against the ideological mysticism of the Hegelian and speculative philosophy in general."[30] It was Engels, already a materialist and a communist, who gave a special impetus to Marx's interest in economics; he now began the serious study of the subject that was to continue as long as he lived. Altogether, the Paris year may have been the most important period in Marx's life.

But the long arm of the Prussian Government reached him in the French capital. When copies of the *Deutsch-Französische Jahrbücher* were received by the Berlin police, the Prussian Minister of Interior, Count Adolf Heinrich von Arnim-Boytzenburg, placed Marx's name on a proscription list. Noting that the "whole tone of that journal" constituted "attempted high treason and *lèse majesté*," von Arnim-Boytzenburg ordered his police authorities "to arrest, and seize the papers of, Dr. Arnold Ruge, Carl [*sic*] Marx, Heinrich Heine, and Ferdinand Coelestin Bernays as soon as they cross our side of the frontier."[31]

In the meantime Prussian agents dogged Marx's footsteps in Paris and reported his activities to Berlin. A few months after the suspension

---

29. See *Karl Marx on Revolution*, pages 154–242, 332–372.
30. Marx to Nicolai Frantzevich Danielson, October 7, 1868.
31. See page 183.

of the *Deutsch-Französische Jahrbücher*, Marx published two articles in *Vorwärts!*, a German-language journal in Paris, that were sharply critical of Prussia and its monarchy.[32] The Prussian ambassador, Karl Eduard Arnim, protested to the French Government, then under the leadership of the historian and politician François Guizot, and as a result *Vorwärts!* editor Bernays was sentenced to two months in Sainte Pélagie prison and a fine of 300 francs. Marx's turn came next. The Prussian King sent the distinguished German scientist, Alexander von Humboldt, on a special mission to King Louis Philippe; von Humboldt carried with him a lengthy letter from Frederick William IV and a "splendid porcelain vase" as a gift. Louis Philippe assured von Humboldt that he would clear Paris of German radicals and atheists, and an order soon went out for the expulsion of a number of them, including Bernays, Heine, and Ruge. Marx, who had been forewarned several days earlier, received the order of expulsion on January 25; it had a grace period of a week. On February 1 he left Paris for Brussels.

In Brussels "Karl Marx, Dr. of philosophy, twenty-six years old," respectfully petitioned King Leopold I for permission to settle there with his wife (temporarily left behind in Paris). Leopold did not reply, but in the following month Marx, who like other foreigners had to register with the *Sûreté Publique*, was asked to sign a pledge not to write anything about contemporary Belgian politics. He did so. In protest against the government in Berlin he also formally renounced his Prussian citizenship. Stateless, he remained under constant police surveillance[33] but was not otherwise interfered with.

The Belgian capital was then the home of a circle of foreign radicals. Most of them were German, but Bakunin was also now in Brussels, and there was a sprinkling of émigrés of various nationalities. Marx, soon joined by Engels, became active among them. The two men founded a Communist Correspondence Committee, to maintain contact with communists in other countries. Marx contributed to the *Deutsche-Brüsseler-Zeitung*, a radical German-language newspaper published twice a week in Brussels, and continued his literary collaboration with Engels. In 1846 they completed the exuberantly polemical *German Ideology*, and at the end of 1847 they wrote for the German Communist League, which they had organized in June of that year, the historic *Manifesto of the Communist Party*.[34]

---

32. "Critical Marginal Notes on the Article 'The King of Prussia and Social Reform. By a Prussian.'" See *Karl Marx on Revolution*, pages 7–22.

33. Police reports on Marx are to be found in the Amsterdam Institute for Social History, MS, E17.

34. The *Manifesto* was published anonymously in German, in London, February 1848. The first English translation, by Helen MacFarlane, appeared in the Chartist weekly, *The Red Republican*, in 1850; here Marx and Engels were mentioned as the authors for the first time. For the text see *Karl Marx on Revolution*, pages 79–107.

In February of 1848 revolutions began to break out in Europe. News of the uprising in Paris led to demonstrations in Brussels, and the enthusiastic Marx urged German workers there to join their Belgian brethren. Having recently inherited some 6,000 francs from his father's estate, he contributed about 5,000 to buy arms. This was reported to Belgian police and on the night of March 3 they invaded Marx's home and took him to jail. The following day he was ordered to leave Belgium immediately.

Marx went back to Paris, where he had been invited by Ferdinand Flocon, a journalist and member of the Provisional Government there. Insurrections soon broke out in Germany, including Berlin and Cologne, and Marx decided to return home to help spread the revolution.

Arriving in Cologne April 11, he applied for citizenship and permission to remain in the city. The latter was granted and, with the help of Engels, Marx began raising money to organize a revolutionary newspaper.

The whole situation was now very different from what it had been in 1842–43. Germany was in a state of rebellion, partly nationalistic, partly democratic, partly radical. Even autocratic Prussia felt the revolutionary tremor. An all-German *Nationalversammlung* (National Assembly) met in Frankfurt in May, 1848, to draft a democratic constitution for a united Germany. The work of the "Unifiers" finally ended in frustration, but in the meantime the German atmosphere was permeated with revolutionary strivings.

Marx, too, was different from his *Rheinische Zeitung* days, when he had struggled in defense of freedom of the press within the established order and in a liberal "bourgeois" framework. Now, five years later, he was a communist and a leader of the Communist League, which was dedicated to revolutionary activism. His interest was no longer in freedom as it might be obtained through a middle-class democratic system—assuming it could be obtained at all in the autocratic German states—but in the overthrow of the whole social order. In his 1848–49 articles in the *Neue Rheinische Zeitung*, Marx was to call the National Assemblies in Frankfurt and Berlin "parliamentary cretinism."[35]

The turmoil of the year 1848—when there was fighting on the barricades not only in revolutionary Paris but also in such seemingly conservative monarchical capitals as Berlin and Vienna—seemed to Marx proof that Germany, as well as the rest of Europe, was on the verge of a thorough revolution.[36] He and Engels had visualized it, pro-

---

35. Engels, "Marx and the *Neue Rheinische Zeitung*, 1848–1849," in *Der Sozialdemokrat*, March 13, 1884.
36. See the section on Germany in *Karl Marx on Revolution*.

phetically as it were, in the *Communist Manifesto* at the beginning of 1848.

The instrument for the hastening, crystallization, and encouragement of the revolution was to be the *Neue Rheinische Zeitung* in Cologne, a resurrection of the title of the old *Rheinische Zeitung*, with the word *Neue*—New—added to it. The paper's subtitle was "Organ of Democracy," which it was not, at least not in the accepted Western (including Anglo-American) sense. In Marxian terminology "democracy" connoted the "proletariat," a term that embraced the entity known as "the people," meaning the actual or potential revolutionary lower classes, which obviously comprised many people. Years later, no less a specialist on the subject than Lenin said of the *Neue Rheinische Zeitung* that "to this very day [1914] it remains the best and unsurpassed organ of the revolutionary proletariat."

The journal, originally scheduled to appear on July 1, came out one month earlier because of the expectation of "new and insolent" reactionary press laws, as the first issue (June 1) announced. It was undercapitalized at 13,000, out of a projected 30,000, from shares sold, at 50 Taler each, to members of the Communist League, of whom there were two or three hundred in Cologne and the Rhineland, and to unsuspecting noncommunists.

The latter, amounting to about half of the shareholders, were soon alienated, particularly after the *Neue Rheinische Zeitung* showed its contempt for the Frankfurt National Assembly, on which German democrats and nationalists pinned their hopes for a parliamentary system and for national unity. In an unsigned article of June 23, 1848 (written by Engels), the Assembly was accused of "cowardice." In later years Engels recalled with some pride: "The very first number began with an article[37] ridiculing the nothingness of the Frankfurt Parliament, the aimlessness of its long-winded speeches, the superfluousness of its cowardly decisions. It cost us half of our shareholders." Middle-class supporters of the newspaper were further antagonized when it castigated the brutality with which General Louis-Eugène Cavaignac suppressed the June 23 uprising in Paris.[38] All this dried up local sources of desperately needed cash for the *Neue Rheinische Zeitung*, necessitating fund-raising expeditions. One such excursion, in August-September, 1848, took Marx as far as Vienna and Berlin and raised 1,950 Taler from Polish democrats, most of which went to pay immediate debts (including a 500-Taler installment on the printing press). The *Neue Rheinische Zeitung* was to be chronically short of money. In mid-November of 1848, half a year after the paper first

---

37. Engels, "The Frankfurt Assembly," June 1, 1848.
38. Articles by Engels published June 26, 28, 29, 1848.

appeared, Marx wrote to Engels: "I have not yet received one penny from the newspaper." When the *Neue Rheinische Zeitung* was liquidated, in May, 1849, Marx, after selling the printing machine and his own furniture, borrowed an additional 300 Taler to pay the typesetters, office employees, editorial personnel, and paper suppliers. Altogether the *Neue Rheinische Zeitung* cost him some 7,000 Taler from his own pocket.

The newspaper started with an editorial board of six,[39] all of them former members of the Communist League (which had dissolved to join a "democratic society"). Each member tended to write his specialty. Wilhelm Wolff, a Silesian, for example, wrote on agriculture. Georg Weerth, a poet, composed *feuilletons*. Weerth's most famous, or notorious, piece was the anonymously published "Life and Exploits of the Famous Knight Schnapphahnski [Snatch-Rooster-ski]," a satire on a powerful Prussian Junker general, Prince Felix Maria von Lichnowski. There was a publisher, Hermann Korff. Marx himself was editor in chief, in control of everything, including finances. His "dictatorship" of the *Neue Rheinische Zeitung* was, in Engels' words, "gladly accepted by us all."

Next to Marx, Engels was the most important staff member; he was also the bluntest and roughest political writer on the paper. Even after he fled Cologne, early in October, upon the issuance of an order for his arrest, he continued his contributions from abroad. Engels wrote the bulk of the editorials and much else besides. Altogether, he and Marx between them contributed some 227 articles, a number of them in several installments. As an organ dedicated to revolution, the *Neue Rheinische Zeitung* also published reportage from cities in rebellion, such as Berlin, Paris, Prague, and Vienna.

Conflict with the authorities began at once. In addition to Engels' piece on the Assembly, the first issue of the *Neue Rheinische Zeitung* carried Marx's attack on General Hans Gustav von Hüser, the Prussian commandant in nearby Mainz, accusing him and the government in Berlin of designs to disarm the people's militia and to turn the "Germans into even greater slaves" than before.[40] From then on the paper directed a steady drumfire of criticisms, exposures, and sarcasms not only at government policies but also at the assorted democrats and liberals who, both in the hapless Prussian Assemblies in Berlin (occasionally broken up and into by the King's troops) and the National

---

39. Heinrich Bürgers, a journalist; Ernst Dronke, a journalist; Frederick Engels; Georg Weerth; Ferdinand Wolff, a journalist; Wilhelm Wolff ("Lupus"), a journalist and later (when he lived in England, where he remained a close friend of Marx and Engels) a teacher.

40. "Hüser," June 1, 1848. See *Karl Marx on Revolution*, page 429.

Assembly in Frankfurt, were striving—with monumental incompetence and futility, as it turned out—to transform the prevailing German autocracies into a parliamentary system. The Prussian authorities soon moved against the militant *Neue Rheinische Zeitung* and its editor.

The immediate occasion was an article exposing highhanded police tactics in the arrest of Friedrich Anneke, a Cologne communist. What gave particular offense to the authorities, in the persons of Herr Staatsprokurator (State Prosecutor) Hecker and Herr Oberprokurator (Chief Prosecutor) Zweiffel—with whom Marx was soon to engage in a running duel—was the broad hint that one of the arresting policemen was drunk:

> Between six and seven in the morning seven gendarmes entered Anneke's home, immediately manhandled the maid in the entrance hall and sneaked silently up the stairs. Three remained in the vestibule, four broke into the bedroom, where Anneke and his pregnant wife were sleeping. Of these four pillars of justice, one was reeling, at this early hour already more or less filled with "spirit," the water of true life, the burnt water.[41]

A charge of police drunkenness was almost tantamount to *lèse majesté* in the eyes of the police. Chief Prosecutor Zweiffel and the gendarmes felt themselves properly insulted and haled Marx and his publisher into court for "slander." After two hours of interrogation the examining magistrate, the Chief Prosecutor, and a police commissioner raided the offices of the *Neue Rheinische Zeitung* and found what they thought, wrongly, was a manuscript copy of the incriminating article—whose authorship Marx had refused to divulge. Police investigation and harassment, with Marx summoned before the magistrate for interrogation, continued for several weeks.

Two weeks after the article on Anneke came out, on July 20, Marx took up the question of a reported new censorship law pending in Berlin. He attacked it as a repetition of the old "Napoleonic press despotism." His comments on the censorship now differed from those he had written in defense of freedom of the press half a dozen years earlier. This time the tone and approach were not philosophical or theoretical but bluntly combative.

> From the day this law goes into effect, the [Prussian] officials can commit any despotism, any tyranny, any illegality, with impunity; they can coolly flog or order to be flogged, arrest and hold without a hearing; the only effective control, the press, has been made ineffective. The day this law goes into effect the bureaucracy can cele-

---

41. See "Arrests," page 112.

brate a festival of joy ... In fact, what remains of freedom of the
press, when that which deserves public contempt can no longer be
exposed to public contempt?[42]

Because of the fluid revolutionary situation in Berlin and other
German cities the government took no immediate steps against Marx
and his newspaper. That summer Marx helped organize so-called
democratic associations in Cologne and the rest of the Rhineland to
carry on revolutionary agitation among workers and peasants. On
September 25 a revolt broke out in Cologne and martial law was declared. Two days later the city's radical newspapers,[43] including the
Neue Rheinische Zeitung, were closed at the order of the military
commandant. They were permitted to reopen two weeks later, on
October 12.

Early in October the Prosecutor's office began to move against
the editors of the *Neue Rheinische Zeitung*. Arrest warrants were
issued for some of them, who, like Bürgers, Dronke, and Engels, fled
the city. At the beginning of November, Marx, accompanied by a
friendly crowd, was summoned to court for a renewed hearing. In
the middle of the month news came from Berlin that, in the prevailing turmoil of the capital, the government had suspended all but the
conservative newspapers there, had disarmed the people's militia, and
had driven out the National Assembly at bayonet point. The Assembly
moved to a hotel and unanimously voted the suspension of taxes.
Whereupon Marx issued an extra: "NO MORE TAXES!" The extra concluded: "From this day on, all taxes are therefore suspended! ! ! Taxpaying is high treason, tax avoidance is the first duty of the citizen!"[44]

Toward the end of November Marx underwent two more court
hearings and was afterward put under three indictments. They included the "crimes" of having insulted Herr Oberprokurator Zweiffel
and the gendarmerie in reporting the Anneke affair; of having satirized
the Junkers in the "Schnapphahnski" piece; and of "incitement to
rebellion" in the antitax campaign. They were combined into two
cases, one dealing with "insult" and the other with "rebellion." Trial
for both, set for December 20, was postponed (for lack of evidence)
to February 7, 1849.

When the jury trial before the Court of Assizes opened, the room
was filled with Marx's supporters. The "insult" case came first. After

---

42. See "The Prussian Press Bill," page 121.
43. *Neue Kölnische Zeitung für Bürger, Bauern und Soldaten*, a communist
paper; *Zeitung des Arbeiter-Vereins zu Köln*, also a communist paper; and *Der
Wächter am Rhein*, a radical journal.
44. See page 130, footnote.

the prosecutor and the defense attorney had presented their statements, Marx rose and spoke for about an hour. He did not defend
himself. He attacked, almost contemptuously, both the tactics and the
law used by Chief Prosecutor Zweiffel, who built his case on Article
222 of the old Napoleonic *Code Pénal*, which dealt with resistance to
authority. The Article spoke of *"outrages par paroles"—oral offenses—*
by the resister. Marx argued that it did not apply to the written or
printed word. As for injury done to the honor and sensibilities of
offended officials who resort to Article 222, Marx pointed out that it
was not a measurable quantity:

> What is honor, what is sensitivity? What is injury in regard to
> them? This depends entirely on the individual with whom I have to
> deal, on the level of his education, on his prejudices, on his conceit.
> There is no other yardstick to measure the *noli me tangere* [touch
> me not], the pompous vanity of an official who deems himself
> incomparable.

Marx concluded his speech, to the accompaniment of applause in
court, with a peroration for revolution and a call for a fighting press
to expose injustice and destroy the existing order:

> I regard it as a real sacrifice when we decide to break a lance with
> *these* opponents [prosecutors and gendarmes]. But once and for all
> it is the duty of the press to speak up for the oppressed in its im-
> mediate vicinity. . . . It does not suffice to fight general conditions
> and the higher authorities. The press must decide to enter the lists
> against *this* particular gendarme, *this* procurator, *this* district admin-
> istrator. . . . The first duty of the press, therefore, is *to undermine
> all the foundations of the existing political system.*[45]

The following day, February 8, the case of incitement to rebellion
was taken up, under Article 367 of the *Code Pénal*. The prosecution
was denied its victim. That day the jury brought in a verdict of not
guilty for Marx and for his publisher, Hermann Korff.

The struggle with the authorities did not cease, of course, but
one episode did have an amusing twist. On the last day of February
the *Neue Rheinische Zeitung* printed an anonymous notice to the
effect that a local garrison officer, von Uttenhoven, Captain of Company 8, Infantry Regiment 16, was black-marketeering in firewood.
Whereupon two noncoms went to Marx's home to demand satisfac-
tion for the "insult" to their entire company. Marx, apparently forewarned, prepared himself with a pistol. According to the story later

---

45. See "The Role of the Press . . . ," page 135.

told by the Marxist theorist Karl Kautsky, who heard it from Engels: "Marx met them in his dressing gown, in the pocket of which he had put an unloaded pistol in such a way that the butt stuck out. This was enough for the noncoms to give up their argument and withdraw meekly, despite the fact that they wore sidearms." Marx then protested sharply to the town commandant, Colonel Engels (no relation to Frederick), that his soldiers behaved like "bands of robbers."

A month later the Prussian Minister of Interior wrote to Franz August Eichmann, governor of the Rhine Province, that Marx should be expelled from Cologne. Fearing trouble from radicals, Eichmann counseled delay and advised that at the first opportune moment the *Neue Rheinische Zeitung*'s firebrand editor be driven out of Prussia altogether. The chance was not long in coming. On May 10 the *Neue Rheinische Zeitung* published an article by Marx that constituted a savage indictment not only of Prussia's reigning monarch—"Herr von Hohenzollern"—but also of the whole Hohenzollern dynasty, past and present. He enumerated the historic examples of the "breaches of faith, the perfidies, the legacy huntings by which this family of corporals" had made itself great.[46] In his harsh castigation, Marx quoted the caricature from Heinrich Heine's poem *"Der Wechselbalg"* ("The Changeling; or Monster"):

A child with a big pumpkin head,
with long sideburns and gray pigtails,
with spidery-long but strong little arms,
with a gigantic gizzard but short entrails,
a monster....[47]

Government action against Marx and the *Neue Rheinische Zeitung*, which was then dying of financial malnutrition, was drastic. An order for his expulsion from Prussia, drafted on May 11, was handed to Marx by the Cologne police director, Wilhelm Arnold Geiger, five days later. Marx had just enough time to prepare the last issue of the now "meager" *Neue Rheinische Zeitung*, which came out on May 19. This final issue was printed in red ink. Marx's last article in it rang with furious defiance:

We are ruthless, we demand no consideration from you. When our turn comes, we will not gloss over our terrorism. But the royalist ter-

---

46. "The Deeds of the House of Hohenzollern," May 10, 1849. See *Karl Marx on Revolution*, pages 477–81.

47. "*Ein Kind mit grossem Kürbiskopf,/ Mit langem Schnurrbart, greisem Zopf,/ Mit spinnig langen, doch starken Ärmchen,/ Mit Riesenmage, doch kurzen Gedärmchen,/ Ein Wechselbalg....*"

rorists, the terrorists by the Grace-of-God-and-of-Right, are brutal, contemptible, and vulgar in practice, cowardly, covert, and deceitful in theory, and *dishonorable* in both.[48]

The poet Ferdinand Freiligrath contributed a more poetic farewell. The last two stanzas of his verse were:

When the last Crown breaks like glass
in battle's lightnings and flames,
when the people speak their final "Guilty,"
we will stand together again.

With the word, the sword,
On the Danube, on the Rhine,
The throne-smashing people, the rebel,
Will be a loyal companion for all time![49]

The *Neue Rheinische Zeitung* thus came to an end, with its editors and contributors exiled and scattered.

Marx, joined by Engels, traveled through southwest Germany urging revolt. They encountered a resounding lack of enthusiasm. In Bingen they were arrested by Hessian troops, taken to Frankfurt, and released. They were two young men in search of a successful revolution, which they were never to find in their lifetimes.

Early in June the intellectual twins separated. Engels, the more athletic and activist of the two, went to Kaiserslautern, the temporary capital of Baden, to join the forces of its threatened provisional government. He participated in some losing skirmishes, a military experience that was later to win him among his friends, including the Marx family, the affectionate title "the General."[50] Marx betook himself to Paris, city of chronic revolutions, home of indefatigable radicals.

It was a dismal time to be in Paris. Cholera was raging and there were long lines of hearses rushing to the cemeteries as a frightened population watched. Much of the proletariat was discontented with Guizot's conservative-bourgeois government. Marx, living on the Left

---

48. See "The Suppression of the *Neue Rheinische Zeitung* under Martial Law," page 152.

49. *"Wenn die letzte Krone wie Glas zerbricht,/ In des Kampfes Wettern und Flammen,/ Wenn das Volk sein letztes 'Schuldig!' spricht,/ Dann stehn wir wieder zusammen!/ Mit dem Wort, mit dem Schwert, an der Donau,/ am Rhein,/ Eine allzeit treue Gesellin/ Wird dem Throne zerschmetternden Volke sein/ Die Geachtete, die Rebellin!"*

50. See, for example, *Mohr und General. Erinnerungen an Marx und Engels (Moor and General. Recollections of Marx and Engels)* (Dietz Verlag, Berlin, 1970).

Bank under an alias,[51] immediately noted that the city was a "revolunary crater" and made contact with insurgent elements. Always the optimist, he informed Engels, temporary soldier in insurgent Baden, that in a few days he expected to have "several revolutionary journals at my disposal."[52]

A brief uprising in June was easily suppressed, and Marx's turn came next. In the middle of July he was handed an order of expulsion from Paris to Morbihan, in Brittany; he considered the place an "unhealthy" swamp and was sure the government order was a "masked attempt at murder." After five weeks of postponement, Marx, once more "without a sou," left France. On August 24, 1849, he went to London, at that time a gathering place for continental refugees, where he was to live in exile for the rest of his life.

His days as a fighting journalist ended when Marx was thirty-one. The articles he wrote in the decade 1852–62 as London correspondent for the *New-York Daily Tribune* and briefly the Vienna *Presse* were no longer crusading journalism, but primarily factual and expository reportage. (For his American journalism during this period, see *Karl Marx on America and the Civil War*, Volume II of The Karl Marx Library.) After that, the only more-or-less paying profession he ever had came to an end.

For the rest of his life Marx was absorbed primarily in economic research for his masterpiece, *Capital*, but he still found time occasionally to protest against press distortions, especially in the areas that concerned him most deeply, including the First International and the defense of the Paris Commune (see *Karl Marx on the First International*, Volume III of The Karl Marx Library), and all aspects of the development of European socialism.

The articles and letters in this volume, all translated by the editor, are essentially as Marx wrote them. Among the minor alterations are the elimination of italics for some words and phrases, primarily those that Marx was in the habit of underlining in nineteenth-century polemical fashion. Brief explanations and translations (Marx was multilingual and peppered his writing with Latin, French, English, and other phrases) are given in brackets. Footnotes are the editor's except for those otherwise signed.

---

51. "M. Ramboz," 45, Rue de Lille.
52. Marx to Engels, June 7, 1849.

Chronology:
Marx as a Newspaperman*

1818

MAY 5   *Birth of Karl Marx, in Trier, Rhenish Prussia.*

1841

APRIL 15   *Receives Ph.D. degree from Jena University, in absentia.*

1842

JANUARY 15–   *Writes "Remarks on the Latest Prussian Censorship*
FEBRUARY 10   *Instruction," which because of censorship difficulties in Germany is published in Switzerland, in Arnold Ruge's* Anekdota zur neuesten deutschen Philosophie und Publizistik, *February, 1843.*

MAY 5   *Begins a series of six articles on debates over freedom of the press in the Rhenish Landtag, in the Cologne* Rheinische Zeitung *(May 5, 8, 10, 12, 15, 19).*

MID OCTOBER   *Becomes editor in chief of the* Rheinische Zeitung, *at age twenty-four, and moves to Cologne from Bonn.*

NOVEMBER   *Meets Frederick Engels, soon to become his lifelong friend and collaborator, for the first time in the office of the* Rheinische Zeitung.

---

* For a complete chronology of Marx's life, see *Karl Marx on Revolution,* Volume I of The Karl Marx Library, pages xxxi–liv.

1843

JANUARY 1–16   *Publishes a series of seven articles on the suppression of the* Leipziger Allgemeine Zeitung, *in* Rheinische Zeitung *(January 1, 4, 6, 8, 10, 13, 16).*

MARCH 17   *Resigns from* Rheinische Zeitung, *which is finally suppressed by the censorship (April 1).*

LATE OCTOBER   *Moves to Paris, to become coeditor, with Arnold Ruge, of* Deutsch-Französische Jahrbücher.

1844

LATE FEBRUARY   *Publishes first double issue of* Deutsch-Französische Jahrbücher, *to which he contributes two articles,* "Critique of Hegel's Philosophy of Law" *and* "On the Jewish Question."

MARCH 26   *Suspension of* Deutsch-Französische Jahrbücher, *after break with Arnold Ruge.*

AUGUST 7, 10   *Publishes anti-Ruge article,* "The King of Prussia," *etc., in* Vorwärts, *a twice-weekly German-language publication in Paris.*

AUGUST 28   *Meets Engels for second time, in Paris, and begins permanent working relationship.*

1845

FEBRUARY 3   *Expelled from Paris, moves to Brussels, where he remains, as a writer* (The Holy Family, *1845;* The German Ideology, *completed 1846;* The Poverty of Philosophy, *1847) and communist activist, for more than three years.*

1847

JANUARY 3–
FEBRUARY,
      1848   *Writes for* Deutsche-Brüsseler-Zeitung, *a radical German-language paper in Brussels.*

1848

LATE JANUARY   *Completes, in collaboration with Engels,* Manifesto of the Communist Party.

FEBRUARY 24	Manifesto *appears for first time, in German, in London.*
MID APRIL– JUNE 1	*After revolutionary outbreaks in Germany, returns to Cologne from Brussels (April 11), works on plans to establish the daily,* Neue Rheinische Zeitung.
JUNE 1	*Publishes first issue of* Neue Rheinische Zeitung, *starting with 6,000 subscribers, with Marx as editor in chief.*
EARLY JULY	Neue Rheinische Zeitung *investigated by police for radicalism.*
JULY 20	*Publishes "The Prussian Press Bill," in* Neue Rheinische Zeitung, *attacking censorship.*
SEPTEMBER 26	Neue Rheinische Zeitung *suspended under martial law, one day after outbreak of revolution in Cologne.*
OCTOBER 5	Neue Rheinische Zeitung *resumes publication.*
NOVEMBER 14, 20, 23, 26	*Marx appears in court on charges of* lèse majesté *and incitement to rebellion.*
DECEMBER 2	*Summoned to court again.*
DECEMBER 6	*Indicted for incitement to rebellion.*
DECEMBER 20– 21	*Court trial. Decision postponed.*

1849

FEBRUARY 7–8	*Tried in Cologne court and acquitted by jury.*
MAY 16	*Receives order of expulsion from Prussia.*
MAY 19	*Publishes last issue of* Neue Rheinische Zeitung.
JUNE 3	*Arrives in Paris.*
AUGUST 24	*Leaves Paris, after being ordered out, for London, where he will live for the rest of his life.*

1850

MARCH 6	*Publishes, in collaboration with Engels, first issue of* Neue Rheinische Zeitung. Politisch-Ökonomische Revue, *printed in Hamburg in an edition of 2,500 copies, and dated January, 1850.*

LATE MARCH   *Second issue of the* Revue, *dated February, 1850.*

APRIL 17   *Third issue of the* Revue, *dated March, 1850.*

MAY 19   *Fourth issue of the* Revue, *dated March–April, 1850.*

NOVEMBER 29   *Fifth-Sixth issue—the last one—of the* Revue, *dated May–October, 1850.*

1851

AUGUST 7   *Invited by Charles Anderson Dana to write for New-York Daily Tribune.*

1852

AUGUST 21   *Publishes first article—"The Elections in England: Tories and Whigs" (translated into English by Engels)—in* Tribune, *August 21.*

OCTOBER 2–23   *Reprint of* Tribune *article in Chartist weekly, the* People's Paper *(October 2, 9, 16, 23).*

1853

FEBRUARY 18   *Publishes "Capital Punishment . . ." in* Tribune. *This is the first article Marx wrote in English, all the preceding ones having been translated by Engels.*

OCTOBER 19–   *Publishes a series of articles, "Lord Palmerston," in*
JANUARY 11,   Tribune *(October 19, November 4, 21, 1853; Janu-*
1854   *ary 11, 1854). The series, in slightly changed form, also appeared in the* People's Paper *(October 22, 29, November 5, 12, 19, December 10, 17, 24, 1853), and as a brochure in 1853 and 1854.*

1854

SEPTEMBER 9–   *Publishes a series of eight articles, "Revolutionary*
DECEMBER 2   Spain," *in New-York Daily Tribune (September 9, 25, October 20, 27, 30, November 24, December 1, 2).**

---

* For complete text of these articles see *Karl Marx on Revolution* (Volume I of this series), pp. 586–629.

1855

JANUARY 2–
OCTOBER 8
Publishes 112 articles (some in collaboration with Engels) in Neue Oder-Zeitung, *a Breslau daily; a few of the same articles also appear in* New-York Daily Tribune.

1856

APRIL
Publishes a series of four articles, "The Fall of Kars," in the People's Paper (*April 5, 12, 19, 26*).

1857

SEPTEMBER–
APRIL, 1858
Writes sixteen articles—eight in collaboration with Engels—all but one of them biographical, for New American Cyclopaedia, *published in New York City; articles appear in Vols. II (1857), III (1858), and IV (1859).*

1859

JULY 3
Becomes temporary editor of Das Volk, *a radical German-language weekly in London.*

AUGUST 20
Das Volk *ceases publication.*

1861

JANUARY–
OCTOBER 11
Because of U.S. Civil War, New-York Daily Tribune *suspends Marx's correspondenceship, printing none of his articles for the first time in about nine years.*

OCTOBER 11
Publishes "The American Question in England" in New-York Daily Tribune; *this is Marx's first article in that paper in the year 1861. For the rest of the year the* Tribune *publishes only seven more of his articles.*

OCTOBER 25
Begins writing for Die Presse, *a Vienna daily, starting with article, "The North American Civil War."*

1862

MARCH 10   *Publishes last article, "The Mexican Imbroglio," in*
                New-York Daily Tribune, *thus ending a ten-year*
                correspondenceship for that paper. In that period
                Marx contributed a total of approximately 356 arti-
                cles to the Tribune, *a number of them signed by him,*
                many of them unsigned ("From Our London Corre-
                spondent"), several in collaboration with Engels, and
                almost one-third used as anonymous "leaders," or
                editorials by the Tribune.

DECEMBER 4   *Publishes last article, "English Neutrality—The Situ-*
                ation in the Southern States," in Die Presse. *Alto-*
                gether Die Presse, *in the thirteen months that Marx*
                wrote for it, published about thirty-five of his arti-
                cles, most of them relating to the U.S. Civil War.*

                Thus the year 1862 marks the end of Marx's career
                as full-time journalist. Henceforth his writing for
                newspapers was sporadic and intermittent. Suffering
                from numerous chronic illnesses which frequently in-
                terrupt his work, Marx thenceforth devoted all the
                energies he could muster to the First International,**
                and to research on and writing Capital, *in addition to*
                occasional pieces connected with radicalism.

1883

MARCH 14   *Marx died at his home in London.*

---

* For text of these articles, see *Karl Marx on America and the Civil War*
(Volume II of this series), pp. 87–235.
** See *Karl Marx on the First International*, Volume III of this series.

THE PRESS,
THE CENSORS,
AND THE FIRST
RHEINISCHE ZEITUNG

Debates on Freedom of the
Press and Publication*

O NE FINE spring morning in Berlin, to the astonishment of Germany's whole writing and reading public, the *Preussische Staats-Zeitung*[1] published its *self-confessions*. Of course it chose a genteel, diplomatic, not precisely entertaining form of confession. It gave itself the appearance of wanting to hold up the mirror of confession to its sisters; it spoke, mystically, only of other Prussian newspapers, while actually it meant itself, as the Prussian newspaper par excellence.

This fact leaves room for sundry explanations. Caesar spoke of himself in the third person. Why should not the *Preussische Staats-Zeitung* also speak of itself in the third person? Children who speak of themselves are in the habit of saying, not "I," but "George," etc. Why shouldn't the *Preussische Staats-Zeitung* also make use of *Vossische*,[2] *Spenersche*,[3] or any other sacred name, in place of its own "I"?

And now the new Censorship Instruction has come out.[4] Our newspapers thought they would have to adopt the appearance and the conventional trappings of freedom. The *Preussische Staats-Zeitung*, too, was obliged to wake up and have some sort of liberal—or at least independent—idea.

---

* This series of six articles appeared in the *Rheinische Zeitung* May 5, 8, 10, 12, 15, 19, 1842. The Landtag, or Provincial Diet, in which the debates took place sat in Düsseldorf from May 23 to July 25, 1841.

1. The *Preussische Staats-Zeitung*, or *Staats-Zeitung* for short, a Berlin daily, was the semiofficial organ of the Prussian Government in the 1840s.

2. *Vossische Zeitung*, an independent Berlin daily.

3. *Spenersche Zeitung*, a pro-government Berlin daily.

4. See "Remarks on the Latest Prussian Censorship Instruction," page 89.

The first necessary condition of freedom, however, is self-awareness, and self-awareness is an impossibility without self-confession.

It was therefore firmly assumed that the *Preussische Staats-Zeitung* wrote self-confessions; if we remember that we see here the semiofficial press child's first awakening to self-awareness, all puzzles will resolve themselves. One will then be convinced that the *Preussische Staats-Zeitung* "utters many a great word with composure," and remain uncertain only whether one should admire the composure of the greatness or the greatness of the composure.

Hardly had the Censorship Instruction come out, hardly had the *Staats-Zeitung* recovered from this blow, when it erupted with the question: "What use has a greater freedom from censorship been to you Prussian newspapers?"

Evidently it wants to say: What use has my strict observance of the censorship been all these years? What has become of me, despite the most painstaking and all-round vigilance and tutelage? And what will become of me altogether? I have not learned to walk, and a sportive public expects *entrechats* from the hip-bone lame! So it will be with you too, my sisters! Let us confess our weaknesses to the Prussian people, but let us be diplomatic in our confession. We do not exactly tell them that we are uninteresting. We tell them that if the Prussian newspapers are uninteresting to the Prussian people, the Prussian state is uninteresting to the newspapers.

The bold question of the *Staats-Zeitung*, and the even more daring answer, are mere preludes to its awakening, dreamlike indications of the text it will convey. It awakens to consciousness, it speaks its mind. Hearken to Epimenides![5]

It is known that the first theoretical activity of reason, still wavering halfway between sensing and thinking, is *counting*. Counting is the child's first free theoretical act of reason. *Permit us to count*, the *Preussische Staats-Zeitung* calls out to its sisters. *Statistics* is the first political science! I understand the head of a man if I know how many hairs it produces.

Do unto others as you would have them do unto you. And how could we dignify ourselves, and especially myself, the *Preussische Staats-Zeitung*, better than by statistics! Not only that I appear as frequently as any French or English newspaper, but also that the statistics will show that I am less read than any other newspaper in the civilized world. Take away the officials, who have to interest themselves in me with some displeasure, discount the government offices which a semiofficial organ may not ignore, and who, I ask, reads me?

---

5. Epimenides was an ancient Cretan shepherd who, according to legend, awoke from fifty-seven years of sleep to find himself possessing the gifts of prophecy and priestcraft.

Calculate what I cost and calculate what I bring in, and you will admit that it is not lucrative to express great ideas with composure. Do you see how striking statistics is, how counting makes superfluous any more far-ranging intellectual operations! Hence, do count! Tables of figures instruct the public without stirring up any emotions.

And the *Staats-Zeitung* with its statistical importance not only puts itself beside the Chinese and the universal statistician Pythagoras, but it also shows that it has been affected by the great contemporary natural philosopher[6] who once wanted to present the differences among animals, etc., in rows of figures.

Thus even when it appears to be quite concrete, the *Preussische Staats-Zeitung* is not without modern philosophical principles.

The *Staats-Zeitung* is many-sided. It does not content itself with holding to figures of *time* quantity. It pushes its recognition of the quantitative principle further, speaking also of the right of *geometrical* quantity. Space is the first thing whose size impresses a child. It is the first magnitude of the universe that the child experiences. Hence it considers a grown man to be a great man, and the childish *Staats-Zeitung* tells us that *thick* volumes are disproportionately better than *thin* ones, or even than single papers, *newspapers*, that issue only a single sheet daily.

You Germans can now, for a change, speak out at length! Write really prolix books about political institutions, really thorough books that nobody reads except the author and the reviewer—but keep in mind that your newspapers are not books. Keep in mind how many sheets go into a thorough work in three volumes! Hence do not seek the spirit of the day in the newspapers, which want to supply you with statistical tables, but seek it in books, whose spatial magnitude already guarantees their thoroughness.

Keep in mind, you good children, that "learned" things are what is involved here; go to the school of thick books and you will at once take a fancy to us newspapers because of our airy format and our gentlemanly nonchalance, which are truly refreshing after the heavy volumes.

To be sure! To be sure! Our time does not possess that real sense for greatness that we so admire in the Middle Ages. Look at the paltry, pietistic little tracts, look at our philosophical systems in small octavos, and then turn your gaze to the twenty gigantic folios of Duns Scotus. You don't have to read the books; the adventurous look of them touches your heart, strikes your senses like some Gothic building. These naturally gigantic works physically affect the mind, which feels itself oppressed by their mass, and the sense of oppression is the be-

---

6. Lorenz Oken, a German naturalist.

ginning of awe. You do not possess the books, they possess you. To them you are an accident, and so also, in the opinion of the *Preussische Staats-Zeitung*, should the people be to their political literature.

So the *Staats-Zeitung* is not without historical, purely medieval principles, even though it expresses itself modernly.

If, however, the theoretical thinking of the child is quantitative, its judgment, as well as its practical thinking, is chiefly practical-sensate. The sensate condition is the first bond that ties it to the world. The *practical senses*, preferably nose and mouth, are the first organs with which it *judges* the world. The childish *Preussische Staats-Zeitung*, therefore, judges the worth of newspapers, that is, its own worth, with the *nose*. Just as one Greek thinker[7] considered arid souls the best, so the *Staats-Zeitung* considers the "good-smelling" newspapers the "good" newspapers. It cannot praise enough the "literary perfume" of the *Allgemeine Augsburger*[8] and the *Journal des Débats*.[9] Praiseworthy, rare naïveté! Great, all-great Pompey!

After the *Staats-Zeitung* has thus, through a few expressions deserving of thanks, afforded us deep views into the state of its soul, it ends by summarizing its political opinion in one great reflection whose point is the major discovery:

"That in Prussia the public administration and the whole organism of the state are separated from the political spirit, hence they cannot have any *political* interest either for the newspaper or for the people."

Thus, according to this view of the *Preussische Staats-Zeitung*, the public administration in Prussia does not have the political spirit, or the political spirit does not have the public administration. Indelicate for the *Staats-Zeitung* to assert what its severest opponent could not improve upon, that the actual political life is without political spirit, and that the political spirit does not exist in the actual state!

But we must not let ourselves forget the childish-sensate standpoint of the *Preussische Staats-Zeitung*. It tells us that in discussing railways one must think only of rails and ways; in discussing trade agreements, only of sugar and coffee; in discussing leather factories, only of leather. Of course, the child stops with the sensate perception; it sees only the particular. The invisible nerve threads which connect the particular with the general—which everywhere, as also in the state, animate the material parts into an intellectual whole—these do not exist for the child. The child believes the sun revolves around the earth; the general revolves around the particular. The child, therefore, does not believe in the *spirit* [*Geist*] but in *ghosts* [*Gespenster*].

---

7. Heraclitus, whom Marx discussed in his doctoral dissertation.
8. *Allgemeine Zeitung*, a daily published in Augsburg from 1810 to 1882.
9. A Paris daily founded in 1789.

Thus the *Preussische Staats-Zeitung* holds the political spirit to be a French ghost; and it believes it can exorcise the ghost by incantations about leather, sugar, bayonets, and figures.

Still, it will occur to our readers that we set out to discuss the "proceedings of the Landtag," and instead they have been presented with the "innocent angel," the senile press child—the *Preussische Staats-Zeitung*—and with a repetition of the precocious cradle song with which it and its sisters seek again and again to lull themselves into salutary winter sleep.

But doesn't Schiller say:

What cannot be seen by the reason of an intelligent man
The brain storm of a childish mind easily can.[10]

The *Preussische Staats-Zeitung* has reminded us in a brain storm that we in Prussia have Landtags as good as those in England, and that the daily press *may* discuss their proceedings, if it *can;* for the *Staats-Zeitung*, in a great classical self-awareness, is of the opinion that what the Prussian newspapers lack is not the *may*, but the *can*. The latter we gladly accept from it as a privilege, in that we immediately, without further explication of its potency, take the liberty of putting its brain storm into reality.

The publication of the proceedings of the Landtag will become a fact only if they are treated as "public acts," that is, subjects for the press. The latest Rhineland Landtag affects us closely.

We begin with its "debates over freedom of the press" and must remark beforehand that, while our own concrete view of this question occasionally appears as that of a participant, in subsequent articles we will report and discuss the course of the proceedings more as historical observers.

The very nature of the proceedings conditions this difference in presentation. For in all other debates in the Landtag we find that the various opinions are on the same level. In the press question, on the other hand, the opponents of a free press have an advantage. Apart from the slogans and commonplaces in the air, we find among these opponents a *pathological emotion*, a passionate prejudice, which gives them a *real*, not an imaginary, position toward the press, while in general its defenders in the Landtag have no real relationship to their protégé. They have never come to know the freedom of the press as a *necessity*. For them it is a matter of the head, in which the heart plays no role. For them it is an "exotic" plant which they relate to merely as "amateurs." Hence it happens that the outstandingly "good" principles of the opponents are met with vague, much too generalized

---

10. From Schiller's *"Die Worte des Glaubens"*: *"Und was kein Verstand der Verständigen sieht,/ Das übet in Einfall ein kindlich Gemüt."*

arguments, and the stupidest idea considers itself important so long as its foundation is not destroyed.

Goethe once said that the painter portrays successfully only those female beauties whose types he has, at least at some time or other, loved as living individuals.[11] Press freedom too is a beauty—even if not precisely a female one—which one must have loved in order to be able to defend it. What I truly love—this is a Being whose existence I feel as a necessity, as one of which I have a need, without which my own Being cannot have a fulfilled, satisfied, or complete existence. The defenders of the freedom of the press seem to be fulfilled without the existence of freedom of the press.

The "liberal opposition" reveals the high-water mark of a political assembly, just as the opposition in general reveals the high-water mark of a society. At a time when it is philosophical audacity to doubt the reality of ghosts, when it is paradoxical to come out against witchcraft trials, such a time is the legitimate time of ghosts and witchcraft trials. A land like ancient Athens, which treated sycophants, parasites, as public buffoons, fawners, they being exceptions to the common sense of the people, is a land of independence and self-reliance. A people which, like all peoples of the best periods, has the right to think and to speak the truth, and yet defends court jesters, can only be a people of dependence and un-selfness. A popular assembly in which the opposition assures us that freedom of the will belongs to the essence of man is, to say the least, not a popular assembly of freedom of the will. The exception proves the rule. The liberal opposition demonstrates how far the liberal position, and freedom, have become concretized.

So having remarked that in the Landtag defenders of freedom of the press are by no means on top of their subject, we can say that this is even more true of the Landtag in general.

Nevertheless, we take up this point of the proceedings, not only out of a special interest in freedom of the press, but also out of a general interest in the Landtag. For we find the specific spirit of the Estates nowhere more clearly and fully expressed than in the debates on the press. By preference, in the opposition to freedom of the press, as in the opposition to *general freedom* of the mind in any given sphere, the individual interests of the particular Estates, the natural one-sidedness of their character, appear most blunt and ruthless, and show their teeth simultaneously.

The debates bring us a polemic of the princely Estates against a free press, a polemic of the knightly Estates, a polemic of the city

---

11. Goethe, *Verschiedenes über Kunst*, Chapter 2: "That which the artist has not loved, does not love, he should not portray, cannot portray."

Estates, so that it is not the *individual* who polemicizes, but the Estates. What other mirror, therefore, could reflect the inner character of the Landtag more faithfully than the debates on the press?

We begin with the opponents of a free press, and particularly with one moderate speaker from the princely Estates. We do not go into the substance of the first part of his speech, "Press freedom and censorship are both evils," etc., because this theme was treated more thoroughly by another speaker; but we cannot forgo the peculiar argumentation of this speaker.

"Censorship" is "a lesser evil than the mischief of the press." "This conviction was established little by little in our Germany" (one asks oneself which part of Germany that is), "so that laws about it were promulgated by the Federation, and accepted by Prussia."[12]

The Landtag debated freeing the press from its bonds. The bonds themselves, the speaker exclaims, the chains the press suffers under, prove that they are not designed for freedom of movement. The press's fettered existence shows its essence. The laws against freedom of the press refute freedom of the press.

This is a diplomatic argument against all reforms, and most decisively expresses the classical theory of a certain school.[13] Every restriction on freedom is a factual, irrefutable proof that the rulers have been convinced that freedom must be restricted, and this conviction then serves as a norm for subsequent convictions.

It was once laid down that the earth does not revolve around the sun. Was Galileo refuted?

Thus also in "our Germany" a conviction shared by individual princes was once legally established that serfdom was a characteristic of certain human bodies; that truth could be most clearly conveyed by surgical operations, that is, torture; that the flames of hell were already demonstrated to the heretic by the flames of this earth.

Was not lawful serfdom a factual proof against the rational vagary that the human body was not an object of negotiation and possession? Did not natural torture refute the hollow theory that truth was not drawn from bloodletting, that the stretching of the spine on the martyr's rack does not produce frankness, that convulsions are not a confession?

Thus, the speaker said, the fact of censorship refutes freedom of the press—which is factually correct, a truth of such actuality that topography could measure its size, in that it ceases to be factual and true at certain junctures.

"Neither in speech nor in writing," we are told further, "neither

---

12. This and other quotations are from the *Sitzungs-Protokolle des sechsten Rheinischen Provinzial-Landtags* (Coblenz, 1841).

13. The Historical School of Law, which came into being in Germany at the end of the eighteenth century.

in our Rhineland province nor in all of Germany, does the true and more noble intellectual development appear to be fettered."

The noble, melting-sweet voice of truth in our press is a gift of the censorship.

We now turn the previous argument of the speaker against himself; we give him, instead of a rational cause, a decree. In the latest Prussian Censorship Instruction it is officially announced that the press has hitherto been subject to too many restrictions, and that it has yet to attain a true national content. The speaker sees that convictions in "our Germany" are fickle.

But what illogical paradox, to consider censorship responsible for our own better press!

The greatest orator of the French Revolution, whose *voix toujours tonnante* [ever thundering voice] is still reverberating in our time, the lion whom one must have heard roar to cry out to him, as did the people, "Well roared, Lion!"[14]—Mirabeau—trained himself in prison. Are prisons therefore the colleges of oratory?

It is a truly lordly prejudice that because the German mind has become a wholesale merchant despite all intellectual customs houses, the closing of the customs houses and the cordons have made it a wholesale merchant. Germany's intellectual development took place, not *because of*, but *despite*, censorship. If the press is stunted and made miserable within censorship, this is brought out as an argument against a free press, although it shows only an unfree press. If, despite the censorship, the press preserves its inherent character, this is credited to the censorship, even though the press speaks only for the spirit and not the fetters.

For the rest, the "true, and more noble development" is due to other circumstances.

At the time of the strict observance of censorship, from 1819 to 1830 (later on, censorship was itself censored by the conditions of the time and some unusual convictions that developed in a large part of Germany, if not in "our Germany"), our literature went through its *"Evening Paper period,"* which one can call true and noble and intellectual and rich in development with the same justification as that of the editor of the *Evening Paper*, a born "Winkler,"[15] being humorously called "Hell,"[16] although we cannot glorify him with even the luminosity of a swamp at midnight. This *"Krähwinkler"*[17] of the

---

14. From Shakespeare's *A Midsummer Night's Dream*, Act V, Scene 1.
15. Karl Gottlieb Theodor Winkler (pseudonym, Theodor Hell), a journalist. Marx uses the name as a pun, for *Winkler* means a pettifogger or shady dealer.
16. The German word *hell* means "clear," "bright," "light," or "luminous."
17. A double pun: crow corner—hick town.

business establishment "Hell" is the prototype of the literature of that period, and that Lenten time will convince the next generation that if a few saints could endure forty days without nourishment, the rest of Germany, although not at all saintly, learned to live for twenty years without any intellectual consumption or production. The press became *vile*, and the only thing one is not sure about is whether the deficiency of reason surpassed the deficiency of character, whether the deficiency of form surpassed the deficiency of content, or vice versa. For Germany, criticism [*Kritik*] would achieve its highest point if it could prove that that period never existed. Philosophy, the only field of literature in which a living spirit still pulsed, ceased to speak German, because the German language had ceased to be the language of thought. The mind spoke in incomprehensible, mysterious words, because comprehensible words were no longer permitted to be understandable.

Now as regards an example of Rhineland literature—and, of course, any example is of some concern to the Rhenish Diet—one could wander through all the five government districts with Diogenes' lantern and never encounter "that man." We do not consider this to be a deficiency of the Rhine Province, but rather a proof of its practical-political sense. The Rhine Province can engender a "free press," but it lacks the adroitness and illusions to create an "unfree" one.

The recently ended literary period, which we can designate as the "literary period of the strict censorship," is thus the evident, the historic, proof that censorship has, indeed, homogenized the development of the German mind in a disastrous, irresponsible way, so that it is not, as the speaker thinks, destined to become *magister bonarum artium* [teacher of the fine arts]. Or does one understand the words "noble, and true press" to mean a press that wears its chains decorously?

When the speaker permits himself to "recall a well-known adage about the small finger and the whole hand," we take the counterpermission to ask whether it is not most fitting for the dignity of a government to give its people not only a *single* hand, but both hands?

Our speaker, as we have seen, has dismissed the question of the relationship between censorship and intellectual development in a casually genteel, diplomatically sober manner. Even more decisively does he represent the negative side of his position in his attack on the historic formation of freedom of the press.

Regarding the existence of freedom of the press in other countries: "England cannot provide the standard, because there historically, for hundreds of years, relationships have developed that are peculiar to England's situation, and they cannot be brought forth in any other country by the application of theories." "In Holland, freedom of the press could not protect it from oppressive national debt, and it contributed largely to the introduction of a revolution which had as its consequence the loss of half of that country."

We skip France, to which we will return later.

"In Switzerland, finally, is one to find there an Eldorado bestowed on it by the freedom of the press? Does one not remember with disgust the stories in their newspapers about raw party squabbles, in which the names of the parties, properly reflecting their scant human dignity, are separately identified, like beastly bodies, as men of horn and claw, and with their downright slanderous speeches make themselves despised by their neighbors!"

The English press does not represent freedom of the press at all, because it rests on *historical foundations*. The press in England has merit *only* because it is historical, not as a press at all, for it should have established itself *without* historical foundations. History has the merit, not the press. As if the press did not belong to history, as if the English press did not have to fight hard, and often barbaric, battles under Henry VIII, Mary the Catholic, Elizabeth, and James, in order to wrest for the English people its historical foundations!

And does it not, on the contrary, speak for freedom of the press, when the English press, enjoying the greatest liberty, operates on historic foundations without destructiveness? Still, the speaker is not consistent.

The English press does not bear witness for the press in general *because* it is English. The Dutch press speaks against the press in general, *even though* it is only Dutch. In the former case all the advantages of the press are vindicated on the basis of its historical foundations; in the latter, the lack of historical foundations is charged to the press. In the one case, the press is not credited with its share in the historical consummation; in the other, history is not to have its share in the deficiency of the press. Just as the press in England is entangled with her history and peculiar position, so it is in Holland and Switzerland.

Should the historical foundations be reflected, raised, or developed by the press? The speaker reproaches it with all of this.

He censures the Dutch press because it is historical. It should have prevented history, it should have preserved Holland from oppressive national debt. What an unhistorical demand! The Dutch press could not prevent the age of Louis XIV; the Dutch press could not prevent the English Navy under Cromwell from rising to top rank in Europe; it could not exert any magic in any ocean to save Holland from the painful role of becoming the arena of the Continent's belligerent powers; it could not, no more than all the censors in Germany together could annul Napoleon's bids for power.

But has a free press ever increased a national debt? When under the Orléans Regency all of France lost herself in Law's financial frenzy, who opposed that fantastic period of storm and stress except a few satirists, who, indeed, drew not bank tickets but Bastille tickets.

The demand that the press should protect a country from national debt—which can be carried further, so as to make it pay the debts of individuals too—reminds one of that littérateur who had a grudge against his doctor because the latter had cured two of his bodily illnesses but not the typographical errors in his writings. Freedom of the press promises as little as the doctor to make a person or a people perfect. The press itself is not perfect. It is trivial to slander the good because it is a specific good and not a universal good at the same time, that it is *this* and *no other* good. Indeed, if the press were everything in everything, it would make all other functions of a people, and the people itself, superfluous.

The speaker reproaches the Dutch press with the Belgian Revolution.

No man with any historical education at all would deny that the separation of Belgium and Holland was incomparably more historical than their union.

The press in Holland brought about the Belgian Revolution. Which press? The reform or the reactionary one? It is a question that we can also raise in France, and when the speaker censures the clerical Belgian press, which was at the same time democratic, he also censures the clerical press in France, which was at the same time absolutist. Both contributed to the overthrow of their governments. In France it was not freedom of the press, but censorship, that did the revolutionizing.

But apart from that, the Belgian Revolution *appeared* at first as an intellectual revolution, a revolution of the press. Otherwise, the assertion that the press made the Belgian Revolution makes no sense. Is that something to be censured? Should a revolution be concretized immediately? Beat instead of speak? A government can concretize an intellectual revolution; a material revolution must first intellectualize a government.

The Belgian Revolution is a product of the Belgian mind. Hence the press, the freest form in which mind evidences itself nowadays, had its share in the Belgian Revolution. The Belgian press would not have been a Belgian press if it had kept at a distance from the Revolution, but likewise the Belgian Revolution would not have been Belgian if it had not been at the same time a revolution of the press. The revolution of a people is *total*, that is, each sphere rebels in its own way; so why not also the press as press?

The speaker censures the Belgian press; not the press, he censures Belgium. And here we find the jumping-off point for his historical view of freedom of the press. The national character of a free press—

and it is well known that an artist does not paint great historic tableaux with watercolors—the historical individuality of a free press, which makes it the press peculiar to its own national spirit—is repugnant to the speaker from the princely Estates; rather, he demands that the newspapers of the various nations be the press of *his* views, the press of the *haute volée* [high society], and that they revolve around single individuals instead of spiritual worldly entities, nations. This demand appears undisguised in the judgment on the Swiss press.

As an introduction we allow ourselves one question. Why didn't the speaker consider the fact that the Swiss press of the Voltairean Enlightenment appeared in the person of Albrecht von Haller? Why didn't he remember that if Switzerland is not precisely an Eldorado, yet in the person of a Herr von Haller it produced a prophet who, in his *Restoration of Political Science*, provided the foundation of the "noble, and true" press of the *Berlin Political Weekly?*[18] By their fruits ye shall know them. And what soil on earth outside of Switzerland can produce fruit of this juicy legitimacy?

The speaker blames the Swiss press for having adopted the "beastly" party names of the "horn-and-claw men"; in brief, for speaking Swiss to the Swiss, who live with oxen and cows in a certain patriarchal harmony. *The press of that country is the press of that country.* There is nothing to be said about this. At the same time, however, a free press reaches beyond the limitation of a country's particularism, as is likewise proven by the Swiss press.

In regard to the "beastly" party names we remark that religion itself dignifies the "beastly" as symbol of the spiritual. Our speaker will in any case reject the Indian press, which in religious enthusiasm celebrates the cow Sabala and the ape Hanuman. He will reproach the Indian press for the Indian religion, as he reproached the Swiss press for the Swiss character. But there is one press which he will hardly subject to censure; we mean the *holy press*, the Bible; and doesn't the latter divide all mankind into two great parties, the *goats* and the *sheep?* Does not God himself characterize his own relationship to the houses of Judah and Israel in the following way: I am a moth to the house of Judah and a mite to the house of Israel? Or, what is closer to us seculars, isn't there a princely literature which transforms all of anthropology into zoology—we mean the heraldic literature? That contains more curiosities than the horn-and-claw men.

What, then, did the speaker criticize in freedom of the press? *That the deficiencies of a people are at the same time the deficiencies of its press;* that it is the most ruthless expression, the manifest aspect of the historic spirit of a people. Did he prove that the spirit of the

18. *Berliner Politisches Wochenblatt,* a Berlin weekly published from 1831 to 1841.

German people is excluded from this great natural privilege? He proved that every people expresses *its* spirit in *its* press. Shouldn't that which, according to the speaker's own assurance, is found among the beast-attached Swiss be proper for the philosophically trained spirit of the Germans?

Finally, does the speaker mean that the national deficiencies of a free press are not likewise the national deficiencies of the censors? Are the censors exempt from the historic totality, untouched by the spirit of their time? Alas, this might be the case, but what sane man would not excuse the sins of the nation and the era in the press, rather than the sins against the nation and the era in the censorship?

We remarked at the outset that it was the special status of the various speakers that polemicized against freedom of the press. The speaker from the princely Estates first formulated diplomatic reasons. He proved the impropriety of freedom of the press out of *princely convictions*, which were clearly enough expressed in censorship laws. He thought that the more noble, true development of the German mind was created by restraints imposed from *above*. Finally, he polemicized *against all peoples* and with aristocratic reserve rejected freedom of the press as the indelicate, indiscreet, self-centered speech of a nation.

The speaker from the knightly Estates, to whom we come now, did not polemicize against peoples but against the people. In freedom of the press he contested *human freedom*; in the law of the press, *the law*. Before he went into the question of press freedom itself he took up the question of the unabridged and daily publication of the Landtag debates. We follow him step by step.

"The first of the proposals for publication of our deliberations suffices." "It is in the hands of the Landtag to make wise use of the granted permission."

Precisely this is the *punctum quaestionis* [point in question]. The province believes that it controls the Landtag only when the publication of its debates is no longer left to the caprice of its wisdom, but has become a legal requirement. We would have to designate the new concession as a new retrogression if it were so interpreted as to leave publication to the caprice of the Landtag.

Privileges of the Estates are not the law of the province. Rather, the laws of the province cease precisely where they become the privileges of the Estates. Thus the Estates of the Middle Ages absorbed into themselves all the rights of the country and turned them into special prerogatives against the country.

The citizen does not want to recognize law as a privilege. Can he consider it a law when new privileges are added to old privileges?

The rights of the Landtag are in this sense no longer rights of the province, but *rights against the province*, and the Landtag itself would be the province's most conspicuous injustice if there were any mystical assertion that it was the province's foremost right.

How far the speaker from the knightly Estates has fallen into this medieval conception, how ruthlessly he has fought for the privileges of the Estates against the rights of the country, the course of his speech will show.

"The extension of this permission" (the publication of the debates) "can proceed only from inner conviction, not from external influences."

A surprising turn! The influence of the province on *its* Landtag is designated as external, being in contrast to the sensitive inwardness of the Estates, whose highly irritable nature calls out to the province: "*Noli me tangere!*" ["Touch me not!"] This elegiac flourish of the "inner conviction" as against the raw, external, unjustified north wind of "public conviction" is the more remarkable since the proposal was designed to convert the inner conviction of the Estates into an external one. Indeed, here too we find illogicality. Where it appears to the speaker the more suitable, the area of ecclesiastical controversies, he challenges the province.

"We," the speaker continues, "will permit it" (the publication) "where we consider it useful, and restrict it where its extension would be considered by us useless or even quite harmful."

We will do what *we* want. *Sic volo, sic iubeo, stat pro ratione voluntas.* [This I wish, this I command; in place of reason, the will suffices.] This is the language of absolute despotism, which, indeed, in the mouth of a modern Estates gentleman has a pathetic aftertaste.

Who are "we"? The Estates. The publication of the debates is for the province and not for the Estates, but the speaker knows better. The publication of the proceedings is also a *privilege* of the Estates, which have the right, if they find it proper to do so, to endow their wisdom with the many-voiced echo of bad journalism.

The speaker knows only the province of the Estates, not the Estates of the province. The Estates have a province where the privilege of their activities extends, but the province has no Estates through which it could become active itself. To be sure, the province has the right, under prescribed conditions, to create those gods, but soon after the creation it must, like the servitors of fetishism, forget that the gods are its own handiwork.

In this connection it is not to be ignored that a monarchy without a Landtag is worth no more than a monarchy with a Landtag, for if the Landtag does not represent the provincial will, then we place more confidence in the public intelligence of the government than in the private intelligence of landowners.

We have here the peculiar spectacle, possibly rooted in the heart of the Landtag, that the province has to fight, not through but with, its representatives. According to the speaker, the Landtag does not consider the general rights of the province its exclusive privilege—for in that case the daily unabridged publication of deliberations would be a new right of the Landtag, because it is a right of the country—but, rather, the country should consider the privileges of the Estates as its exclusive right. Why not also the privileges of any class of officials whatever, or of the nobility, or the priests!

Yes, our speaker states frankly that the privileges of the Estates decline in proportion as the rights of the province increase.

"Desirable as it appears to him that in this assembly freedom of discussion take place and an anxious weighing of words be avoided, it appears to him equally necessary that, in order to maintain this freedom of the word and this candor of speech, our words should in time be judged only by those for whom they are intended."

The speaker concludes that, precisely because freedom of discussion is desirable in our assembly—and what liberties would not be desirable for us?—precisely because of that, freedom of discussion is not desirable in the province. Because it is desirable that we speak without intimidation, it is even more desirable to keep the province in the imprisonment of secrecy. *Our* words are not *intended* for the province.

One must acknowledge the tact with which the speaker showed that, by the unabridged publication of its debates, the Landtag would be turned from a privilege of the Estates to a right of the province; that he, having become the direct object of the public spirit, had to decide to be a realization of the public spirit; and that, placed in the light of general consciousness, he had to relinquish his particular Being in favor of the general.

But when the knightly speaker mistook personal privileges and individual freedoms that are opposed to the people and the government for general rights, and thereby incontestably expressed the exclusive spirit of his Estates, his interpretation turned the spirit of the province upside-down, even though he had turned its general demands into personal desires.

Thus the speaker seems to assume the curiosity of the province about "our words" (the personalities of the Estates) to be personal avidity.

We assure him that the province is in no way curious about the "words" of the Estates or of individual persons, and only such words can rightly be called "their" words. Rather, the province demands that the words of the Estates be transformed into a publicly under-standable voice of the country.

The question is whether the province is to have a *consciousness about its representation*, or not! Should a new secrecy of representation be added to the secrecy of government? Even in the government the people are represented. Their new representation by the Estates is entirely pointless precisely because of the Estates' specific character—in that they act, not for the province but for themselves; in that they represent nothing but themselves. A representation removed from the consciousness of its electorate is no representation. What I don't know doesn't hurt me. It is a senseless contradiction that the function of the state, which by preference represents the autonomy of the individual provinces and even their formal cooperation, is deprived of cognizance—a senseless contradiction that my personal action is to be the unknown act of another.

But a publication of the Landtag deliberations that depends on the caprice of the Estates is worse than none, because when the Landtag gives me, not what it is, but what it wants to appear to me to be, I take it for what it makes itself out to be, as merely a semblance, and it is bad when a semblance has lawful existence.

Yes, even the daily unabridged publication in print—can one call it unabridged and *public?* Is it not an abridgment when one substitutes writing for speech, plans for pensions, paper action for real action? Or does publication consist only of referring the *real* matter to the public and not, rather, of referring it to the *real public*—that is, not the imaginary reading public, but the living, actual public?

Nothing is more contradictory than that the highest public activity of the province is secret, that while the doors of the courts of the province are open to private proceedings, its own proceedings must stop at the door.

Hence an unabridged publication of the Landtag deliberations, in its real, logical sense, cannot be anything but the *full disclosure of the Landtag.*

Our speaker, on the contrary, goes on to see the Landtag as a sort of coffeehouse: "With most of us, a good personal understanding is based on long-standing acquaintanceship in which we find ourselves despite differences of opinion, a relationship which is inherited by the newcomers.

"Precisely because of this we are mostly able to honor the value of our word, and this happens the more freely, the fewer the *external* influences allowed to work—influences that may be useful only if they come up in the form of well-meaning advice, but not in the form of pronounced judgments, of praise or of blame, that seek to have an effect on our personalities through publicity."

The gentleman speaker speaks from the heart.

We are so cozy together, we talk so unrestrainedly, we weigh the *value* of our respective words so precisely—should we then let the judgment of the province alter this, our so patriarchal, so genteel, so comfortable position, which would perhaps put less value on our words?

Thank God for this. The Landtag cannot bear daylight. At night, in private life, we feel cozy. When the whole province has the confidence to entrust its right to single individuals, it goes without saying that these single individuals are so condescending as to accept the trust of the province; but it would be real extravagance to demand that they should requite like with like and trustingly submit themselves, their achievements and their personalities, to the judgment of the province, which has first given them a judgment of consequence. At any rate, it is more important that the personality of the Estates should not be endangered by the province than that the interest of the province should be endangered by the personality of the Estates.

We want to be reasonable, and also very gracious. To be sure, we—and we are a species of government—allow no pronouncing of judgment, no commendation, no censure; we allow the public no influence on our *persona sacrosancta* [sacrosanct person], but we permit well-meaning advice, not in the abstract sense that it is well-meaning for the country, but in the full-toned sense that it has a passionate tenderness for the person of the Estates, a special opinion of its superiority.

One could think, to be sure, that if the public is detrimental to our good understanding, then our good understanding of the public must be detrimental to it. But this sophistry forgets that the Landtag is the Diet of the Estates and not the Diet of the province. And who could manage to resist the most striking of all arguments? If, constitutionally, the province appoints the Estates to represent its universal intelligence, it has by that very act entirely handed over its own judgment and reason, which are now exclusively incorporated in the chosen deputies. It is said that great discoverers are killed, or, what is no legend, are buried alive in fortresses, as soon as they communicate their discovery to the despot. So also the political reason of the province always falls on its own sword the moment it has made the great discovery, so that the Estates, of course, rise again, Phoenix-like, in the following elections.

After these cheerfully importunate descriptions of the danger that threatens the personalities of the Estates from outside—that is, from the province—by the publication of the Landtag's deliberations, the speaker concludes his diatribe with the major thought which we have pursued up to now:

"Parliamentary freedom"—a very high-sounding phrase—"finds itself in its first period of development. It must, under protection and nursing, acquire the inner strength and autonomy that are absolutely necessary before it can be exposed, without disadvantage, to outer storms."

Here again the old unfortunate antithesis between the Landtag as the *inner* and the province as the *outer*.

Of course, we have long been of the opinion that parliamentary freedom stands at the beginning of its beginning, and the present speech has itself convinced us anew that the *primitiae studiorum* in the *politicis* [original study of politics] is far from complete. In no way do we mean by this—and the present speech again confirms our opinion—that the Landtag should be given a longer term to ossify itself *against* the province. The speaker perhaps understands by parliamentary freedom the freedom of the old French *parlements*. According to his own admission, there is among the Estates a long-standing acquaintanceship whose spirit extends, like an epidemic inheritance, to the *homines novi* [new men]—but still no time for publicity? The twelfth Landtag can give the same answer as the sixth, but with the decisive change that it is much too independent to let the genteel privilege of secret deliberations be torn from it.

Indeed, the development of parliamentary freedom in the old French sense—the independence vis-à-vis public opinion, the stagnation caused by the caste spirit—evolved most completely in isolation, but one cannot give warning too soon against this development. A genuine political assembly thrives only under the great protection of the public mind, just as life thrives under the protection of open air. Only "exotic" plants, plants that are transplanted into a foreign climate, require the protection and nursing of the hothouse. Does the speaker consider the Landtag an "exotic" plant in the free and clear atmosphere of the Rhine Province?

As our speaker from the knightly Estates—with almost comical earnestness, and almost melancholy dignity, and almost religious pathos—developed the postulate of the high wisdom of the Estates as they evolved from medieval freedom and independence, the uninformed person is surprised to see how the question of freedom of the press has sunk from the high wisdom of the Landtag to the average unwisdom of the human species; from the independence and freedom of the privileged Estates as recommended by authority to the principle of the unfreedom and dependence of human nature. We are not surprised to encounter one of the Christian-knightly, modern-feudal figures—in short, the romantic principle personified—that are so numerous nowadays.

These gentlemen, because they do not wish to consider freedom as a natural gift of the universal sunlight of reason, but as a super-natural gift of a particularly favorable constellation of the stars—viewing freedom, as they do, only as an individual characteristic of certain persons and Estates—are for the sake of consistency obliged to subsume universal reason and universal freedom under the evil sentiments and phantoms of "logically ordered systems." To save the special freedom of privilege, they proscribe the universal freedom of human nature. But because the bad spawn of the nineteenth century that infected the consciousness of these modern knights was incomprehensible to them—since it made no sense to assume that internal, essential, universal characteristics could be tied up with external, accidental, particular oddities in certain human individuals (that is, potentially common to all individuals)—they necessarily took refuge in the miraculous and the mystical. Furthermore, because the real position of these gentlemen in the modern state in no way corresponds to the conception that they have of their position—because they live in a world that lies beyond reality, because imagination is their head and their heart, because they are dissatisfied with practice—they necessarily seize upon theory, but only the theory of the Beyond, religion, which, however, receives at their hands a polemical bitterness fertilized by political tendencies, more or less consciously becoming a wish for the mantle of saintliness which is very worldly and at the same time very fantastic.

Thus we will find that our speaker contraposes his practical demands to an imaginary, mystical-religious theory; his real theories to a smart-aleck, pragmatically sly experience drawn from the most superficial practice; human reason to superhuman saintlinesses; and the real saintliness of ideas to the caprice and unbelief of inferior points of view. The more genteel, more nonchalant, and hence more sober language of the speaker from the princely Estates now becomes pathetic twistedness and fantastically extravagant unctuousness, a pathos which privilege used to come nearer to avoiding.... [19]

We have given the quotation at length in order not to weaken its pathetic impression on the reader.

The speaker placed himself *à la hauteur des principes* [at the height of principles]. To combat freedom of the press, one must defend the permanent immaturity of the human species. It is an altogether tautological assertion that the unfreedom of man's Being contradicts the freedom of his Being. Malicious skeptics might be so foolhardy as to disbelieve what the speaker says.

If the immaturity of the human species is the mystical argument against freedom of the press, then, at any rate, censorship is a highly understandable measure against the immaturity of the human species.

---

19. A long quotation from the speaker is omitted here.

What develops is imperfect. Development only ends with death. Hence the real conclusion from this would be to kill man to save him from this state of imperfection. So at least the speaker concludes, in order to kill freedom of the press. For him, true education consists in keeping man swaddled in the cradle throughout his life, because as soon as he begins learning to walk he falls down, and he learns to walk only by falling down. But if we all remain swaddled children, who will swaddle us? If we all lie in the cradle, who will rock it? If we are all jailed, who will be the keeper?

Man is by nature imperfect, as an individual and in the mass. *De principiis non est disputandum.* [There is no arguing over principles.] Granted! What follows from this? That the reasoning of our speaker is imperfect, governments are imperfect, the Landtags are imperfect, freedom of the press is imperfect, every sphere of human activity is imperfect. If, therefore, one of these spheres should not exist because of its imperfection, then nobody has the right to exist, and man altogether has no right to exist.

Granting the principle of human imperfection, then we know from the first that all human institutions are imperfect; then there is nothing more to be said, nothing for and nothing against, for imperfection is not their specific character, not a mark of differentiation.

Why should only a free press be perfect amid all these other imperfections? Why does an imperfect Estates system demand a perfect press?

If everything human is by nature imperfect, should we therefore throw everything together pell-mell, admire everything alike, good and bad, truth and lie? The logical consequence would be that in looking at a painting I would see only blurs but no color, confusing crisscross lines but no drawing; in viewing the world I would see human relations only in their most external aspects, being incapable of judging the value of things. For how can I make a judgment from a viewpoint that sees the whole world as undifferentiated flatness where all existence is imperfect? This viewpoint is itself the most imperfect of all the imperfections that surround it. We must therefore measure the essence of inner ideas by the existence of things themselves, and not let ourselves be misled by instances of one-sided and trivial experience, since as a consequence of the latter all experience disappears, all judgment is suspended, all cows are black.

From the standpoint of the Idea, it is self-evident that freedom of the press has an entirely different justification from censorship, in that the former is itself an aspect of the Idea, of freedom, a positive good; whereas censorship is an aspect of unfreedom, a polemic of the viewpoint of semblance as against the viewpoint of essence, a mere negation.

No! No! No! the speaker cries out meantime: I don't blame the appearance, I blame the essence. Freedom is the infamy of press freedom. Freedom **gives** possibility to evil. Hence freedom is evil.

Evil freedom!

> He stabbed her in a thicket dark as a mine,
> and sank her body in the deep Rhine![20]

But:

> This time I must talk to thee, please,
> Lord and Master, listen to me in peace![21]

Does not freedom of the press exist in the land of censorship? The press in general is a consummation of human freedom. Hence where there is a press there is freedom of the press.

In the land of censorship, to be sure, the state has no freedom of the press, but a member of the state, the *government*, does have it. Apart from the fact that official government publications have complete freedom of the press, doesn't the censor exercise absolute freedom of the press everyday, if not directly, then indirectly?

The writers are at the same time his secretaries. When the secretary does not express the opinion of authority, the latter strikes out the patchwork. Hence the censorship writes the newspapers.

The censor's cross-strokes are for the press what the straight strokes—the *Kuas*[22]—of the Chinese are for their thought. The *Kuas* of the censors are the categories of literature, and as is well known, categories are the typical soul of more extensive content.

Freedom is so very much of the essence of man that even its opponents realize it, in that they fight its reality; they want to appropriate the most costly jewel, which they will not consider the jewel of human nature.

No man fights against freedom; at most, he fights against the freedom of others. Hence every kind of freedom has always existed, at one time as a particular prerogative, at another, as a general right.

The question has only now acquired a *consistent sense*. One does

---

20. "*Er hat sie erstochen im dunklen Hain,/ Und den Leib versenket im tiefen Rhein!*"—a paraphrase of Ludwig Uhland's poem "*Die Rache.*"

21. "*Diesmal muss ich zu dir reden,/ Herr und Meister, hör' mich ruhig!*"—a paraphrase of Goethe's poem "*Der Zauberlehrling.*"

22. Symbols representing natural phenomena, made of three straight and broken lines.

not ask whether freedom of the press should exist, for it always exists. One asks whether freedom of the press is the privilege of individual men or whether it is the privilege of the human spirit. One asks whether the non-right of the one side should be the right of the other. One asks whether "freedom of the mind" has a greater right than "freedom against the mind."

If, however, a free press and freedom of the press are to be rejected as the consummation of "universal freedom," then censorship and a censored press are even more the consummation of a particular freedom, for how can the species be good if the genus is bad? If the speaker had been consistent, he would have rejected, not the free press, but the press. According to him, the press would be good only if it were not the product of freedom, that is, not a human product. Either animals or gods would be completely entitled to the press.

Or should we perhaps—the speaker dare not voice this—place the government and himself under divine inspiration? When a private person boasts of divine inspiration there is, in our society, only one speaker who officially refutes it—the doctor of mental illness.

English history has sufficiently demonstrated how the claim of divine inspiration at the top produces the counterclaim of divine inspiration at the bottom, and Charles the First ascended the scaffold because of divine inspiration from the bottom.

To be sure, our speaker from the knightly Estates, as we will hear later, goes so far as to portray censorship and freedom of the press, a censored press and a free press, as two evils, but he does not get to the point of characterizing the press in general as an evil.

On the contrary. He divides the whole press into a "good" and a "bad" press. Of the bad press, we are told what is incredible, that its object is wickedness and the widest possible spreading of this wickedness. We overlook the fact that the speaker trusts our credulity too much when he demands that we accept his word about professional wickedness. We can only remind him of the axiom that everything human is imperfect. Therefore would not even the bad press be imperfectly bad—hence good—and the good press imperfectly good—hence bad?

But the speaker shows us the reverse side. He maintains that the bad press is better than the good one, for the bad always finds itself on the offensive, the good on the defensive. Now he himself had told us that man's development ends only with his death. Of course he did not say very much with this except that life ends with death. But when the life of man is development and the good press is always on the defensive—"warding off, reserved, firm"—doesn't it thereby constantly oppose development, that is, life itself? Either this good defensive press is wicked or development is wicked, in which case the speaker's previous assertion that the object of the "bad press is the widest possible spreading of bad principles and the widest possible furtherance of bad ideas" loses its mystical incredibility in a rational interpretation; the widest possible spreading of principles and the widest possible furtherance of ideas is bad in a bad press.

The relationship between a good and a bad press becomes even more peculiar when the speaker assures us that the good press is impotent and the bad press omnipotent; for the former would then be without any effectiveness on the people, while the latter would be irresistible. To the speaker, the good press and the impotent press are identical. Does he then want to maintain that the good is impotent or that the impotent is good?

He contraposes the siren song of the bad press to the sober voice of the good. After all, it is with a sober voice that one sings best and most effectively. The speaker seems to be acquainted only with the sensual heat of passion, not with the hot passion of truth, or the victory-conscious enthusiasm of reason, or the irresistible affect of moral forces.

Under the ideas of the bad press he includes "the pride that recognizes no authority in Church and State," the "envy" that predicts the abolition of the aristocracy, and other things, to which we will revert later. For the time being we content ourselves with the question of how he knows this isolated idea to be good. If the general forces of life are bad—and we heard it said that the bad is omnipotent in its effectiveness on the masses—then *what* and *who* is justified in appearing to be good? It is an arrogant assertion: My individuality is good, the few existences that correspond to my individuality are good, and the wicked, bad press does not want to recognize this. The bad press!

Having at the outset changed his attack on freedom of the press to an attack on freedom, the speaker now changes it to an attack on the good. His fear of the bad turns out to be a fear of the good. He therefore bases censorship on an acceptance of the bad and a rejection of the good—or is it not true that I despise a man when I say to him at the outset that his adversary in battle is bound to be victorious because, while he himself may well be a very sober fellow and a very good neighbor, he is nevertheless a very bad hero who, although he carries consecrated arms, does not know how to handle them; and that although he and I, both of us, may be thoroughly convinced of his perfection, the world would never share this conviction because, while his ideas may be good, his energy is wretched?

Much as the speaker's distinction between the good and the bad press makes any refutation superfluous, since it gets engulfed in its own contradictions, we should not ignore the main point, that the speaker has put the question altogether falsely and has made a basis of what he should have first proved.

If one wants to speak of two kinds of press, the distinction must be derived from the essence of the press itself, not from outside considerations. Censored press or free press, one or the other must be the good or the bad press. It is over just this that one debates—whether the censored press or the free press is good or bad, that is, whether it corresponds to the essence of the press to have a free or an unfree existence. To make the bad press a refutation of the free press is to maintain that the free press is bad and the censored one is good, which is precisely what has to be proved.

Lowly opinions, personal chicaneries, and infamies, these the censored press shares with the free press. That it produces individual products of this or that sort does not, therefore, constitute its distinction as a species; even in a swamp, flowers grow. The question here is the essence, the inner character, that separates the censored press from the free press.

The free press that is bad does not correspond to the essence of its character. The censored press with its hypocrisy, its characterlessness, its eunuch language, its doglike tail wagging, embodies only the inner conditions of its existence.

A censored press is still bad even when it produces good products, for these products are good only insofar as they exhibit a free press within a censored one, and insofar as it is not in their character to be products of a censored press. A free press is still good even when it produces bad products, for these products are apostates from the nature of a free press. A castrated man is still a bad male, even if he has a good voice. Nature continues good, even if it brings forth abortions.

The essence of a free press is the characterful, reasonable, ethical essence of freedom. The character of a censored press is the characterless ogre of unfreedom; it is a civilized monster, a perfumed abortion.

Or does one need further proof that freedom of the press corresponds to the essence of the press and that censorship is a contradiction of it? Is it not self-evident that outer restrictions on intellectual life are not part of its inner character if they deny such life instead of affirming it?

To really justify censorship the speaker should have proved that censorship belongs to the essence of freedom of the press; instead he proved that freedom does not belong to the essence of man. He rejects the whole species to retain a good genus, for freedom is, after all, the essential species of the whole intellectual existence, hence also of the press. To abolish the possibility of evil, he abolishes the good and realizes the bad, for the human good can be only that which is a realization of freedom.

We will therefore consider a censored press bad, so long as it is not proved to us that censorship emanates from the essence of freedom of the press itself.

But even granting that censorship is born together with the nature of the press—although no animal, still less an intellectual being, comes into the world with chains—what follows therefrom? That freedom of the press as it exists on the official side, and censorship too, also need censorship. And who is to censor the government press except the people's press?

To be sure, another speaker thought that the evil of censorship would be abolished if it were tripled—the censorship placed under provincial censorship and provincial censorship in turn under Berlin censorship—and the freedom of the press made one-sided and the censorship many-sided. So many circumlocutions in order to live! Who is to censor the Berlin censorship? Now, to return to *our* speaker.

At the very beginning he informed us that no light would come from the struggle between the good and wicked press, but may we now ask: Doesn't he want to make the "useless" struggle permanent? According to him, isn't the struggle between censorship and press a struggle between a good and a bad press?

Censorship does not abolish the struggle; it makes it one-sided; it makes a secret struggle out of an open one; out of a struggle of principles it makes a struggle of nonviolent principles with unprincipled violence.

True censorship, rooted in the very essence of freedom of the press, is *criticism;* that is the court the press creates out of itself. Censorship is criticism as government monopoly; but doesn't criticism lose its rational character when it proceeds, not openly but secretly, not theoretically but practically; when it does not judge parties but becomes itself a party; when it does not use the sharp knife of reason but the blunt scissors of caprice; when it wants to apply criticism but not to suffer it; when it disavows itself while offering itself; when, finally, it is so uncritical as to confuse individual with universal wisdom, dicta of power with dicta of reason, ink spots with sun spots, the crooked lines of the censor with mathematical constructions, and striking blows with striking arguments?

In the course of this presentation we have shown how the visionary, unctuous, soft-hearted mystique of the speaker turns into the hardheartedness of a petty-smart pragmatism and into the narrow-mindedness of an idealess experience-calculus. In his arguments about the relationship between the censorship law and the press law, and preventive and repressive measures, he spares us this trouble, since he himself goes on with the conscious application of his mystique. . . .[23]

The speaker is not fortunate in his comparison. He is overcome by a poetic exaltation the moment he depicts the omipotence of evil. We have already heard the voice of the good impotently, because soberly, counterechoing the "siren song of evil." Now the evil becomes "Greek fire," while the speaker has no comparison for truth, and if we were to make a comparison with his "sober" words for him, it would be that truth is like flint which strikes sparks when it is struck. It is a fine argument for slaveholders to cudgel humanity out of the Negro, an admirable maxim for the legislator to enact repressive laws against truth so that it will thereby pursue its object more boldly. The speaker seems to have respect for the truth only when it becomes "natural" and demonstrates itself "palpably." The more dikes you put up against truth, the more efficiently you maintain truth! Always dammed up!

But let's let the sirens sing!

The speaker's mystical "imperfection theory" has finally borne its earthly fruit; it has thrown its moonstones at our heads. Let us look at the moonstones!

Everything is imperfect. Censorship is imperfect, press law is imperfect. By this essence is it known. Concerning the rightness of its *idea* nothing further is to be said; there is nothing left for us but, from the standpoint of the lowest empiricism, to determine by probability calculation on which side most dangers lurk. It is a purely temporal difference whether the rules themselves prevent the evil through censorship or whether the evil is repeated through the press law.

One sees how the speaker, through the hollow phrase "human imperfection" is able to get around the essential, inner, characteristic difference between censorship and press law, and to transform the controversy from a question of principle into a question of the market place, whether more bluenoses are to be got by the censorship or by the press law.

But when press law and censorship law are contraposed, then what is involved is not the consequences but the reason, not their individual application but their universal equity. Montesquieu already teaches that despotism is more comfortable in its application than lawfulness, and Machiavelli maintains that the bad has better consequences for princes than the good. So if we do not want to preserve the ancient little Jesuitical aphorism that the good objective—and we doubt the good of the objective itself—sanctifies bad means, we must above all examine whether censorship is in its essence a *good* means.

The speaker is right when he calls the censorship law a preventive measure; it is a precautionary measure of the police against freedom.

---

23. A long quotation is omitted.

But he is wrong when he calls the press law a repressive measure. It is the rule of freedom itself to make exceptions in moderation. The censorship regulation is no law. The press law is no regulation.

In a press law, freedom punishes. In a censorship law, freedom is punished. The censorship law is a suspect law against freedom. The press law is a vote of confidence which the press gives itself. The press law punishes the misuse of freedom. The censorship law punishes freedom as a misuse. It treats freedom as a criminal—or is it, in every sphere, considered a penalty of honor to be under police surveillance? A censorship law has only the *form* of a law. A press law is a *real* law.

A press law is a real law because it is the positive essence of freedom. It regards freedom as the normal condition of the press, the press as an essence of freedom, and therefore comes in conflict with abuse by the press only in the exceptional case when it opposes its own principle and thereby suspends itself. Freedom of the press as press law prevails against attempts on itself, that is, against press abuse. A press law declares freedom to be the nature of the violator. Hence what it has done against freedom it has done against itself, and this self-injury seems to it a penalty which is a recognition of its freedom.

Thus the press law, far from being a repressive measure against freedom of the press, is merely a means to discourage repetition of violation through a penalty; one should, rather, view the lack of press legislation as the exclusion of freedom of the press from the sphere of lawful freedom, for lawfully recognized freedom exists in the state as law. Laws are not repressive measures against freedom, any more than the law of gravity is a repressive measure against movement; the law of gravity propels the eternal motions of the heavenly bodies but, as a law of falling, kills me if I violate it by trying to dance in the air. Rather, laws are positive, clear, universal norms, in which freedom has won an impersonal, theoretical existence independent of the caprice of any individual. A law text is the Bible of freedom of a people.

The press law is therefore the legal recognition of freedom. It is *law*, because it is the positive Being of freedom. It must therefore be in existence even if it is never applied, as in North America, whereas censorship can never become lawful, any more than slavery, even if it exists a thousand times as law.

There are no real preventive laws. The law prevents only as command. It becomes active law only when it is violated, for it is true law only when within it the unconscious natural law of freedom has become the conscious law of the state. Where law is real law—that is, where it is the essence of freedom—it is the real essence of the freedom of man. Hence laws cannot prevent man's activities, for they are, after all, the inner life laws of his behavior, the conscious mirror images of his life. Thus law steps back before the life of man as a life of freedom; and until his real action shows that he has stopped obeying the natural law of freedom, the law of the state compels him to be free, just as physical laws emerge as alien only after my life has ceased to be the life of these laws, when it is *sick*. Hence a preventive law is a senseless contradiction.

Therefore preventive law has no measure within itself, no rational rule, for rational rule can emanate only from the nature of the thing, in this case, freedom. Preventive law must be unlimited, for if the prevention of freedom is to be successful, it must be as large as its subject, that is, boundless. The preventive law is therefore the contradiction of an *unlimited limitation*, and it ceases to operate, not by necessity, but by the accident that sets bounds to caprice, as the censorship demonstrates daily *ad oculos* [before one's eyes].

The human body is by nature mortal. Hence sickness cannot be avoided. Why does a man submit to a doctor only when he is sick, and not when he is well? Because it is not only the sickness that is an evil, but also the doctor. Through medical guardianship life is recognized as an evil and the human body as an object of treatment by medical colleges. Is death not preferable to a life that has only preventive measures against death? Does not free movement also belong to life? What is any illness but life restrained in its freedom? A perpetual doctor would be a disease, in that one would not even have the prospect of dying, but must go on living. If life should die, death could not live. Does not the mind have greater right than the body? Indeed, this has often been so interpreted—that bodily motion is harmful and is to be withdrawn from the free motion of the mind. Censorship takes as its starting point the consideration that sickness is a normal state, and freedom is a sickness. It constantly assures the press that it [the press] is sick, and no matter what proof of the health of its physical constitution may be, it must permit itself to be treated. But censorship is not even a doctor to literature, applying various remedies according to the sickness. It is a country surgeon who knows only a single mechanical, universal remedy for everything—the scissors. And it is not even a surgeon who purposes my health; it is a surgical aesthete who considers superfluous everything in my body that displeases him, irritates him, or affects him with distaste; it is a quackery that pushes back a skin eruption in order not to have to see it, without regard to whether it could rebound on the more sensitive internal organs.

You consider it unjust to capture birds. Is not the cage a preventive measure against birds of prey, bullets and storms? You consider it barbaric to blind nightingales, and you don't think it barbaric to gouge out the eyes of the press with the points of censorship pens? You consider it despotic to cut the hair of a man against his will, but every day the censorship cuts into the flesh of intellectual individuals, and passes only heartless bodies, bodies without reaction, sanctified bodies, as healthy!

We have shown how the press law is a right and the censorship a wrong. But the censorship itself admits that it is not an end in itself, that it is not a good in and by itself, that therefore it rests on the principle: "The end sanctifies the means." But an end that needs unholy means is no holy end, and cannot the press also adopt the principle and boast: "The end sanctifies the means"?

The censorship is thus no law but a police measure, but it is itself a *bad police measure*, because it does not achieve what it wants and it does not want what it achieves.

If the censorship law wants to *prevent* freedom as something displeasing, it achieves its opposite. In the country of censorship, every forbidden piece of writing—that is, printed without the censor—is an event. It passes as a martyr, and there is no martyr without a halo and devout followers. It passes as an exception, and the more freedom continues to be of value to man, the more it becomes an exception to the general unfreedom. Every mystery corrupts. Where public opinion is a mystery to itself, it is from the outset corrupted by all writings that formally break through the mysterious bounds. The censorship makes all forbidden writing, good or bad, extraordinary writing, while freedom of the press robs all writing of special importance.

If the censorship is honest it averts caprice and makes caprice into a law. It cannot prevent a danger that is greater than itself. The danger to the life of every Being consists in losing itself. Hence unfreedom is the intrinsic fatal danger for man. Consider for the moment that, ethical consequences apart, you cannot enjoy the advantages of a free press without tolerating its discomforts. You cannot pluck the rose without its thorns! And what do you lose by a free press?

The free press is the omnipresent open eye of the spirit of the people, the embodied confidence of a people in itself, the articulate bond that ties the individual to the state and the world, the incorporated culture which transfigures material struggles into intellectual struggles and idealizes its raw material shape. It is the ruthless confession of a people to itself, and it is well known that the power of confession is redeeming. The free press is the intellectual mirror in which a people sees itself, and self-viewing is the first condition of wisdom. It is the mind of the state that can be peddled in every cottage, cheaper than natural gas. It is universal, omnipresent, omniscient. It is the ideal world, which constantly gushes from the real one and streams back to it ever richer and animated anew.

The course of the presentation has shown that censorship and press law are as different as caprice and freedom, as formal law and real law. But what applies to essence also applies to appearance. What rightly applies to both applies to their application. As press law and censorship law are different, so also is the position of the judge and the position of the censor in regard to the press.

Of course, our speaker, his eyes turned heavenward, sees far beneath him the earth as a contemptible dust heap, and so he does not know what to say about any flower except that it is dusty. Thus here also he sees only two measures that in their application are equally capricious, for to him caprice is action according to individual conception, individual conception cannot be separated from intellectual things, etc., etc. If the conception of intellectual things is individualistic, what right does one intellectual viewpoint have over another, the opinion of the censor over the opinion of the writer? But we understand the speaker. To prove the right of censorship he takes the memorable roundabout way of depicting censorship and press law both as being in their application unlawful because, since he knows everything worldly to be imperfect, for him there remains only one question—whether caprice should stand on the side of the people or on the side of the government.

His mystique changes into libertinism, in that he places law and caprice on the same level and sees only a formal distinction where ethical and legal antitheses are concerned, for he does not polemicize against the press law but against *the law*. Or does any law exist that carries within itself the necessity of being applied in *each individual case* in the legislator's sense and *absolutely* excluding every *caprice*? It takes incredible audacity to call such a senseless task the *philosopher's stone*, for only the most extreme ignorance can posit it. Law is universal. The case that has to be decided according to law is individual. To subsume the individual under the universal requires a judgment. The judgment is problematical. The *judge* is also part of the law. If laws were self-applying, then courts would be superfluous.

But everything human is imperfect! Hence: *Edite, bibite!*[24] Why do you demand judges, since judges are human? Why do you demand laws, since laws can be executed only by human beings and everything carried out by human beings is imperfect? Relinquish yourselves to the good will of the master! Rhineland justice is as imperfect as the Turkish! Hence: *Edite, bibite!*

What a difference there is between a judge and a censor!

The censor has no law as his master. The judge has no master

---

24. Eat and drink!—a Latin phrase from a German student song.

but the law. But the judge has the duty to interpret the law in an individual case as he *understands* it after conscientious examination; the censor has the duty to understand the law as it is officially *interpreted* for him in an individual case. The independent judge belongs neither to me nor to the government. The dependent censor is himself an organ of the government. With the judge, at most only the unreliability of a single mind is involved; with the censor, the unreliability of a single person. The judge is confronted with a specific violation of the press; the censor, with the spirit of the press. The judge judges my action according to a definite law; the censor not only punishes the crime, he also *creates* it. When I am placed before the court, I am accused of violating an existing law, for if a law is supposed to have been violated, it does after all first have to exist. Where there is no press law, no law of the press can be violated. The censorship does not accuse me of violating an existing law. It condemns my opinion because it is not the opinion of the censor and his master. My open act that is willing to expose itself to the world and its judgment, to the state and its law, is judged by a concealed, merely negative power, which does not know how to constitute itself as a law, which shies away from the light of day, which is not bound by any universal principles.

A censorship law is an impossibility, because it wants to punish, not offenses, but opinions; because it cannot be anything other than what the censor formulates; because no state has the courage to formulate in legal, universal principles that which it can do in practice through its organ the censor. This is also why the administration of censorship is entrusted, not to the courts, but to the police.

Even if censorship were factually the same as justice, it would remain primarily a fact, without being a necessity. But to freedom belongs not only *what*, but very much also *how* I live, not only that I act in freedom, but also that I act freely. What distinguishes the master builder from the beaver, if not the fact that the beaver is a master builder with a pelt and the master builder is a beaver without a pelt?

Redundantly, our speaker once more returns to the effects of freedom of the press in countries where it really exists. As we have already recited this theme at great length, we will touch here only on the French press. Apart from the fact that the deficiences of the French press are the deficiencies of the French nation, we do not find the evil where the speaker seeks it. The French press is not too free; it is not free enough. It is not subject to intellectual censorship, to be sure, but subject to a material censorship, the high security deposit. This affects the press materially, because it pulls the press out of its true sphere into the sphere of big business speculations. In addition, big business speculations need big cities. Hence the French press is concentrated in a few points, and when material force is thus concentrated, does it not work demonically, as intellectual force does not?

But if you insist on judging freedom of the press not according to its idea but according to its historical existence, why not seek it out where it exists historically? Natural scientists seek to establish a natural phenomenon in its purest condition by means of experiments. You need no experiments. You find the natural phenomenon of freedom of the press in North America in its purest, most natural forms. But if North America has great historic foundations for freedom of the press, Germany has even greater ones. Literature, and the intellectual formation of a nation growing out of it, are after all not only the direct historical foundation of the press, but also its own history. And what other nation in the world can boast of these most direct historical foundations of freedom of the press as much as the German nation?

But, our speaker interrupts again, but woe to Germany's morality if its press became free, for freedom of the press effects "an inner demoralization that seeks to undermine the higher destiny of man, and with it the foundation of true civilization."

It is the *censored* press that has a demoralizing effect. The potent vice, hypocrisy, is inseparable from it, and out of this, its basic vice, flow all its other defects, for even the capacity for virtue is lacking in its revolting vice of passivity, even if viewed aesthetically. The government hears only its own voice; it knows that it hears only its own voice; and yet it fixes itself in the delusion that it hears the voice of the people, and demands from the people that it likewise fix itself in this delusion. The people, for their part, therefore sink partly into political superstition, partly into political heresy, or, entirely turned away from political life, they become a *private mob*.

Insofar as the press daily extols the creations of the government's will, whereas God himself said about his own creation only on the sixth day, "And, behold, *it was* very good," insofar as one day necessarily contradicts the other, the press lies constantly and has to reject even the consciousness of the lie and to cast off its own shame.

Insofar as the people are obliged to consider free writings illegal, they accustom themselves to regard the illegal as free, freedom as illegal, and the legal as the unfree. Thus censorship kills the political spirit.

But our speaker fears freedom of the press for "private individuals." It does not occur to him that censorship is a constant attack on the rights of private persons and even more so on ideas. He gets into pathos over endangered personalities, but should we not get into pathos over the endangered public welfare?

We cannot contrast our views and his more sharply than by contraposing his definitions of "bad opinion" to ours.

Bad opinion is "the pride that recognizes no authority in Church and State." And should we not consider a bad opinion that which does not recognize the authority of reason and law? "It is envy that preaches the abolition of everything that the mob calls aristocracy"; and we say it is envy that wants to abolish the eternal aristocracy of human nature, freedom, an aristocracy which even the mob does not doubt.

"It is spiteful, malicious joy that delights in personalities, whether lie or truth, and peremptorily demands from the public that no scandal of private life remain unexposed."

It is spiteful, malicious joy that extracts the gossip and personalities from the great life of nations, misjudges reason in history, and preaches only the scandal of history to a public that is incapable of judging the matter; that stresses single aspects of phenomena and personalities; that peremptorily demands mystery so that every blemish of public life remain veiled.

"It is the impurity of the heart and the imagination that is titillated by obscene pictures."

It is the impurity of the heart and the imagination which titillates itself with obscene pictures of the omnipotence of evil and the impotence of good; it is imagination whose sin is pride; it is the impure heart that hides its worldly arrogance in mystical pictures. "It is despair over one's own salvation that wants to deafen the voice of conscience by a denial of God." It is despair over one's own salvation that makes personal weakness into mankind's weakness to shift it from one's own conscience; it is despair over the salvation of mankind that forbids it to follow its inherent natural laws, and which preaches immaturity as a necessity; it is hypocrisy that makes God into a hollow pretext without a belief in his own reality, the omnipotence of the good; it is selfishness that puts private salvation higher than the salvation of the whole.

These people despair over mankind in general and canonize individuals. They project a frightening picture of human nature and demand that we genuflect before the icon of a few privileged individuals. We know that the individual person is weak, but we know at the same time that the totality is strong.

Finally the speaker recalls the words about gratification that echo from the branches of the Tree of Knowledge, whose fruits we barter away today as then: "Ye shall not eat of it... In the day ye eat thereof, then your eyes shall be opened, and ye shall be as gods, knowing good and evil."[25]

---

25. Genesis 3:3, 5.

Although we doubt that the speaker has eaten of the Tree of Knowledge, that we (the Rhineland Estates) have bartered with the devil—at least Genesis tells us nothing about it—nevertheless, we agree with the speaker's opinion that the devil did not lie to us then, for God himself says, "Behold, the man is become as one of us, to know good and evil."[26]

In fairness, we let the speaker state the epilogue to his speech: "Writing and speaking are mechanical accomplishments."

Tired as the reader may be of these "mechanical accomplishments," for the sake of completeness we must, in addition to the princely Estates and the knightly Estates, also let the town Estates spit at freedom of the press. We have before us here the opposition of the bourgeois, not the *citoyen* [citizen].

The speaker from the town Estates believes that he joins Sièyes with the bourgeois observation: "Freedom of the press is a beautiful thing, so long as bad people do not meddle with it." "On the other hand, no proven means has been found hitherto," etc., etc.

The viewpoint that calls freedom of the press a thing is already something to commend for its naïveté. One can generally reproach this speaker with anything except a deficiency of prosaicness or an excess of imagination.

So freedom of the press is a beautiful thing, perhaps something that embellishes the sweet habit of existence, an agreeable, a gallant thing? But then there are bad people who misuse language for lying, the head for intrigues, the hands for stealing, the feet for desertion. It is a beautiful thing for speaking and thinking, for hands and feet, for good language, pleasant thinking, capable hands, most excellent feet—if only there were no bad people who misuse them! Not even a small remedy has yet been discovered against this.

"Sympathies for a constitution and freedom of the press must necessarily be weakened when one sees how in that country" (France) "they are tied up with constantly changing conditions and an anxious ignorance about the future."

Thus we first come to the world-shaking discovery that the earth is a *mobile perpetuum* [perpetual motion]—at which many a peaceful German grabbed his nightcap and sighed over the constantly changing conditions of the Motherland, and an anxious ignorance of the future made him sick of a house that stands on its head every moment.

Freedom of the press *causes* "changeable conditions" as little as the astronomers' telescope causes the pertpetual motion of the planetary system. Wicked astronomy! What a fine time it still was when the earth, like some respectable bourgeois, sat in the center of the uni-

---

26. *Genesis* 3:22.

verse, serenely smoked its clay pipe, which it did not even have to light itself, since the sun, the moon, and stars, like so many faithful night lights and "beautiful things," danced around it.

He who to destroy what he himself built is not ready
Will always remain on this earth which is never steady

says Hariri,[27] who was no native Frenchman but an Arab.

The following notion quite definitely speaks for the speaker's Estates: "The true, honest patriot cannot suppress the feeling that a constitution and freedom of the press are not for the benefit of the people, but only to satisfy the ambition of a few individuals and the rule of parties."

It is well known that a certain psychology explains the whole as being made up of small causes and, from the correct view that everything a human being fights for is of interest to him, proceeds to the incorrect view that there exist only "small" interests, only interests of stereotyped egotism. It is known, moreover, that this kind of psychology and anthropology is found particularly in cities, where it is regarded as a mark of intellectual subtlety to see through the whole world and find, sitting behind the passage of the cloud of ideas and facts, only very petty, envious, intriguing puppets who pull the strings. But it is also known that if one looks too deeply into the mirror one falls on *one's own head*, and so also the anthropology and worldly knowledge of these clever people is chiefly a mystifying clout on the head.

The position of the speaker is also marked by superficiality and indecisiveness. "A feeling for independence speaks for freedom of the press" (that is, in the sense of the man who makes the motion), "but it must give a hearing to reason and experience."

If the speaker had finally said that his reason was for freedom of the press but his feeling for independence was against it, his speech would have been a complete genre picture of urban reaction.

He who has a tongue and speaks not,
Who has a blade and fences not,
What good is he, when a creature he is not?[28]

We now come to the defenders of freedom of the press and begin with the main motion. We pass over the more general statements,

---

27. "*Wer nie was er gebaut, zerstört, der steht stät/ Auf dieser ird'schen Welt, die selbst nicht stät steht.*" Marx's quotation from the medieval Arab writer Hariri is taken from Friedrich Rückert's *Die Verwandlungen des Abu Seid von Serug, oder die Makamen des Hariri* (2nd ed., 1837).
28. "*Wer eine Zung' hat und spricht nicht,/ Wer eine Kling' hat und ficht nicht,/ Was ist der wohl, wenn ein Wicht nicht?*"

which are strikingly well put in the introductory remarks of the motion, to take up immediately the characteristic standpoint that is peculiar to this motion.

The mover of the motion wants the "freedom of the press trade" not to be excluded from the "general freedom of the trades," as is still the case, and wherein the internal contradiction appears as a classic inconsistency.

"The work of arms and legs is free, that of the head is under tutelage. Under the tutelage of greater heads, no doubt? God forbid; this does not happen with the censors. To him whom God gives an office he also gives intellect!"

It strikes one in the first place that freedom of the press is subsumed under freedom of the trades. But we cannot quite reject the opinion of the speaker. Rembrandt painted the Mother of God as a Dutch peasant woman, why cannot our speaker depict freedom in a form with which he is safe and familiar?

No less can we deny the speaker's arguments as containing a relative truth. If one considers the press itself only as a trade, a greater freedom is due to it, the trade of the head, than to the trade of arm and leg. The emancipation of the arm and leg becomes humanly significant only by the emancipation of the head, for it is well known that arms and legs become human arms and legs through the head they serve.

Original as this speaker's point of view may appear at first glance, we must nevertheless ascribe to it the absolute merit of the unsupported, foggy, and misty ratiocination of those German liberals who think they honor freedom when they place it in the starry sky of imagination instead of the solid ground of reality. It is these arguers of the imagination, these sentimental enthusiasts who see every contact of their ideal with common reality as a profanation, whom we Germans have partly to thank for the fact that freedom has hitherto remained a fancy and a sentimentality.

Germans are generally inclined to sentiment and excess; they have a *tendre* [affection] for the music of the spheres. It is therefore to be welcomed when the great question of the Idea is demonstrated to them from a hardy, realistic standpoint borrowed from the immediate environment. Germans are by nature most devout, most submissive, most reverential. Out of sheer respect for ideas, they do not put them into realization. They consecrate to them a cult of worship but they do not cultivate it. Hence the intention of the speaker is to familiarize the German with his own ideas, to show him that they are not unapproachable but of immediate interest, and that the language of the gods is to be translated into the language of men.

It is well known that the Greeks believed they saw their Apollo,

Athena, and Zeus in the Egyptian, Lydian, and even Scythian gods, and that they ignored what belonged exclusively to the foreign cults as a nonessential. So it is also no lapse that the German views the unknown goddess of freedom of the press as one of his familiar goddesses, and accordingly calls her freedom of the trades or freedom of property.

Precisely because we do recognize and appreciate the standpoint of the speaker, we subject it the more to a sharper criticism.

"One might well think: A continuation of the guild system alongside freedom of the press, because the trade of the head has a higher potential, comparable to the older seven free arts, can be taken into consideration; but a continuation of unfreedom of the press alongside freedom of the trades is a sin against the holy ghost."

To be sure! The subordinate form of freedom is by itself declared illegal if the higher form is unauthorized. The right of an individual citizen is a folly if the right of the state is not recognized. If freedom in general is justified, it goes without saying that a facet of freedom is the more justified the greater the splendor and the development of essence that freedom has won in it. If a polyp is justified, because the life of nature gropes darkly in it, why not a lion, in whom life storms and roars?

However, correct as the object may be of considering the higher aspect of law as proven by a lower aspect, it is reversed in application, which makes the lower sphere the measure of the higher one and turns its own rationally limited inner laws into something comic because it interpolates the pretention that it is not the law of its own sphere but of a superior one. It is as if I wanted to force a giant to live in the house of a pygmy.

Freedom of the trades, freedom of property, of conscience, of the press, of the courts, are all species of the same genus, *freedom without a family name.* But how entirely erroneous it is to forget difference in oneness and to make a definite species the measure, the norm, the sphere of the other species? It is intolerance of a species of freedom that would tolerate the others only when they have apostatized from themselves and declared themselves its vassals.

Freedom of the trades is only freedom of the trades and no other freedom, for in it the nature of the trade forms itself unhindered according to its own inherent rules; freedom of the courts is freedom of the courts, if the courts promote the inherent rules of the law, and not those of another sphere, such as religion. Every definite sphere of freedom is the freedom of a definite sphere, just as every definite way of life is the way of life of a definite entity. Would it not be topsy-turvy to demand that the lion arrange the rules of his life according to those of the polyp? How false would be my conception of the unity and interconnection of the bodily organism if I concluded: Since arms and legs are active in their own way, then eyes and ears, those organs that tear man away from his individualism and make him the mirror and echo of the universe, should have an even greater right to activity, that is, to become arm-and-leg activity raised to a higher power?

As in the planetary system each individual planet revolves around the sun in such a way that the planet moves around itself, so in the system of freedom each of its worlds circulates only around the central sun of freedom in such a way that it circulates around itself. To make freedom of the press a class of freedom of the trades is to defend it in such a way as to kill it with the defense; for do I not do away with the freedom of a person when I demand that he should be free in the manner of another person? The press calls out to the trades: Your freedom is not my freedom. Just as you obey the laws of your sphere, so I want to obey the laws of my sphere. To be free in your manner is, to me, identical with unfreedom, just as the carpenter would hardly feel himself edified if, when he demands freedom for his trade, he is given the equivalent of the freedom of the philosopher.

We want to state the speaker's thought bluntly. What is freedom? Answer: Freedom of the trades; just as though a student, if asked, What is freedom? were to answer: *A free evening.*

With the same justification as for this kind of freedom of the press, one could subsume every species of freedom under freedom of the trades. The judge follows the trade of the law; the preacher, the trade of religion; the father of a family, the trade of bringing up children. But have I thereby expressed the essence of the law, of religion, or of ethical freedom?

One could turn the matter around and call freedom of the trades a species of freedom of the press. Do the trades work only with hand and foot, and not also with the head? Is the language of the word the only language of thought? Does not the mechanic with his steam engine speak very perceptively to my ear, the bed manufacturer very clearly to my back, the cook very understandably to my stomach? Is it not a contradiction that all these sorts of freedom of the press are permitted, but not the one that by means of printer's ink speaks to my mind?

To defend the freedom of a sphere, and even to comprehend it, I must conceive it in its essential character, not in external relationships. But is the press true to its nature, does it act according to the nobility of its nature, *is it free,* if it is degraded to a trade? The writer, to be sure, must earn a living in order to exist and be able to write, but he must in no way exist and write in order to earn a living.

When *Béranger* sings:

Je ne vis, que pour faire des chansons,
Si vous m'ôtez ma place, Monseigneur,
Je ferai des chansons pour vivre,[29]

there is in this threat of his an ironic indication that the poet falls
out of his proper sphere as soon as poetry becomes a means.

The writer in no way considers his works as a means. They are
ends in themselves; they are so little a means for him and for others
that he sacrifices his existence for their existence when necessary, and
otherwise, just as the preacher of religion makes it his principle "To
obey God more than man," among the latter of whom he is himself
encased within his human needs and desires. In contrast, you have a
tailor from whom I order a Parisian dress coat who brings me a Roman
toga because it is more in keeping with the eternal laws of beauty!

The first freedom of the press consists in not being a trade. The
writer who reduces it to a material means deserves as a penalty for
this inner unfreedom the outer one, censorship; or rather, his very
existence is already a penalty.

Of course the press is also a trade, but this is not the business of
the writer, but of the printers and book dealers. The question under
consideration is not freedom of the trades but freedom of the press.

Our speaker does not content himself with considering freedom of
the press as being assured by freedom of the trades, he demands that
freedom of the press should subject its own laws to the laws of
freedom of the trades. He even polemicizes against the rapporteur
of the committee who asserts a higher view of freedom of the press,
and he ends with the kind of demand that can only have a comical
effect, for humor enters the moment the laws of a lower sphere are
applied to a higher one, just as, in reverse, it becomes comical when
children affect poignancy.

He speaks of "competent and incompetent authors." This he understands to mean that the exercise of an imparted right in the freedom of
the trades is always tied to a condition that is more or less difficult
to fulfill, according to the yardstick of the trade. "Understandably,
masons, carpenters, and architects have to fulfill conditions from
which other trades are free." His motion "applies to a right in particular, not in general."

First, who is to confer the competence? Kant did not confer on
Fichte the competence of a philosopher, Ptolemy did not confer on
Copernicus the competence of an astronomer, Bernard of Clairvaux

---

29. *"I live only to make songs,/ If you take away my place, sir,/ I will make
songs in order to live."*

did not confer on Luther the competence of a theologian. Every scholar considers his critic an "incompetent author." Or should non-scholars decide who is a competent scholar? Clearly one would have to leave the decision to the incompetent authors, for the competent ones cannot be judges of their own cause. Or should competence be tied to an Estate? The shoemaker Jakob Böhme was a great philosopher. Many a professional philosopher is only a great shoemaker.

For the rest, when one talks about competent and incompetent authors one must not be content with making a differentiation among persons; one must further divide the trade of the press into different trades; one must issue different trade licenses for the different spheres of writing activity. Or should the competent writer write about everything? The shoemaker is, as a matter of course, more competent to write about leather than the jurist. Likewise, the day laborer is more competent to write about whether one should work on holidays or not than the theologian. Let us therefore tie competence to particular material conditions, so that every citizen would be a competent and incompetent writer at the same time, competent in matters of his profession and incompetent in everything else.

Apart from the fact that in this way the world of the press, instead of being a link among people in general, would be the real means of separation, so that the difference among the Estates would be intellectually fixed and literary history would sink to the level of the natural history of a particular race of animals; apart from the boundary conflicts and collisions which could not be settled or avoided; apart from the fact that stupidity and narrow-mindedness would be made into a law for the press, for I consider the intellectuality and freedom of the particular only in connection with the whole, that is, not in their separation from each other—apart from all this, since reading is exactly as important as writing, there are also bound to be competent and incompetent readers, a natural conclusion that was drawn in Egypt, where the priests, the competent authors, were at the same time the only competent readers. And it is very fitting that only the competent authors be given permission to buy and read their own writings.

What illogicality! Once a privilege predominates, the government has the full right to maintain that it is the *only competent authority* on its own commissions and omissions, for if, outside of your own particular profession, you consider yourself competent as a citizen to write about the most general matters, about the state, should not other mortals, whom you want to exclude, also be competent as human beings to pass judgment on something very particular, namely, your competence and your writings?

There would arise the absurd contradiction that the competent author would be able to *write* about the state without censorship, but the incompetent one could write about the competent author only with censorship.

Freedom of the press would surely not be attained by your recruitment of a herd of official writers from your own ranks. The competent authors would then be the official authors, and the struggle between censorship and freedom of the press would be transformed into a struggle between competent and incompetent writers.

Hence a member of the Fourth Estate rightly points out "that, if any press compulsion is to continue, it should be the same for all, that is, that in this respect no class of citizens should be accorded more rights than any other."

Censorship brings us all into subjection, just as in a despotism everybody is equal, if not in worth, then in unworth; its kind of press freedom wants to introduce oligarchy into the mind. At best, censorship declares a writer to be inconvenient, unsuitable within the boundaries of its domain. Freedom of the press proceeds on the presumption of anticipating world history, sensing in advance the voice of the people which alone has hitherto judged which writer was "competent," which "incompetent." Solon presumed to judge a man only at the end of his life, after his death, a view that fails to judge a writer before his birth.

The press is the commonest way of communicating to individuals their intellectual Being. It knows no respect for the person, but only respect for intelligence. Do you want to ban administratively the intellectual ability to communicate external symptoms? What I cannot be for others I am not and cannot be for myself. If I cannot be a mind for others I cannot be one for myself, and do you want to give single individuals the privilege of being minds? Just as everybody learns to write and read, so everybody must be *allowed* to write and read.

And *for whom* is there to be the division of writers into "competent" and "incompetent"? Obviously not for the truly competent, for they would prevail anyway. Is it to be for the "incompetent," who would want to protect and impose themselves by an external privilege?

But this palliative would not make even the press law dispensable, for as a speaker from the peasant Estates remarks: "Cannot the privileged one also transgress his competence and become punishable? In that case, a particular press law would be necessary, whereby one would run into the same difficulties as in a general press law."

When the German looks back to his history, he finds one main reason for his slow political development—the miserable literature of the "authorized writers" before Lessing. The scholars by profession, by trade, by privilege, the doctors and other "octors," the unprincipled university writers of the seventeenth and eighteenth centuries with their stiff pigtails and their genteel pedantry and their trivial micrological dissertations—these put themselves between nation and intellect, between life and science, between freedom and people. It was the "unauthorized" writers who made our literature. Gottsched and Lessing—try to choose between an "authorized" and an "unauthorized" author!

In general we do not love that "freedom" which has currency *only* in the plural. England is proof in historical life-size of how dangerous for "freedom" the restricted horizon of "freedoms" is.

"*Ce mot des libertés,*" says Voltaire, "*des privilèges, suppose l'assujetissement. Des libertés sont des exemptions de la servitude générale.*"[30]

If, moreover, our speaker wants to exclude *anonymous* and *pseudonymous* writers from freedom of the press and subject them to censorship, we remark that the name does not belong to the matter in the press, but that where a press law exists the publisher, and thereby also the anonymous and pseudonymous writer, is subject to the courts. Besides, when Adam named all the animals in Paradise, he forgot to give names to German newspaper correspondents, and nameless they shall remain in *saeculum saeculorum* [all eternity].

If the mover of the motion sought to restrict the subject of the press to *persons*, so other Estates want to restrict the *material substance* of the press, the sphere of its operations and Being; and there thus emerges an unintellectual bargaining and haggling over how much freedom the freedom of the press should have.

One of the Estates wants to restrict the press to a discussion of material, intellectual, and ecclesiastical conditions in the Rhine province; another desires "community papers," the names of which would indicate their limited content; a third even wants each province to have *only one paper* in which to be candid!

All these efforts remind one of the gymnastics teacher who proposed that the best method to teach jumping was to bring the pupil to a big pit and show him with a thread how far across the pit he should jump. It goes without saying that the pupil was first to train himself in jumping and was not to leap across the whole pit the first day, but the thread was to be moved farther away from time to time. Unfortunately, at the first lesson the pupil fell into the pit, and has been lying there ever since. The teacher was a German, and the pupil called himself "Freedom."

Judging by the predominant normal type, therefore, the defenders of freedom of the press in the Sixth Rhineland Landtag differ from their opponents not in content but in degree. The ones oppose, the

---

30. "This talk about freedoms, about privileges, presupposes subjection. Freedoms are exemptions from general servitude."

others defend limitation on the special position of the press. The ones want the privilege to be on the side of the government only, the others want to divide it among several individuals; the ones want the whole, the other the half of censorship; the ones want three-eighths press freedom, the others want none at all. God protect me from my friends!

Entirely different from the general spirit of the Landtag are the speeches of the reporters and a few members from the peasant Estate.

One reporter remarks, among other things, "In the life of nations, as well as of individual persons, there comes a time when the fetters of too long a tutelage become unbearable, when independence is being striven for, and when everybody wants to be responsible for his own actions. At that point censorship has outlived itself; there, where it still prevails it is regarded as an odious coercion to be forbidden to write that which is said publicly."

Write as you speak, speak as you write, so the elementary school teachers are already teaching us. Later they say, Speak what is prescribed to you, and write what you have said.

"As often as the irresistible passage of time develops a new, important interest, or brings forth a new need for which existing laws do not contain sufficient regulations, new laws must regulate this new condition of society. Such is fully the case here."

This is the genuinely historical view as against the imaginary one, which the judgment of history kills so as to show afterwards the bones of the historical worship of relics.

"The task" (of a press code) "may, of course, not be so easily accomplished; the first attempt to be made will perhaps remain very incomplete! But all states will be indebted to the legislator who will first occupy himself with this, and under a king like ours, the Prussian Government will perhaps be given the honor of pioneering along this path, which alone can lead to the desired end."

How isolated this valiant, dignified, decisive opinion stood in the Landtag our whole presentation has shown; this emerges from the superfluous remarks of the chairman to the reporter rapporteur. And finally there is the indignant but striking speech by a member of the peasant Estate:

"They circle around the question before us like a cat around warm porridge." "The human mind must develop itself freely *according to its own inherent laws* and then be permitted to communicate what it has achieved, otherwise a clear, live stream would become a pestilential swamp. If ever a people were fit for freedom of the press, it is surely the quiet, genial German, who needs a goad against his phlegmatism rather than the intellectual strait jacket of censorship. The denial of free communication of his thoughts and feelings to his fellow men has much resemblance to the North American solitary confinement of prisoners, which in its full harshness often leads to insanity. If a man is not allowed to criticize, his praise has no value; similarly, his inexpressiveness is like Chinese painting, which lacks shadow. Let us not, after all, find ourselves in the same company as that somnolent nation!"

If we now take a look at the press debates as a whole, we cannot overcome the desolate, unpleasant impression that an assembly of representatives of the Rhine Province produces, oscillating as it does between the deliberate obduracy of privilege and the natural impotence of a half-liberal vacillation hither and yon; we cannot avoid remarking disapprovingly about the virtually complete lack of general and wide-ranging viewpoints, and the slovenly superficiality with which the matter of a free press was debated and put aside. So we ask ourselves once again whether the press was too far from the Estates and whether it had too few real contacts with them, rather than whether they could defend freedom of the press with the thoroughness and serious interest needed for the occasion?

Freedom of the press handed its petition to the Estates with the most delicate *captatio benevolentiae* [running after a favor].

At the very beginning of the Landtag a debate arose in which the chairman remarked that the printing of the Landtag proceedings, very much like other writings, was subject to censorship, but that here he would take the place of the censor.

Did not in this one point the matter of freedom of the press collapse together with the freedom of the Landtag? This collision is the more interesting because here was laid down to the Landtag itself the proof that with the lack of freedom of the press, all other freedoms are illusory. Every facet of freedom conditions every other, just as every organ of the body does. As soon as a specific freedom is put in question, freedom in general is put in question. As soon as one facet of freedom is repudiated, freedom itself is repudiated, and it can lead only a mere semblance of life, since afterwards it is pure chance which object unfreedom takes over as the dominant power. Unfreedom is the rule and freedom the exception of chance and caprice. Hence nothing is more perverse than, when a *particular* Being of freedom is involved to think that this is a *particular question*. It is a general question within a special sphere. Freedom remains freedom, be it expressed in the blackness of print, or in real estate, or in conscience, or in a political assembly; but the loyal friend of freedom, whose sense of honor is already injured when he has to vote: *Should freedom be or not be?*—this friend is taken aback by the specific material in which freedom appears, he mistakes the genus for the species, he forgets freedom for the press, he believes he passes judgment on an alien Being and he sentences his own Being. Thus the Sixth Rhineland Landtag has sentenced itself, in that it has pronounced judgment on freedom of the press.

The very wise, practical bureaucrats, who privately and falsely consider themselves what Pericles aloud and rightly boasted about himself: "I am a man who, in his knowledge of the needs of the state, as well as in the art of how to develop them, can compare with anybody"[31]—these hereditary leaseholders of political intelligence would shrug their shoulders and remark with oracular gentility that the defenders of freedom of the press are threshing empty chaff, because a *mild* censorship is better than a *harsh* freedom of the press. We reply to them what the Spartans Sperthias and Bulis said to the Persian satrap Hydarnes: "Hydarnes, your advice to us has not been weighed equally on both sides. For the one you advise has already been tried; the other you have not tried. Specifically, you know what it is to be a vassal; but you have not yet tried freedom, to find out whether it is sweet or not. For if you had tried it, you would have advised us to fight for it not only with lances but also with axes."[32]

---

31. Thucydides, *Peloponnesian War*, Book 2.
32. Herodotus, *History*, Book 7.

The Leading Article
in the *Kölnische Zeitung**

W HETHER it was Hermes[1] himself—or his son, the goat god Pan, who wrote the ailing article in No. 179 we shall let the reader decide, remembering that the Greek Hermes was the god of eloquence and logic: "To spread philosophical and religious views through the newspapers or to combat them in newspapers seems to us equally inadmissible. ..."

The state, according to the author, not only has the right but also the duty "to silence *unprofessional* prattlers." He means the opponents of his views, for he has long come to an agreement with himself that he is a *professional* prattler.

It is a question, therefore, of further sharpening the censorship in religious matters, of a new police measure against the nearly suffocated press: "In our opinion, the state can be reproached with undue leniency rather than with excessive severity."

But the leading article has second thoughts. It is dangerous to reproach the state, so he addresses himself to the authorities; his accusation against freedom of the press is transformed into an accusation against the censors; he accuses the censors of applying "too little" censorship: "Thus far a blameworthy leniency has been shown, not, to be sure, by the state, but by 'individual authorities,' in letting the new philosophical school permit itself the most disgraceful attacks on Christianity in public papers and in other printed works not intended exclusively for a scientific reading public."

Again the author pauses and again he has second thoughts; less

---

* From "The Leading Article in No. 179 of the *Kölnische Zeitung*," published in the *Rheinische Zeitung*, July 10, 1842.
1. Carl Heinrich Hermes, political editor of the *Kölnische Zeitung*. Marx is playing with his classical name.

than eight days ago he found too little freedom of the press in the freedom of the censorship; now he finds in the compulsion of the censors too little compulsion by the censors. This has to be set right again: "As long as censorship exists, its most urgent duty is to cut out such repulsive excrescences of boyish insolence as have repeatedly offended our eyes in recent days."

Stupid eyes! Stupid eyes! And the "stupidest eye will be offended by an expression which can only be intended for the powers of comprehension of the broad masses."

If the more relaxed censorship allows repulsive excrescences to appear, what about freedom of the press? If our eyes are too weak to bear the "arrogance" ["*Übermut*"] of what has been censored, how can they be strong enough to bear the "courage" ["Mut"] of the free press?

"As long as censorship exists, its most urgent duty is to ..." And when it no longer exists? The sentence must be interpreted: It is the most urgent duty of the censorship to exist as long as possible.

And again the author has second thoughts: "It is not our function to act as public prosecutor and therefore we refrain from any more precise specification."

What divine kindness there is in the man! He refrains from "more precise specification," whereas only with quite precise, quite distinct examples could he prove and show what *his* view aims at; he utters but vague, half-whispered words of suspicion; it is not his function to act as *public* prosecutor, it is his function to be a *concealed* prosecutor.

For the last time the unhappy man thinks better of it: that it is his function to write leading liberal articles, to play the "loyal friend of freedom of the press." He therefore throws himself into the final position: "We could not refrain from protesting against a procedure which, if it is not a result of accidental negligence, can have no other aim than to compromise in public opinion the movement for a freer press, and to give the game to the opponents who fear to lose by playing fair."

The censorship—so teaches this champion of freedom who is as bold as he is penetrating—if it is not merely the English leopard with the inscription "I sleep, wake me not," has engaged in this "negligent" procedure to compromise the movement for a freer press in public opinion.

Is there still any need to compromise a press movement that draws attention of the censorship to "accidental negligence" and which expects to get its reputation in public opinion from the "censor's penknife"?

This movement can be called "free" only insofar as the shameless license is sometimes called "free"; and isn't it the shamelessness of unwisdom and hypocrisy to try to pass as a defender of the freer press movement and at the same time to teach that the press will fall into the gutter the minute two gendarmes stop holding it up?

What do we need the censorship for, why do we need this leading article, when the philosophical press compromises itself in public opinion? The author, of course, wants in no way to limit "the freedom of scientific research": "In our day, scientific research is rightly allowed the widest and most unlimited scope." The following pronouncement will show what a conception of scientific research our man has: "A sharp distinction must be made between what the freedom of scientific research requires, which can but benefit Christianity itself, and what lies beyond the limits of scientific research."

Who should decide the limits of scientific research if not scientific research itself! According to the leading article, limits should be prescribed to scientific research. The leading article thus knows an "official reason" which does not learn from scientific research but teaches it, and which, like a scholarly Providence, prescribes the length every hair should have to transform a scientific beard into a world beard. The leading article believes in the scientific inspiration of the censorship....

The Cabinet Order About the Daily Press*

Cologne, November 15

Today's *Kölnische Zeitung* publishes the following Royal Cabinet Order which during the past month has been sent to all higher administrators:

I have often pointed out the necessity of meeting the bad tendency of the daily press—to mislead public opinion on general affairs by dissemination of untruths or distorted facts—by immediately publishing the rectifying truth in the same papers that were guilty of reporting such falsehoods. It is not enough to leave the counteraction against a daily newspaper's endeavors to corrupt public opinion to other papers that are directed by a better spirit, and to wait for them to do so. Just where the poison of corruption has been poured out, there it must be rendered harmless; this is not only the duty of the authorities to the reading public to which the poison had been administered, but is at the same time the most effective of all means of destroying the tendencies of deception and lies wherever they appear—in that the editorship is forced to publish judgment against itself. For this reason, I have ascertained to my displeasure that these proper and necessary means to curb the degeneracy of the press have been applied little or not at all. Insofar as the existing laws regarding the unquestioned acceptance of all factual reports sent to them by official authority, and without any comment or introductory remarks, are not sufficiently established, I await from the Ministry of State proposals for the necessary supplementation. If, however, they are now sufficient for the purpose, I desire that the same be energetically taken in hand by my authorities for the protection of right and truth, and recommend this, in addition to the Ministries

---

* *Rheinische Zeitung*, November 16, 1842.

themselves, particularly to the direct care of the governors, whom the Ministry of State is to supply with directions.

The more earnestly it lies in my heart that freedom of expression, in its noble, loyal, candid, and dignified disposition, no matter where it is declared, be not stunted, and that the public discussion of truth be restricted as little as possible, the more unrelentingly must be kept down the spirit that uses the weapon of lies and subornation, so that freedom of expression cannot be misused and cheated of its fruits and blessings.

(Signed) Friedrich Wilhelm

We hasten to report to our readers the above royal Cabinet Order, since we see in it a *guarantee* to the Prussian press. Every loyal paper can only consider it an important support on the part of the government when untruths or distorted facts, which in their reporting the editors, despite the greatest caution, cannot always avoid, will be rectified by an authentic source. Through these official elucidations the government guarantees the daily press not only a certain historical correctness of factual content, but, what is more important, also recognizes the great importance of the press by a positive participation which will always reject the negative participation of prohibition, suppression, and censorship in ever more narrow confines. At the same time the Royal Cabinet Order proceeds from the presupposition of a certain independence of the daily press, without which neither the tendencies of deception, lies, and pernicious efforts, and even less so noble, loyal, candid, and dignified tendencies, could nowhere emerge and establish themselves in the newspapers. This royal presupposition of a certain independence of the daily press is the *most superior guarantee of this independence,* and should be greeted by the Prussian newspapers as an unambiguous expression of the royal will.

The Suppression of the
Leipziger Allgemeine Zeitung[*]
in Prussia

Cologne, December 31, 1842

THE GERMAN PRESS begins the New Year under seemingly clouded auspices. The recent prohibition of the *Leipziger Allgemeine Zeitung* in the Prussian states refutes strikingly enough all the complacent dreams of the credulous about great concessions for the future. Since the *Leipziger Allgemeine Zeitung*, which comes out under Saxon censorship, is suppressed because of its discussion of Prussian affairs, our hopes for censorship-free discussion of our internal affairs are suppressed at the same time. This is a factual consequence that no one will deny.

The main reproaches against the *Leipziger Allgemeine Zeitung* were approximately as follows: "It prints rumor after rumor, at least half of which later prove to be false. Added to this, it does not stick to facts but pries into motives; and no matter how often its judgment may be wrong, it always expresses it with the same poignancy of infallibility and the most hate-filled passion. Its direction is unsteady, 'indiscreet,' 'unprepared'—in a word, a bad exercise."

Assuming that all these accusations are well founded, are they accusations against the capricious character of the *Leipziger Allgemeine Zeitung*, or are they not rather accusations against the necessary character of a young, newly arisen people's press? Is it a question of the existence of only a certain kind of press, or a question of the nonexistence of a real press, that is a *people's press?*

The French, the English, and all other newspapers began in the same way as the German, and each one of them deserved and received the same reproaches. The press is nothing, and can be nothing, if it is

---

[*] This series of six articles was published in the *Rheinische Zeitung*, January 1, 4, 6, 8, 10, 13, 1843.

not the loud and, naturally, "often the passionate and, in its expressions, exaggerated and blundering daily thinking and feeling of a people that really thinks itself to be a people." This is why it is like life itself, always becoming, never ending. It stands among the people and honestly sympathizes with all its hopes and fears, its loves and hates, joys and sorrows. What it learns hopefully or fearfully it communicates loudly and judges vehemently, passionately, one-sidedly, as the mood and thoughts of the moment dictate. The errors of fact and judgment it publishes today it refutes tomorrow. The press is the intrinsic "spontaneous" politics that its opponents generally love to cultivate.

The recent reproaches against the young press contradict each other in the same breath. Look, they say, what firm, steady, definite politics the English and French papers have. These papers are based on actual life, their views are the views of an existing ready-made power; they do not indoctrinate the people, they are the actual doctrines of the people and its parties. You, however, do not express the ideas, the interests of the people; you *make* them first, or rather, shove them into the people. You create the party spirit. You are not its creation.

Thus the press is reproached for the fact that there exist no political parties and, at the same time, because it wants to remedy this deficiency and create political parties. But it is self-evident. Where the press is young the people's spirit is young, and the loud daily political thinking of a recently awakened people's spirit is bound to be more unprepared, more formless, more rash than a political spirit that had grown great and strong and self-assured in political struggles. Above all, the people, whose political sense has just awakened, ask less for the *factual* correctness of this or that event than for the *moral* soul which animates it; fact or fable, it remains an embodiment of the thoughts, fears, and hopes of a people, a *true* fairy tale. The people see this, they see their own Being reflected in the Being of the press, and if this were not the case they would consider it unessential and unworthy of attention, for the people do not let themselves be deceived. No matter how the young press may compromise itself daily and be imbued with bad passions, the people see in it their own condition and they know that despite all the poison that malice and unreason drag in, its essence always remains true and pure and the poison passing through the constantly moving, constantly full stream will become truth and healing medicine. The people know that their press bears their sins, humbles itself for them, and, forgoing its own glory, distinction, pride, and irrefutability, exhibits the rose of a moral spirit within the thorn of the present.

We must therefore view the reproaches made against the *Leipziger Allgemeine Zeitung* as reproaches against the youthful people's press, hence against the actual press, for it goes without saying that the press cannot become real without going through the necessary stages of development rooted in its essence. But we must declare the rejection of the people's press a rejection of the people's political spirit. Yet in the beginning of our article we characterized the auspices of the German press as seemingly clouded. And so it is, for the struggle against an existence is the first form of recognition of its actuality and its power. And only the struggle can convince the government, as well as the people and the press itself, of the actual and necessary right of the press. Only struggle can show whether the press is a concession or a necessity, an illusion or a truth.

Cologne, January 3

In its issue of December 31 the *Kölnische Zeitung* published an article by a correspondent datelined "Leipzig, the 27th," which reported almost gleefully the suppression of the *Leipziger Allgemeine Zeitung*, whereas the cabinet order that decreed the suppression of this paper, and which can be found in the *Staats-Zeitung*[1] that arrived here yesterday, is dated December 28. The mystery is easily solved by the observation that the news of the suppression of the *Leipziger Allgemeine Zeitung* reached the post office here on December 31, and the *Kölnische Zeitung* saw fit not only to *write* the article here but also to make the good city of Leipzig appear to be the home of its *own voice*. The "mercantile" imagination of the *Kölnische Zeitung* was "nimble" enough to exchange concepts. It saw the residence of the *Kölnische Zeitung* in Leipzig, while the residence of the *Leipziger Zeitung* in Cologne has become an impossibility. If after thinking it over the *Kölnische Zeitung* should want to defend its fantasy as dry and truthful fact, it would force us to report, in connection with its fictitious correspondence from Leipzig, still another fact, namely, "that it exceeded all bounds of decency and, in the eyes of all moderate and thoughtful people, committed an incomprehensible indiscretion."

In regard to the suppression of the *Leipziger Allgemeine Zeitung* itself, we have voiced our opinion. We did not challenge the deficiencies of the *Leipziger Allgemeine Zeitung* as being without reality but we did maintain that those deficiencies, which emanate from the *essence* of the people's press, must be tolerated in the course of its development, if there is to be a course of development at all.

The *Leipziger Allgemeine Zeitung* is not the whole German press, but it is a necessary and integral part of it. The various elements which make up the nature of a people's press must find their appro-

---

1. The *Allgemeine Preussische Staats-Zeitung*, a semiofficial Berlin daily.

priate expression in the natural development of each paper. Thus the whole body of the people's press will divide itself into different newspapers, each reciprocally complementing the other; thus, for example, in one political science will predominate and in another political practice, in one new thought, and in another new fact. Only by preserving the elements of the people's press in their unhindered, independent, and one-sided development, and by expressing itself in various organs, can a "good" people's press be formed, that is, a people's press that unites within itself harmoniously all *true* moments of the *people's spirit*, so that each newspaper contains the actual moral soul, just as the fragrance and soul of the rose is in every leaf. But for the press to achieve its destiny, it is necessary that its destiny not be prescribed from outside, and that it be given the same recognition one is accustomed to give a plant—a recognition of its own *inner laws*, which must not and cannot be denied arbitrarily.

Cologne, January 5

We have had to listen to a great many abstractions about the difference between a "good" and a "bad" press. Let us once and for all illustrate the difference with an example!

The *Elberfelder Zeitung*,[2] in an article datelined Elberfeld, January 5, characterizes itself as a "good paper." The January 5 issue of the *Elberfelder Zeitung* brings the following news: "Berlin, December 30. The suppression of the *Leipziger Allgemeine Zeitung* has made only a slight impression here."

On the other hand, the *Düsseldorfer Zeitung*,[3] in agreement with the *Rheinische Zeitung*, reports: "Berlin, January 1. The absolute suppression of the *Leipziger Allgemeine Zeitung* has caused the greatest sensation here, since Berliners liked to read that paper," etc.

Which press, then, the "good" or the "bad," is the "true" press? Which one speaks the truth and which the "desired" truth? Which reflects public opinion, and which distorts public opinion? Which one therefore deserves public confidence?

We are little satisfied with the statement in the *Kölnische Zeitung*. In its reply to our remark that it reported the news of the suppression of the *Leipziger Allgemeine Zeitung* "almost gleefully," it confines itself not only to a statistical but also to a typographical error. The *Kölnische Zeitung* must know very well that in the sentence "The mystery is simply solved by the observation that the news of the

---

2. A conservative daily, published in Elberfeld from 1834 to 1904.
3. A liberal daily, published in Düsseldorf from 1826 to 1926.

suppression of the *Leipziger Allgemeine Zeitung* reached the post office here on December 31" the latter was a typo for "December 30." For it was on December 30, at noon, as we can prove if necessary, that the *Rheinische Zeitung*, as well as the *Kölnische Zeitung*, received the news at the post office.

Cologne, January 7

A *moderate* Rhineland paper,[4] as the *Allgemeine Augsburger Zeitung* calls it in its diplomatic language—that is, a paper of moderate talents, very moderate character, and all-too-moderate intelligence— turned around our statement that the *Leipziger Allgemeine Zeitung* is a necessary and integral part of the German people's press to a statement that *lying* is a necessary part of the press. We do not want to take offense from the fact that this moderate paper tore a single sentence from our argument and held that the article in question, as well as a previous one, was not worth its lofty and honorable consideration. As little as we demand of anybody that he jump out of his own skin, so little do we demand of an individual or a party that it jump out of its intellectual skin, that it venture a *salto mortale* [mortal leap] beyond the limits of the horizon of its intelligence—at least of a party whose stupidity passes for holiness. We do not, therefore, discuss what that intellectual denizen of the *Middle Ages* had to do to refute us, we discuss only its actual facts.

First of all, it enumerates the old sins of the *Leipziger Allgemeine Zeitung*: its attitude toward Hanoverian affairs,[5] its partisan polemic against Catholicism (*hinc illae lacrimae!* [hence these tears!] Would our friend take the same position, but in reverse direction, in regard to the mortal sins of the *Münchener Politische Blätter?*[6]), its gossip, etc., etc. We are reminded of an *aperçu* [sketch] from Alphonse Karr's *Les Guêpes.*[7] In it M. Guizot depicts M. Thiers and M. Thiers depicts M. Guizot as a traitor, and unfortunately they are both right. If all the old-style German papers were to be reproached for their past, then the process could revolve only around the formal question of whether they sinned by what they did or what they did not do. We

---

4. The reference is to the *Rhein- und Mosel-Zeitung*, a Catholic daily published in Coblenz between 1831 and 1850.

5. In 1837, when the King of Hanover dismissed seven Göttingen University professors, the *Leipziger Allgemeine Zeitung* defended the latter.

6. A Catholic clerical journal, published in Munich under the title *Historisch-politische Blätter für das katholische Deutschland* (*Historical-Political Papers for Catholic Germany*).

7. *Les Guêpes* (*The Wasps*), a Paris satirical monthly.

will gladly grant our friend the harmless advantage that the *Leipziger Allgemeine Zeitung* was not only a bad paper but that it did not exist at all.

Nevertheless, our incriminated article did not speak of the past but of the present character of the *Leipziger Allgemeine Zeitung*, although, it goes without saying, we would have made no less objections if the *Elberfelder Zeitung*, the *Hamburger Correspondenten*, or the Coblenz-based *Rhein- und Mosel-Zeitung* had been suppressed, for a legal position is not altered by the moral character or even the political and religious opinions of individuals. Rather, there is no doubt that the press is put in an illegal position when its existence is made dependent on its opinions. But so far there has not yet been a code of laws for opinions or a court of justice for opinions.

With honest indignation the "moderate" paper accuses the *Leipziger Allgemeine Zeitung* of falsifying facts, distortions, and lying, and of having held, in its final phase, the lie to be a necessary element of the people's press. And suppose we let this frightful inference pass, and maintain that the lie is a necessary element of the people's press, specifically the German people's press? We do not mean the lie of opinions, the intellectual lie, we mean the lie of facts, the material lie! Stone it! Stone it! our Christian friend would cry. Stone it! Stone it! the chorus would rejoin. But let us not be hasty, let us take the world as it is, let us not be ideologues, and we can give our friend testimony that we are not ideologues. Let the "moderate" paper take a searching look at its own columns, and it will find that like the *Preussische Staats-Zeitung*, like all German and like all newspapers the world over, it reports lies from Paris every day—gossip about pending ministerial changes in France, falsifications hatched by any Paris sheet —which it refutes the next day, or even the next hour! And does the *Rhein- und Mosel-Zeitung* consider a factual lie to be a necessary element in the columns of England, France, Spain, and Turkey, but a damnable capital crime in the columns of Germany or Prussia? Whence this double standard of measures and weights? Whence this dual view of truth? Why must the same paper carry a frivolous and careless piece of news in one column and display the dry irrefutability of an official paper in another? Obviously because for German newspapers there is a French, an English, a Turkish, a Spanish historical time, but not a German time—only a *German timelessness*. But should not the papers rather be commended, and commended for the sake of the country, for calling attention to the feverish interests, the dramatic tensions, that accompany contemporary history in the making, for seizing it from foreign countries and conquering it for the Fatherland! Granted, such newspapers arouse discontent, foment depression of spirit! But they arouse *German* discontent, *German* depression; and they give back to the country the minds that were alienated from the beginning! And what you have is not discontent and depression alone, but also fears and hopes, joys and sorrows; you have above all an awakened genuine interest in the state, a matter of the heart and the home in one's very bones; instead of Petersburg, London, Paris, you have made Berlin, Dresden, Hanover, etc., the capitals on the map of the German spirit—an achievement that is more glorious than the removal of the world capital from Rome to Byzantium.

But if the German and Prussian newspapers that aim to make Germany and Prussia the chief interest of the Germans, to transform the mysterious, priestly Being of the State into a laic institution, open, accessible and belonging to all, making it part of the flesh and blood of the citizens—if they are behind French and English newspapers in factual truth, and if they often behave ineptly and fictitiously, keep in mind that the German knows the state only from hearsay, that closed doors are not eyeglasses, that a secret political system is not a public political system, and do not consider the fault of the state the fault of the newspapers, a fault which the newspapers, in fact, seek to correct.

Thus we repeat again: the *Leipziger Allgemeine Zeitung* is a *necessary and integral part of the German people's press*. It has by preference satisfied direct interest in political facts, as we by preference are interested in political ideas, in connection with which it is self-evident that facts do not exclude ideas nor ideas facts, but what is involved here is the predominant character and the distinctive characteristic.

Cologne, January 9

It would have been against all rules if the "good" press, spearheaded by the Augsburg prophetess Huldah,[8] whose repeated invitation to the dance we will accept later, had not sought to earn its spurs by attacking us from all sides. Today we will deal with our invalid neighbor, the highly esteemed *Kölnische Zeitung! Toujours perdrix!* [Always the (same) partridge!]

To begin with: "Something preliminary," or a "preliminary something," a memorandum we want to send out to help understand today's denunciation, a charming little history of the ways and means by which the *Kölnische Zeitung* seeks to win the "esteem" of the government, asserting "true freedom" in contrast to "arbitrariness" and setting its own inner "limits." The reader who is so inclined will recall how in the No. 4 issue of the *Reinische Zeitung* [January 4] the *Kölnische Zeitung* was accused of having *manufactured* its correspon-

---

8. Huldah, Marx's name for the Augsburg *Allgemeine Zeitung*, is from a Jerusalem prophetess (II Kings 22:14–20; II Chronicles 34:22).

dence from Leipzig, almost gleefully reporting the frequently discussed suppression of the paper there, and how it was dissuaded from a serious defense of its document by the definite threat that otherwise we would have to publish some disagreeable facts regarding its mythical correspondence from Leipzig. The kind reader will recall the *Kölnische Zeitung*'s docile and evasive answer of January 5, our rectifying rejoinder in No. 6 [January 6], and the "suffering silence" which the *Kölnische Zeitung* thereupon found it good to observe. The fact in question is this: the *Kölnische Zeitung* found justification of the suppression of the *Leipziger Allgemeine Zeitung* in a report which "exceeded all bounds of decency and, in the eyes of all moderate and thoughtful people, committed an incomprehensible indiscretion."

This clearly referred to the publication of Herwegh's letter.[9] One could perhaps share this view of the *Kölnische Zeitung* if it had not, a few days earlier, *wanted* to publish Herwegh's letter and been frustrated in its good intentions only by encountering "restraints from outside."

In no way do we want hereby to reproach the *Kölnische Zeitung* with a disloyal hankering, but we must leave it to the public to decide whether it is a conceivable discretion, or whether it is a violation of all the limits of decency and public morality, when one reproaches his neighbor for committing a capital crime when he does what one had in mind to do oneself but was prevented from doing by an outside obstacle. After this explanation it will be understandable why the bad conscience of the *Kölnische Zeitung* replies to us today with a *denunciation*. It says:

"It is maintained there" (in the *Rheinische Zeitung*) "that the uncommonly sharp, almost cutting, in any case disagreeable, tone the press assumed toward Prussia had no other reason than a desire to make itself noticed by and to wake up the government. It is maintained that the people are far ahead of the political institutions, which suffer from intrinsic hollowness; that the people have no confidence in these institutions and even less in any development from the inside out."

The *Kölnische Zeitung* accompanies these words with the following exclamation: "Must one not be amazed that in view of such utterances there should still ring out complaints about insufficient freedom of the press? Can one demand more than the freedom to tell the government to its face that 'all the political institutions are rubbish, and not even good enough to serve as a transition to something better'?"

---

9. On December 24, 1842, the *Leipziger Allgemeine Zeitung* published a letter from the poet Georg Herwegh to King Frederick Wilhelm IV, protesting the prohibition of the distribution of his monthly, *Der Deutsche Bote aus der Schweiz*, on Prussian soil. It was the publication of this letter that led to the prohibition of the *Leipziger Allgemeine Zeitung* in Prussia.

First let us be clear about the ways and means of the citation. The author of the article mentioned[10] asks himself the question exactly why the sharp tone of the press is directed at Prussia. He replies: "I believe the main reason must be found in the following." He does not maintain, as the *Kölnische Zeitung* imputes to him, that there is no other reason; rather, he gives his view only as his *own* belief, his *individual* opinion. Moreover, the author grants what the *Kölnische Zeitung* conceals, that the "upswing of 1840 had thrown itself partly into political institutions, trying to fill them with content and life." Nevertheless, one feels that "the spirit of the people had actually passed them by, hardly touching them, and even in transition to a further development, does not yet know how to discern or really respect them." The author continues, "Whether they are right or not, it is established that the people, as well as the press, have no *full* confidence in the institutions, and even less in the possibility of their evolution from the bottom upward." The *Kölnische Zeitung* changed "no full confidence" into *no* confidence, and from the last part of the cited sentence it left out the words "from the bottom upward," thereby substantially modifying the whole meaning.

The press, the author continues, therefore constantly turned to the government, because what "seemed to be involved was only the forms within which the justified moral will, the ardent desires, and the needs of the people" could confront "the government with free, open, and weighty language." If we put all these passages together, the article in question maintains, is not the *Kölnische Zeitung* saying to the "government's face": "All political institutions are rubbish, not even good enough to serve as a transition to something better"?

Is it a question of *all* political institutions? It is a question only of those political forms in which the "will of the people" can speak out "freely, openly and weightily." And until recently, what have these political forms been? Clearly, only the Provincial Estates. Did the people place any special confidence in the Provincial Estates? Did they expect any great popular development from them? Did the loyalist Bülow-Cummerow consider them a true expression of the people's will? But it was not only the people and the press, but also the government that recognized that political forms themselves were still lacking; or without that recognition, would the latter have had the incentive to create new political forms, Provincial Diet Committees? Not only have we ourselves asserted that such committees in their present form do not suffice, but it has also been asserted in the *Kölnische Zeitung* by a member of such a committee.

The further assertion—that the political forms as *forms* stand in

---

10. "The Prussian Press," an article which appeared in the *Rheinische Zeitung*, January 6, 1843.

opposition to content, that the spirit of the people does not feel "at home" in them as its own forms, and does not know them as the forms of its own life—this assertion merely repeats what has been said by many Prussian and foreign newspapers, but mostly by *conservative* writers, namely, that the bureaucracy is still too powerful, that what actually governs is not the "government," or the whole state, but only a part of it. Whether the present political forms are capable partly of filling themselves with living content and partly of taking on supplementary forms, to this question the *Kölnische Zeitung* should have sought an answer in the Provincial Estates and Provincial Committees in connection with our whole state system, and it would have found there information comprehensible even to its own intelligence. "We do not demand that in popular representation one should make an abstraction of actually existing differences; we demand, rather, that one should recognize the actual differences created and conditioned by the inner structure of the state." "We demand only a *consistent and universal reformation of the fundamental Prussian institutions;* we demand that the real and organic political life should not be abruptly abandoned, so as not to sink back into unreal, mechanical, subordinated, unpolitical spheres of life" (*Rheinische Zeitung*, 1842, No. 345). And how does the honorable *Kölnische Zeitung* quote us? That "all political institutions are rubbish, not even good enough to serve as transition to something better"! It almost seems as if the *Kölnische Zeitung* believes that it can compensate for its own lack of courage by ascribing to others the insolent abortions of its own cowardly and malicious fantasy.

Cologne, January 11

> "*Votre front à mes yeux montre peu d'allégresse!*
> *Serait-ce ma présence, Eraste, qui vous blesse?*
> *Qu'est-ce donc? qu'avez vous? et sur quel déplaisirs,*
> *Lorsque vous me voyez, poussez-vous des soupirs?*"[11]

These words in connection with the neighboring "*Colognese*"![12] The *Kölnische Zeitung* does not disseminate its "alleged denunciation"; it drops its main point, and merely complains that the "management" of the paper has been tangled up in a conflict in a most unpleasant manner. But, dear neighbor, when a correspondent of the *Kölnische Zeitung* identifies one of our Berlin dispatches with the *Rheinische*

---

11. Molière, *Les Fâcheux*, Act I, Scene 5: "*Your brow seems to me to be clouded!/ Would it be my presence, Eraste, that offends you?/ What is it? What troubles you?/ And what misgivings, when you see me, make you sigh?*"
12. The *Kölnische Zeitung*.

Zeitung itself, why should not the *Rheinische Zeitung* retaliate by identifying the Rhineland dispatch of the *Kölnische Zeitung* with the *Kölnische Zeitung* itself? Now, *ad vocem* [in regard to] *fact:* "It" (the *Rheinische Zeitung*) "does not reproach us for a *fact* but an *intention*"!

We do not reproach the *Kölnische Zeitung* only for an intention, but for a *fact of the intention.* A fact, the publication of Herwegh's letter, was changed by the *Kölnische Zeitung* from external accidents into an intention, although its intention had already been changed into a fact. If every thwarted fact were reduced to mere intention, would it thereby become less justifiable? At any rate, it would be an extraordinary virtue that would justify acts by events that thwarted them and reduced them to the mere intention of an act, rather than the act itself. But our loyal neighbor puts the question, not, certainly, to the *Rheinische Zeitung*, who, she darkly suspects, would not be easily "embarrassed" for an answer in its "honesty and scrupulousness," but to that "small portion of the public which is not yet clear as to how much faith to put in the suspicions" (that is: the defenses against suspicions) "of this paper." But, she asks, how does the *Rheinische Zeitung* know "that to this intention" (the publication of Herwegh's letter) "we did not tie another one" (*signo haud probato* [unsubstantiated by any proof]), "that of adding a reprimand which the author's childish petulance deserved?" But how does the *Kölnische Zeitung* know what *intention* the *Leipziger Allgemeine Zeitung* had in publishing the letter? Why not the harmless intention of merely publishing a piece of news? Why not perhaps the loyal intention of bringing the letter to the judgment of public opinion? We have to tell our neighbor an anecdote. In Rome, publication of the Koran is prohibited. A wily Italian knew how to get around it. He published a *refutation* of the Koran, that is, a book which bore on its title page *Refutation of the Koran*, but the content was simply the text of the Koran. And didn't all heretics know how to play this trick? And was not Vanini burned, although in his proclamation of atheism in his book, *Theatrum mundi*,[18] he carefully and ostentatiously presented all counterarguments against it? Did not Voltaire himself, in his *Bible enfin expliquée*,[14] teach religious unbelief in the text and belief in the notes, and did anybody trust the purifying validity of these notes?

But, our honorable neighbor concludes, "Even if we had had such an intention, can our adoption of a piece of writing, which was in any case generally known, be put in the same category as its original publication?"

But, dear neighbor, the *Leipziger Allgemeine Zeitung* too only

---

13. *Amphitheatrum aeternae providentiae* (*Amphitheatre of Eternal Divine Providence*), published in 1615.
14. *The Bible Explained at Last.*

published a piece of writing that had circulated in many copies. "In faith, my lord, you are too wilful-blame."[15]

In the ex cathedra Papal Encyclical of August 15, 1832, "Assumption of the Blessed Virgin," one reads: "It is insanity" (*deliramentum*) "to maintain that all men are to be granted freedom of conscience; freedom of the press cannot be abominated enough."

This sentence takes us from Cologne to Coblenz, to the "moderate" paper, *Rhein- und Mosel-Zeitung*, whose bewailing of our fight for freedom of the press is understandable and explainable by this quotation, strange as it may sound that it should want to be counted "among the very zealous friends of the press." From the "moderate" columns of this paper there leap out, not two lions, but one lion's skin and one lion's cowl, to which we want to call the proper zoological attention. Skin No. 1 expectorates, among other things, as follows:

"On its" (the *Rheinische Zeitung*'s) "part, the struggle is such a loyal one that at the outset it gave us the assurance that in the event of a suppression of the *Rhein- und Mosel-Zeitung* it would side with us for the sake of the 'legality' that is so close to its heart—an assurance that would have been flattering and comforting if the knight embattled against *every* violation of press freedom had not let slip in the same breath an aspersion against the *Münchener Historisch-Politische Blätter*, which, it is well known, has long been prohibited among us."

Strange how at the moment a factual newspaper lie is condemned, it is factually lied about! The passage referred to reads verbatim: "First of all, it enumerates the old sins of the *Leipziger Allgemeine Zeitung:* its attitude toward Hanoverian affairs, its partisan polemic against Catholicism (*hinc illae lacrimae!*) Would our friend take the same position, but in reverse direction, in regard to the mortal sins of the *Münchener Politische Blätter?*"[16] These lines are declared to be a "partisan polemic" against Protestantism by the *Münchener Politische Blätter*. Did we justify its suppression for this? Could we want to justify the "same proceedings," which we considered no cause for the suppression of the *Leipziger Allgemeine Zeitung*, as applying "in reverse direction" to the *Münchener Politische Blätter?* On the contrary! We asked the conscience of the *Rhein- und Mosel-Zeitung* whether it justifies a suppression of one side but does not justify a suppression of the other! We asked it, therefore, whether it condemns the proceedings themselves or rather the tendency of the proceedings. And the *Rhein- und Mosel-Zeitung* answered our question; it answered that, unlike us, it does not condemn partisan religious polemics, but only the partisan political polemics that happen to be so foolhardy as

15. Shakespeare, *The First Part of King Henry the Fourth*, Act III, Scene 1.
16. See the article of January 7, 1843, page 57.

to be Protestant. And thus at the moment when we defended the *Leipziger Allgemeine Zeitung* against the suppression that had "just occurred," mentioning its partisan polemic *with* the *Rhein- und Mosel-Zeitung* against Catholicism, did we not have the right to mention the partisan polemic of the long-prohibited *Münchener Politische Blätter*, *without* mentioning the *Rhein- und Mosel-Zeitung?* To the scanty state of public opinion, the immaturity of unaccustomed daily and vocal political thinking, the character of contemporary history in being, all of which we used to explain *factual* newspaper lies, Number One was gracious enough to add another reason, that of the actual weak-mindedness of a large part of the German press. The *Rhein- und Mosel-Zeitung* has in itself proved how untrue thinking necessarily and unintentionally produces distortions and lies.

Now we come to Number Two, the lion's cowl, for in it the deeper reasons of Number One are going through a more far-ranging process of development. First of all, the lion's cowl informs the public of its uninteresting frame of mind. You expected an "outpouring of anger." But we casually produced a "seemingly elegant snub." The cowl's gratitude for this "unexpected forbearance" is alloyed by the vexatious doubt "whether that unexpected forbearance is to be viewed in fact as a trait of gentlemanliness, or rather as a consequence of spiritual uneasiness and lassitude."

We do not want to expose our pious gentleman to an analysis of how spiritual ease could well produce a reason for spiritual unease, but to go directly to the "content of the refutation in question." The pious gentleman admits to "unfortunately" not being "able to conceal" the fact that, according to his "most moderate intelligence," the *Rheinische Zeitung* sought to hide "its embarrassment behind hollow word fencing," and in order not to permit a "hypocritical humility and modesty" to appear even for a moment, the pious gentleman covers his "most moderate" intelligence with the most striking and irrefutable proofs. He begins as follows:

" 'The old sins of the *Leipziger Allgemeine Zeitung*, its attitude toward Hanoverian affairs, its partisan polemic against Catholicism, its gossip,' etc., well, of course, these cannot be denied; but—in the opinion of our excellent pupil of the great philosopher Hegel—these offenses are completely excused on the ground that other papers have been guilty of the same thing (exactly as if a scoundrel in court could not defend himself more brilliantly than by invoking the bad pranks of his numerous colleagues who are still at large in the world)."

Where did we say that the old sins of the *Leipziger Allgemeine Zeitung* are completely excused on the ground that other papers have also been guilty of the same thing? Where did we even try to "excuse" these old sins? Our real argument, which should be carefully distinguished from the reflection of our argument in the mirror of the "most moderate intelligence," reads thus: To begin with, the *Rhein- und Mosel-Zeitung* has enumerated the "old sins" of the *Leipziger Allgemeine Zeitung*. We then specified those "sins" and continued, "if all the old-style German newspapers were to be reproached for their past, then the process could revolve only around the formal question of whether they offended by what they did or what they did not do. We will gladly grant our friend," the *Rhein- und Mosel-Zeitung*, "the harmless advantage that the *Leipziger Allgemeine Zeitung* was not only a bad paper, but that it did not exist at all."

We therefore do not say that other papers also, we say that *all* German newspapers of the old style, in which we specifically include the *Rhein- und Mosel-Zeitung*, are not *completely* excused, but are rightly subject to the same reproaches. But the *Rhein- und Mosel-Zeitung* may claim the ambiguous advantage of having offended by what it did not do; that is, it may appose its sins of *omission* to the *Leipziger Allgemeine Zeitung*'s sins of *commission*. We can explain to the *Rhein- und Mosel-Zeitung* its passive wickedness by a fresh example. It now vents its fanatical appetite on the defunct *Leipziger Allgemeine Zeitung*, whereas during the latter's lifetime it used to excerpt from it rather than refute it. The picture of our argument which the "most moderate intelligence" strives to clarify for itself needs a small but essential correction. He should not have spoken of a scoundrel who defends himself in court on the ground that other scoundrels are at large. He should have spoken of *two* scoundrels, of whom the one, who has not reformed and has not been imprisoned, triumphs over the other, who has been imprisoned *although* he has reformed.

"Moreover," the "most moderate intelligence" continues, "a legal position is not altered by the moral character or even the political and religious opinions of an individual, and the consequence is an absolutely evil paper, because existence is purely evil, and has a right to such an evil existence (exactly as in all other evils on earth, the *right* to exist cannot be contested, because of man's evil existence)."

It seems, so the pious gentleman wants to convince us, that he not only did not go to the school of a "great" philosopher but not even to that of a "little" one.

The passage our friend has cited in such a wonderfully distorted and muddled way, before it was shattered via the medium of the "most moderate intelligence," actually reads thus:

"Nevertheless, our incriminated article did not speak of the past but of the present character of the *Leipziger Allgemeine Zeitung*, although, it goes without saying, we would have made no less objections if . . . the Coblenz-based *Rhein- und Mosel-Zeitung* had been suppressed, for a legal position is not altered by the moral character or even the political and religious opinions of individuals. Rather, there is no doubt that the press is put in an illegal position when its existence is made dependent on its opinions. But so far there has not yet been a code of laws for opinions or a court of justice for opinions."

Thus we do not maintain that a man cannot be jailed or lose his property or any other *legal* right because of his moral character or his political and religious opinions, the latter assertion of which seems to have particularly incensed our religious friend. We maintain that the legal right of an evil existence should remain unendangered, not because it is evil, but only insofar as its evil remains one of *opinions*, for which there is no court of justice and no code of laws. Thus we appose the existence of evil opinions, for which there is no court of justice, to the existence of evil actions, which, if found to be unlawful, will find their courts of justice and their laws. Hence we maintain that an evil existence, although it is evil, has a right to existence, so long as it is not *unlawful*. We do not maintain, as our sham echo claims, that an evil existence, precisely because it is a "purely evil" existence, cannot be denied "the right to exist." Rather, our worthy well-wisher will have convinced himself that we oppose him and the *Rhein- und Mosel-Zeitung* on account of their evil existence, because we want if possible to change them into good existences, without justifying on our part an attack on the "legal position" of the *Rhein- und Mosel-Zeitung* and its shield bearers. One more proof of the "intelligence level" of our pious zealot:

"When, however, the organ of 'political thought' goes so far as to maintain that such papers as the *Leipziger Allgemeine Zeitung* (and, it goes without saying, particularly the *Rheinische Zeitung*) are 'rather to be commended, and commended for the country's sake,' because, granting that they arouse discontent and depression, the discontents and depressions are *German* discontents and depressions—we cannot help expressing our doubts about this strange way of having deserved well of the country."

In the original this passage reads: "But should not the papers rather be commended, and commended for the sake of the country, for calling attention to the feverish interests, the dramatic tensions, that accompany contemporary history in the making, for seizing it from foreign countries and conquering it for the Fatherland! Granted, such newspapers arouse discontent, foment depression of spirit! But they arouse *German* discontent, *German* depression; and they give back to the country the minds that were alienated from the beginning! And what you have is not discontent and depression alone, but also fears and hopes, joys and sorrows; you have above all an awakened genuine interest in the state, a matter of the heart and the home in one's very bones," etc.

Our Honorable has thus left out connecting middle terms. It is as if we said to him: Best of men! Be grateful to us, we enlighten your intelligence and even if we irritate you a little, it is still *your* intelligence that gains by it—and our friend answers: What! I should be grateful to you because you irritate me! After this proof by the "most moderate intelligence," one will, even without deeper psychological investigations, understand our author's immoderate imagination which has let us move, like cohorts, "through the German countryside, scorching and burning it." At the end our friend throws off his mask. "Ulrich von Hutten and his companions, among whom, as is known, was Luther, will in impotent anger forgive their lion's cowl in the *Rhein- und Mosel-Zeitung.* We can only blush over an exaggeration that ranges us beside such great men and want, because one good turn deserves another, to place our friends alongside Chief Pastor Goeze. Hence we say to him, in the words of Lessing: "And so, very briefly, my knightly renunciation. Write, Herr Pastor, and let others write, as much as the stuff will bear; I too write. If I acknowledge your being right, even in the slightest thing, when you are not right, then I can no longer touch my pen."[17]

---

17. From Lessing's *A Parable.*

Defense of the Mosel-Correspondent*

From the Mosel, in January

NUMBERS 346 AND 348 of the *Rheinische Zeitung* contain two articles by me, one dealing with the firewood emergency in the Mosel region, and the other with the special participation of the Mosel people in the Royal Cabinet Order of December 24, 1841, effecting a more free movement of the press. The latter article is dipped in heavy and, if you wish, crude colors. Whoever becomes directly and frequently aware of the pitiful voice of distress in the surrounding population easily loses that aesthetic tact which knows how to paint the most refined and most modest pictures; perhaps, indeed, he considers it his political duty for a moment to express publicly the language of popular distress which he has found no opportunity to unlearn in his homeland. If it is a question of proving the truth of one's words, the proof can hardly extend to the wording, for in that case every résumé would be untrue, and it would be altogether impossible to convey the sense of a speech without repeating the speech itself. If, for example, one maintained: "The cry of distress of the winegrowers is considered an *insolent shriek*," then in all fairness one could demand only that an approximately correct equation be drawn, that is, the substantiation of a subject that balances to some extent the summary description, "insolent shriek," and makes it a not unfitting designation. If such a test is provided, then what is involved is no longer the *truth* itself but rather linguistic precision; and a judgment on the fleetingly fine nuances of a linguistic expression could hardly be anything but problematical.

The above observations are prompted by two rescripts of Herr Oberpräsident [Lord Lieutenant] von Schaper in No. 352 of the *Rheinische Zeitung*, datelined Coblenz, December 15 [1842], in which

---

* *Rheinische Zeitung*, January 15, 1843.

a number of questions are directed at me about the articles mentioned. The belated publication of my reply is caused chiefly by the content of the questions themselves, in that a newspaper correspondent reports, in the best conscience, the voice of the people as it reaches his ears, without having to be in any way prepared to present the reasons, the causes and the sources, in exhaustive detail. Apart from the loss of time and all the measures such work demands, a newspaper correspondent can consider himself merely a member of a much ramified body in which he freely chooses his own function; and when one person portrays a condition of distress based on a direct impression of public opinion, another person, who may be an historian, will discuss its history, a person of strong feelings, the distress itself, a political economist, the means of its alleviation—demonstrating how this single question can be solved from various sides, some local, some more in connection with the whole political system, etc.

Thus in a lively press the *whole truth* makes its appearance, for if the whole finally emerges, even through occasionally deliberate and occasionally accidental presentation of various individual viewpoints, it is due to the work of the press itself, which prepared the materials for one of its members, that a whole can be fashioned. In this way the press comes into the whole truth by and by, through a division of labor in which it is not one man who does it all but many who do little things.

Another reason for the belatedness of my reply lies in the fact that the editors of the *Rheinische Zeitung*, after the first report I sent in, wanted more supplementary information, and demanded additional materials again after the second and third reports, as well as this concluding report; and finally they requested partly that I supply a report on my sources and partly also they held up publication of my contributions until they could verify my reports on their own.[1]

Furthermore, my reply appears anonymously. In that I follow the conviction that anonymity belongs to the essence of the press, which transforms a newspaper from a collection point of many individual opinions into an organ of a *single mind*. A name separates an article from other articles as firmly as the body of a person separates him from other individuals, thus thoroughly doing away with the article's intention to be only a supplementary member. Finally, anonymity makes not only the speaker himself but also the public more unbiased and more free, in that it does not look at the man who speaks but at the subject he discusses, shifting its yardstick of undisturbed judgment from the empirical person to the intellectual personality.

---

1. While we confirm the above assertions, we remark at the same time that the various reciprocally interpreting letters have made a summary by us necessary.—THE EDITORS OF THE *Rheinische Zeitung*.

Just as I keep silent about my name, so I will name the details of officials and communities only when they are printed as documents and found in bookstores, or when mentioning the name is quite harmless. It is my conviction that the press must denounce *conditions* but not *persons*, unless a public evil could not be assessed otherwise or publicity already dominates the whole public life and has thereby made the German concept of denunciation disappear.

At the end of these prefatory remarks I believe myself entitled to express the just hope that, after reading my *entire* presentation, the Herr Oberpräsident will be convinced of the purity of my intentions and will even ascribe the possible errors to a false view rather than a malevolent disposition. My presentation itself must prove whether I deserved the harsh accusation of slander, as well as the charge of aiming to stir up dissatisfaction and discontent, even as in the case of a continuing anonymity—accusations which must be the more painful since they emanate from a highly admired and beloved man in the Rhine Province.

For an easy survey I have divided my reply into the following rubrics:

A. The Question Regarding the Distribution of Wood.

B. The Relation of the Mosel Region to the Cabinet Order of December 24, 1841, and the More Free Movement of the Press Effected Thereby.[2]

C. The Canker of the Mosel Region.

D. The Vampire of the Mosel Region.

E. Proposals for Relief.[3]

---

2. See page 74.

3. Of the five rubrics, Marx succeeded in discussing only two (A and B); the others were forbidden by the censorship, and the manuscripts are now lost. This article itself was one reason for the suppression of the *Rheinische Zeitung* as of April 1, 1843.

The *Rhein- und Mosel-Zeitung*[*]

Cologne, January 15

THE NUMBER ONE of the *Rhein- und Mosel-Zeitung* of January 11, to whom a few days ago we devoted a few fleeting remarks as the outrider of the lion's article,[1] seeks today to prove by an example how little "it" (the *Rheinische Zeitung*) "in its dialectical superiority is able to comprehend clearly a simple and clearly expressed sentence."

He, Number One, of course never said at all that the *Rheinische Zeitung* had sought to justify the suppression of the *Münchener Politische Blätter*, "but at the moment when it posed as the champion of freedom of the press, it did not take the position of abusing an actually suppressed paper; hence the gallantry with which it sought to enter the lists against a suppression of the *Rhein- und Mosel-Zeitung* does not seem enormous."

Outrider No. 1 overlooks the fact that two reasons could have explained his anxiety about our chivalrous behavior in regard to a possible suppression of the *Rhein- und Mosel-Zeitung*, and both have been answered. The good outrider, we are inclined to think, does not trust our assurance because he sees in the alleged aspersion on the *Münchener Politische Blätter* a hidden justification of its suppression. We could anticipate such a process of thought in the good outrider, the more so as the common man possesses a characteristic cunning of being able to read true meaning in remarks that, as seems to him, have "slipped out" unconsciously. In this case we can reassure the good outrider by proving to him how impossible it is to make a connection

[*] *Rheinische Zeitung*, January 16, 1843.
1. See Marx's dispatch of January 11, 1843 (page 62), in which he describes the *Rhein- und Mosel-Zeitung* as not being two lions, but only one lion's skin and one lion's cowl. The "Number One" referred to is the lion's skin.

between our statement about the *Münchener Politische Blätter* and a justification of its suppression.

Or, as a second possibility, does No. 1 find it dubious and unchivalrous that we reproach an *actually suppressed paper*, like the *Münchener Politische Blätter*, for its partisan polemics against Protestantism? He sees an aspersion in this. And in this case we put a question to the good outrider: "If, at the moment when we defended the *Leipziger Allgemeine Zeitung* against the suppression that had 'just occurred,' and mentioned its partisan polemic along with the *Rhein- und Mosel-Zeitung*'s against Catholicism, did we not have the right to mention the partisan polemic of the 'long suppressed' *Münchener Politische Blätter*, without also mentioning the *Rhein- und Mosel-Zeitung*?" This means: We did not cast an aspersion on the *Leipziger Allgemeine Zeitung* by mentioning the partisan anti-Catholic polemic with the consent of the *Rhein- und Mosel-Zeitung*. Does our statement about the partisan Catholic polemic of the *Münchener Politische Blätter* become an aspersion just because it was so unfortunate as not to have the consent of the *Rhein- und Mosel-Zeitung?*

No. 1 did nothing more than call our statement an aspersion, and since when have we been obligated to take No. 1's word? We said: The *Münchener Politische Blätter* is a Catholic party newspaper, and in this respect it is a *Leipziger Allgemeine Zeitung* in reverse. The outrider *Rhein- und Mosel-Zeitung* says: It is not a party newspaper and no *Leipziger Allgemeine Zeitung* in reverse. It is not "a similar warehouse of untruths, stupid gossip, and derision directed against non-Catholic denominations."

We are not a theological pugilist for one side or the other, but one need only read the cheap, gossipy psychological portrayal of Luther in the *Münchener Politische Blätter,* or what the *Rhein- und Mosel-Zeitung* says about "Hutten and his companions," to decide whether this "moderate" paper's point of view is competent to judge what is and what is not partisan religious polemic.

Finally, the good outrider promises us a "more detailed characterization of the *Rheinische Zeitung.*" *Nous verrons.* [We will see.] The small [Catholic] party between Munich and Coblenz has already discovered that the "political" mind of Rhinelanders must be either exploited for certain unpolitical efforts or suppressed as an "annoyance." Could the *Rhein- und Mosel-Zeitung* see without annoyance its own complete insignificance substantiated by the rapid growth of the *Rheinische Zeitung* throughout the Rhine Province? Is the present moment unfavorable for vexation? We find all this passably superior and only regret that, lacking a more significant organ, that party has to content itself with the good outrider and its seemingly "moderate" paper. From this organ, one can judge the strength of its party.

The Relation of the Mosel Region to the Cabinet Order of December 24, 1841, and the More Free Movement of the Press Effected Thereby*

IN CONNECTION with my article in Number 346 of the *Rheinische Zeitung*, datelined "Bernkastel, December 10," in which I claimed that the people of the Mosel hailed the greater freedom of the press effected by the Most High [Royal] Cabinet Order of December 24 of last year because of their especially oppressed situation, the Herr Oberpräsident [Lord Lieutenant] remarks as follows:

"If that article is to make sense, the Mosel people must have been previously forbidden to discuss frankly and publicly their distress, the causes of the same as well as the remedies. I doubt that this is the case. For in regard to the efforts of the authorities to provide a remedy for the acknowledged distress of the winegrowers, nothing could have been more desirable for them than a discussion of the conditions prevailing there, carried out as openly and frankly as possible." "The author of the above article would therefore oblige me very much if he would have the goodness to cite cases where, even before the publication of the Most High Cabinet Order of December 24 of last year, an open and public discussion of the distress of the inhabitants of the Mosel was prevented by the authorities."

Further on the Oberpräsident remarks, "Moreover, the statement in the above quoted article, that the winegrower's cries for help had long been considered 'insolent shrieks' by the higher authorities, I believe I can say at the outset is an untruth."

My reply to these questions will take the following course. I will seek to prove:

(1) that first, entirely apart from the powers of the press as stated in the Most High Cabinet Order of December 24, 1841, the particular

---

* Published in the *Rheinische Zeitung* in three parts, January 17, 19, 20, 1843.

nature of the distress along the Mosel makes the need for a free press a necessity;

(2) that even if no special obstructions to "open and public discussion" had taken place before the publication of the Cabinet Order in question, my assertion would lose nothing of its correctness, and that the special interest of the Mosel people in the Most High Cabinet Order and in the freer movement of the press which it has effected is understandable;

(3) *that really special* circumstances prevented an "open and public" discussion.

The whole context will then demonstrate to what extent my assertion that "For a long time the authorities had doubts about the desolate situation of the winegrowers and considered their cries of distress insolent shrieks" was truth or untruth.

Ad [about] (1). In the investigation of political conditions one is too easily tempted to overlook the factual nature of relationships and to explain everything as emanating from the will of the acting persons. But there are relationships that determine the actions of private persons as well as those of individual authorities and that are as independent of them as is the manner of breathing. Taking this realistic standpoint at the outset, one will not presuppose a good or a bad law on the one side or the other, but will see relationships in effect that at first glance seem to be merely individuals acting. As soon as it is demonstrated that something was made necessary by conditions, it will no longer be difficult to figure out under which external conditions this thing actually had to come about and under which conditions it could not have come about, even though the need for it was present. One can determine this with almost the same certainty as a cabinet determines under what external conditions substances that are related must form a combination. Hence by our statement that a free press is a necessity because of the particularity of the distress along the Mosel we intend to give our presentation a basis that goes beyond personalities.

The distress of the Mosel region cannot be considered as a simple condition. One must always keep in mind at least two sides, the private condition and the political condition; for as little as the Mosel region lies outside the state, so little does its distress lie outside the political administration. It is the relationship between the two aspects that forms the actual condition of the Mosel region. . . .[1]

Then what is the relation of the administration to the distress of the Mosel? The distress of the Mosel is at the same time a distress of

---

1. *A lengthy exchange of views between a Mosel viticulture society and the local government is omitted.*

government. The *constant* distress of a part of the country—and a distress that began almost unnoticed more than a decade ago, developing gradually and unceasingly to a culmination point, and that is still growing menacingly, may well be called constant—such a constant distress is a contradiction between reality and the maxims of administration, since not only the people but also the government consider the well-being of a countryside as a factual confirmation of the administration. But the administration, in its bureaucratic essence, sees the causes of the distress not in the area of administration but only in the natural and private-bourgeois sector that lies outside the administered area. With the best will, the most eager humanity and the strongest intelligence, the administration, except for momentary and transitory collisions, cannot solve a constant collision between reality and its maxims, for not only is this not its task, but also the best intentions cannot break through an essential relationship or fate at will. The essential relationship is the bureaucratic one, both inside the administrative body itself and in its relation to the administered body.

On the other hand, the private winegrower can hardly fail to recognize that *his* vote is, intentionally or unintentionally, muddied by private interests, and thus the truth of such maxims cannot be presumed absolutely. He will also see that many private interests in the country are suffering, and general administrative maxims cannot be relied upon or reshaped to solve it. If, furthermore, the universal character of a state of distress is asserted, it asserts that well-being is endangered in the way and to the extent that private suffering becomes public suffering and its elimination a duty of the state *against itself*— and thus this assertion of the administered appears to be improper vis-à-vis the administration, since the latter will best judge how far the public well-being is imperiled and must presume a deeper insight into the relationship between the whole and its parts, as well as the parts themselves. The result is that the individual and even many individuals cannot claim to represent the voice of the people; rather, any presentation will always retain the character of a *private* petition of grievances. Finally, even if the conviction of the petitioning private individual were that of the whole Mosel region, the latter itself, as a single administrative unit and as a single section of the country, assumes provincially vis-à-vis the state as a whole the position of a private person, whose convictions and desires must first be measured against general convictions and universal desires.

To solve the difficulties, the administration and the administered both need a third element, which is political without being bureaucratic, an element that does not derive from bureaucratic presuppositions, that is, civic without being directly entangled in private interests and their needs. This complementary element, composed of a political head and a civic heart, is a *free press.* In the realm of the press the administration and the administered can criticize each other's principles and demands as equals, no longer in a subordinate relationship but with equal political worth, no longer as *persons* but as *intellectual powers,* with a basis of reason. The "free press," as it is the product of public opinion, also produces public opinion, and it alone has the power to make a special interest into a general interest; it alone has the power to make the distress of the Mosel region an object of general attention and general sympathy in the Fatherland; it alone has the power to alleviate the misery, if for no other reason than that it distributes the feeling of misery among all.

The press relates itself to the conditions of the people as *intelligence,* but it relates itself to them equally as *mood;* its language, therefore, is not merely the wise language of judgment that hovers over conditions but also the affective language of the conditions themselves, a language which cannot and should not be expected in bureaucratic reports. Finally, the free press carries the people's misery to the foot of the throne, not in a bureaucratically approved form but in its own medium, before which the distinction between administration and administered disappears and which results in a more equally near-standing and more equally far-standing citizenry.

Hence if a more free press was made necessary by the particular distress of the Mosel, when it was a vehement, because *real,* need here, it is clear that there was no necessity for exceptional press obstructions to bring forth this need, but rather, that exceptional press freedom was necessary to satisfy the existing need.

Ad 2. The press that reported the Mosel affairs is, at any rate, only a part of the Prussian political press. Hence to ascertain its condition before the frequently mentioned Cabinet Order it will be necessary to cast a quick glance at the condition of the entire Prussian press before the year 1841.

"Quietly and peacefully," says David Hansemann's *Prussia and France* (2d edition, Leipzig, 1834, p. 262), "quietly and peacefully, general ideas and things are developing in Prussia, the more imperceptibly as the censorship does not permit in the Prussian daily press any thorough discussion of political and even economic questions affecting the state, no matter how decorous and moderate the wording may be. Practically no economic question can be thoroughly discussed, unless its connections with internal and external policy are also investigated, and there are few economic questions, perhaps none at all, that have no such connections. Whether or not this exercise of the censorship is useful, whether or not the censorship could be exercised in this way and under such conditions in Prussia at all, does not come into question. *Suffice it that it is.*"

Remember, furthermore, that Paragraph II of the Censorship Edict of December 19, 1788, states: "But the aim of the censorship is in no way to prevent a decorous, serious, and moderate investigation of truth or to impose on writers *any other* unnecessary and burdensome constraint."

In Article II of the Censorship Edict of October 18, 1819, one reads again: "The censorship should not prevent any serious and moderate investigations of truth, nor impose any unbecoming constraint on writers."

Compare this with the introductory words of the Censorship Instruction of December 24, 1841: "To emancipate the press now from inadmissible restrictions not intended by the Most High [the King], His Majesty the King, through the Royal Ministry of State ... has issued a Cabinet Order specifically disapproving all unbecoming constraints on writing activities, and ... condescended to empower us by indicating to the censors anew the appropriate observation of Article II of the Censorship Edict of October 18, 1819."

Finally, let us recall the following words: "The censor may allow free discussion even of internal affairs. The unmistakable difficulty in finding the proper limits here ought not to discourage the effort to satisfy the real intention of the law, nor lead to anxiety, as has happened often enough already, causing misunderstanding of the intention of the Government."

From all these official utterances it appears that the question of why, in view of the authorities' wishes to hear the Mosel conditions discussed as freely and publicly as possible, censorship obstructions did take place, should, rather, be changed to the general question: Why, despite the "intention of the law," "the intention of the Government," and finally "*the intention of the Most High*," one still had to free the press from admittedly "inadmissible restrictions" in the year 1841, and why one had to be reminded of Article II of the Edict of 1819 in the year 1841? Specifically, in connection with the Mosel region, the question will be formulated, not as to what special press obstructions took place, but rather, what special press favors, *as an exception*, could have inspired this partial discussion of the internal conditions as frankly and publicly as possible?

The following quotation from the above-mentioned Cabinet Order explains most clearly the inner content and character of political literature and the daily press: "In this way, it is to be hoped that political literature and the daily press will recognize their vocation better, acquire a more dignified tone, and abstain in the future from playing upon the curiosity of their readers by printing meaningless reports taken from the correspondence of foreign newspapers, etc., etc.... It is to be expected that this will arouse a greater participation in the interests of the Fatherland, so that patriotism will be enhanced."

The gist of this seems to be that even though no *specific* measures prevented a free and open discussion of Mosel conditions, the *general condition* of the Prussian press itself must have been an insurmountable obstacle to candor as well as to publicity. When we summarize the quoted passages we find the Censorship Instruction says: Censorship was exceedingly nervous and constituted an *external* barrier to a free press; hand in hand with this went an *internal* limitation of the press, which had given up the courage and even the effort to rise above the horizon of mere reporting of the news; finally, the people lost the sense of participation in the interests of the Fatherland and their patriotism, the very elements which are not only the creative forces of a free and open press, but also the only conditions within which a free and open press can function and find popular acceptance, an acceptance which is the life blood of the press, without which it is hopelessly sick.

Hence, on the one hand, if measures taken by the authorities can create an unfree press, it is, on the other hand, beyond the power of the authorities to secure a free and open discussion of special problems, because of the general state of unfreedom of the press; for even frank comments on some matters, filling the columns of the newspapers, could not call forth universal participation and therefore could not achieve true publicity.

Hence, as Hansemann correctly observes, there is probably not a single economic question that does not have some connection with internal and external policy. The possibility of a free and open discussion of the Mosel situation presupposes, therefore, the possibility of a free and open discussion of the entire "internal and external policy." This is not in the power of the individual administrative authorities to offer, but rather, only in the express and decisive will of the King himself, who can take hold firmly and enduringly.

If the open discussion was not free, the free discussion was not open. It confined itself to obscure local sheets, whose horizon, of course, did not and could not extend beyond their own circulation. To illustrate such local discussions we present a few excerpts from various issues of the Bernkastel weekly, *Gemeinnütziges Wochenblatt* [*Public-Utility Weekly*]. Here is one from the year 1835:

"In fall, 1833, a nonresident person in Erden produced 5 ohms [about 40 gallons] of wine. To fill up the cartload [*Fuder*] he bought 2 ohms at a cost of 30 Taler. The cask cost 9 Taler; the grapejuice tax, 7 Taler and 5 silver Groschen; harvesting, 4 Taler; wine-cellar rental, 1 Taler and 3 silver Groschen; woodworker's wage, 16 silver Groschen; the total, not counting construction cost, was a net expense of 51 Taler and 24 silver Groschen. On May 10 the cask of wine was sold for 41

Taler. It is to be remarked additionally that this was good wine and was not sold out of distress, and it did not fall into the hands of usurers" (p. 87). "On November 21, 1835, wine was auctioned off in the market at Bernkastel at 14 silver Groschen—*14 silver Groschen*—per ¾ of an ohm; and on the 27th *ejusdem* [of the same month] 4 ohms together with the cartload, at 11 Taler, to which it is also to be remarked that last Michaelmas it sold at 11 Taler a cartload" (p. 267).

Under date of April 12, 1836, a similar account.

Here are some more extracts from the year 1837: "On the 11th of this month, at public auction before a notary in Kinheim, a young, four-year-old vineyard with 200 plants, properly staked, went at 1½ Pfennig per plant, with the usual form of payment. In the year 1828 the same plant there cost 5 silver Groschen" (p. 47). "A widow at Graach had her crop harvested for half the income, and her share came to 1 ohm of wine, which she disposed of for 2 pounds of butter, 2 pounds of bread, and ½ pound of onions" (in No. 37, *ibid.*). "On the 20th of this month there were forcibly auctioned off: 8 cartloads of 1836 wine from Graach and Bernkastel, partly from the best stock, and 1 cartload of 1835 wine from Graach. They brought in a total of 135 Taler and 15 silver Groschen (including the cask), which makes *circa* 15 Taler per cartload. The cask alone may have cost 10 to 12 Taler. What then is left to the poor grower for his construction cost? Is it not possible to find a remedy for this frightful distress?" (Sent in, No. 4, p. 30.)

One finds here only straightforward accounts which, though occasionally accompanied by an elegiac postscript that is moving in its unvarnished simplicity, nevertheless can hardly be called a free and open discussion of the Mosel conditions.

Therefore, when a segment of the population, and especially the majority, is struck by a shocking and terrifying misfortune, and nobody discusses the misfortune or treats it as a phenomenon deserving to be thought and talked about, the people affected must conclude that others are either not *permitted* or do not *want* to speak out, because they consider the importance of the matter to be illusory. But a cognizance of his misfortune and a sharing of it in spirit is a necessity even for the most uneducated winegrower—even if he merely concludes that with everybody thinking and many speaking about his misfortune, some will take action. Even if a free and public discussion of the Mosel situation had really been permitted, it would not have taken place anyway; and it is clear that people believe only in what exists in *reality*, not in a free press that might exist, but in a free press that actually does exist. The people of the Mosel had already experienced their distress *before* the issuance of the Most High Cabinet Order, had heard doubts about their distress but nothing about a public and free press; but, on the other hand, *after* the issuance of this Cabinet Order, they saw such a press emerge out of nowhere. Thus the conclusion that the Royal Cabinet Order was the sole cause of this press movement—in which the Mosel people, for reasons previously developed, participated directly because it filled a *real* need—seems at least to have been a very popular conclusion. Finally, it seems that even apart from the popularity of this opinion a critical examination would yield the same result. The introductory words of the Censorship Instruction of December 24, 1841, read: "His Majesty the King deigns to *disapprove* explicitly any improper coercion in writing activity, and with the recognition of the value of and the need for free and decent publication . . ." etc.

These introductory words assure the press a special *royal* recognition, hence *political significance*. The fact that a single royal statement was so effective that it could be hailed by the Mosel people themselves as a statement of magic power, as a universal panacea for all ailments, seems to attest to the genuinely royalist sentiment of the Mosel people and to their unmeasured and overflowing gratitude.

Ad 3. We have sought to show that the need for a free press emerged as a necessity from the particularity of the Mosel conditions. We have furthermore shown that before the issuance of the Most High Cabinet Order, the realization of this need was made impossible by the general condition of the Prussian daily press, if not by the special press difficulties. We will finally show that *really special* circumstances were inimical to a free and open discussion of the Mosel conditions. Here too we must first of all emphasize the main point of our presentation and recognize the power of general relationships in the will of the acting persons. In the special circumstances that prevented a free and public discussion of the Mosel conditions, we must see nothing but the actual embodiment and the visible manifestation of the general relationships referred to above, namely, the particular attitude of the administration to the Mosel region, the general state of the daily press and of public opinion, and finally the dominant political spirit and its system. If these conditions were, as it appears, the general, invisible, and compelling forces of the time, it hardly requires mention that they had to act as such, had to become real facts, and had to be expressed as individual acts that *appeared to be* arbitrary. Whoever does not accept this positive viewpoint gets entangled one-sidedly in bitter feelings against personalities who confronted him in the form of the harsh conditions of the time.

To the special press obstructions one must add not only particular censorship difficulties but also special circumstances which made censorship superfluous because they did not allow any subject for censorship to come up even experimentally. Where censorship gets into striking, persistent, and hard collisions with the press, there one can say with considerable certainty that the press has already won in vigor, character, and self-assurance, for only a perceptible action produces a perceptible reaction. Where, on the other hand, there is no censorship because there is no press, although the need for a free and hence potentially censorable press exists, there one must seek *precensorship* in conditions that have already frightened away ideas even in their more unassuming forms.

It is not our aim to give, even approximately, a full account of these special circumstances; to do so would mean writing the history of the Mosel region since 1830. We believe we have carried out our task when we have shown that the free and open word came into conflict with special obstacles in all its forms, in the form of speech, in the form of writing, in the form of print, print *not yet censored* as well as already *censored*.

The spiritlessness and despondency of a suffering population that destroy the moral force necessary for free and open discussion are particularly nourished by the numerous denunciations made necessary by judicial sentences imposed "because of insult to an official in office or in connection with his office."

Such a procedure is still fresh in the minds of many Mosel wine-growers. One citizen, especially popular because of his good nature, said jokingly to the maid of a *Landrat* [prefect] who had freely partaken of the cup on the occasion of the King's birthday the night before, "Last night your master was a little befuddled." Because of this innocent utterance he was publicly haled before the police court in Trier, although, it goes without saying, he was acquitted.

We chose this example because a simple reflection is tied up with it. The *Landräte* are the *censors* in their respective district towns. The prefectural administration, with its subordinate official spheres, is made more powerful by the inclusion of authority over the *local press*. It is already difficult enough to judge in one's own cause, so an incident such as the one mentioned, illustrating a sickly-sensitive conception of the untouchability of officialdom, shows that the very existence of a prefectural censorship is sufficient cause for the nonexistence of a free local press.

Just as artless and unpretentious oral speech leads to the police court, so also the written form of free speech, the petition, even when it is still far removed from publicity in the press, has police-court consequences. In the one instance free speech runs into the untouchability of *official position;* in the other, of the *laws.* . . .[2]

2. After the Cabinet Order of July 6, 1836, 160 peasants from the Trier district presented a petition of economic grievances to their deputy in the Landtag, to be presented to the Prussian Crown Prince. For doing so the deputy was sentenced

Finally, another example will show that a public and free discussion, if it overcomes all obstacles and *exceptionally* reaches the columns of a newspaper, is treated as an exception and thereafter annihilated. A few years ago Kaufmann, professor of public administration in Bonn, published an essay, "On the Distress of the Winegrowers on the Mosel," in the *Rhein- und Mosel-Zeitung;* after circulating for three months in various public newspapers, it was *suppressed* by the Royal Government, a suppression that is still in effect today.

Herewith I believe I have answered sufficiently the questions of the relationship between the Mosel region and the Cabinet Order of December 10, the Censorship Instruction of December 24 based on it, and the freer movement of the press since then. It only remains to substantiate my assertion: "The desolate situation of the winegrowers has long been doubted by the higher authorities and their cries of distress were regarded as insolent shrieks." The questioned sentence can be divided into two parts: "The desolate situation of the winegrowers has long been doubted by the higher authorities," and "their cries of distress were regarded as insolent shrieks."

The first part of the sentence, I believe, needs no further proof. The second part, "their cries of distress were regarded as insolent shrieks," cannot be interpreted precisely from the first part in the way that the Oberpräsident does: "Their cries of distress were regarded as insolent shrieks by the higher authorities." Still, even this interpolation can be applicable, insofar as "higher authority" and "official authority" are taken to mean the same thing.

From the reports submitted heretofore, one is justified in speaking of the winegrowers' "cries of distress" not only in the figurative but also in the literal sense. A government report and criminal-court proceedings have shown that these cries of distress were, on the one hand, regarded as unjustified, and the description of the distress itself as a gross exaggeration based on selfish and egoistic motives; and on the other hand, the complaint against this distress was interpreted as "insolent, disrespectful criticism of the law." That exaggerated cries which ignore the facts stem from evil motives and involve insolent criticism of the law may be called "shrieks," and even "insolent shrieks," is certainly no farfetched or untruthful assertion. That one can be put in place of the other is merely a logical conclusion.

---

to six months' imprisonment for "insolent, disrespectful criticism of the law," although the petition itself was not punishable. The text of the petition is omitted here.

Marginal Notes on the Changes Made in the Ministerial Rescript*

I

THE SAME [*Rheinische Zeitung*] has from its inception followed a reprehensible tendency, etc. Unmistakably there has prevailed in the newspaper a constant intention of attacking the constitution of the state at its foundations, of developing theories aiming at the destruction of the monarchical principle, of sowing in public opinion malicious suspicion of the operations of the government, of inciting one class in the nation against another, of stirring up dissatisfaction with existing legal conditions and of favoring very hostile tendencies against friendly powers. The ideas regarding the alleged shortcomings of the administration, apart from the fact that they were mostly seized out of thin air and have largely dispensed with thoroughness and expertise, have been developed, not in a serious, calm and dignified tone, but in spiteful hostility to the State and its administrative forms and organs.

Clearly, a tendency does not become *reprehensible* by the mere fact that the government declares it to be so. The Copernican cosmos too was not only found reprehensible by the highest authorities of the time but was actually infamous. Furthermore, it is the law everywhere that the plaintiff furnishes the proof. Finally, the *Rheinische Zeitung* is charged with the "unmistakable intention" of committing outrages. But an intention is *recognizable*, hence even more *unmistakable*, only when it is realized in *actions*.

Granting for a moment (which, however, we formally disavow) that all the accusations in the Ministerial Rescript are well founded, it nonetheless follows that in their undefined and ambiguous version they would apply equally to the suppression at will of *any newspaper* with

* Written on February 12, 1843. The Ministerial (Censorship) Rescript was issued January 21, 1843, suppressing the *Rheinische Zeitung* as of April 1, 1843.

as much or as little reason as the suppression of the *Rheinische Zeitung*.

Above all, in the *Rheinische Zeitung* there is supposed to prevail the "unmistakable intention" of "attacking the constitution of the state at its foundations." But as is well known, there unmistakably exists a great difference of opinion about the Prussian constitution and its foundation. Some deny that the foundation has a constitution, and others that the constitution has a foundation.

Stein, Hardenberg, Schön, another Rochow, Arnim, and Eichhorn are of a different opinion. In his lifetime Hegel believed that in his philosophy of law he had laid down the basis of the Prussian constitution, and the German public believed it with him. The government proved this, among other things, by the official dissemination of his writings; but the public did so by its reproach that he was the Prussian state philosopher, as can be read in the old Leipzig *Konversationslexikon*.[1] What Hegel believed then Stahl believes today. In the year 1831 Hegel lectured on the philosophy of law at the special order of the government.

In the year 1830 the *Staats-Zeitung*[2] declared Prussia a monarchy surrounded by republican institutions. Today it declares it a monarchy surrounded by Christian institutions.

In the great difference of opinion on the Prussian constitution and its foundation, it seems natural that the *Rheinische Zeitung* too should have *its* opinion, which, although it may differ from the current government view, nonetheless can cite from Prussian history, as well as many elements of contemporary life and, finally, highly placed authorities.

Far from intending to attack the Prussian constitution at its foundation, the *Rheinische Zeitung*, on the contrary, has attacked, according to its convictions, only the departures from that foundation.

In reference to the suppression of the *Rheinische Zeitung*, an official article in the *Allgemeine Königsberger Zeitung*[3] designates Prussia as the state of liberal sovereignty. This is a definition which is not found in the Prussian *Landrecht* [common law][4] and which lends itself to all kinds of interpretations.

Under "liberal sovereignty" one can understand two things, either

---

1. *Neue eleganteste Conversations-Lexicon für Gebildete aus allen Ständen* (*New and Most Elegant Encyclopedia for the Educated of All Classes*) (Leipzig, 1835), Volume II, page 255: after Hegel came to Berlin in 1818 he "made his philosophy—so to speak—the philosophy of the state."

2. The *Allgemeine Preussische Staats-Zeitung*, founded in 1819, was the semi-official organ of the Prussian Government.

3. The *Königsberger Allgemeine Zeitung*.

4. The Prussian *Landrecht* was a compilation of civil, criminal, ecclesiastical and administrative laws put together in 1794; it was substantially in force until the new code of January 1, 1900.

that freedom is merely the personal disposition of the king, and hence his personal characteristic, or that freedom is the spirit of sovereignty, which therefore is also realized in free institutions and laws, or at least should be so realized. In the first case one has *despotisme éclairé* [enlightened despotism], that is, the *person* of the prince vis-à-vis a whole state made up of spiritless and unfree material. In the latter case, and this was the intention of the *Rheinische Zeitung*, one does not confine oneself to the limits of the prince as a person, but, rather, regards the whole state as his body, so that the institutions are the organs in which he lives and works, so that the laws are the eyes with which he sees.

Furthermore, it is supposed to have been the intention of the *Rheinische Zeitung* to develop "theories aiming at the destruction of the monarchical principle."

One asks again, what does one understand by "monarchical principle"? The *Rheinische Zeitung*, for example, has maintained that the predominance of class differences, a one-sided bureaucracy, censorship, etc., contradict the monarchical principle, and it has always sought to *prove* its assertions, rather than stating them as mere notions. In general, the *Rheinische Zeitung* has never expressed any special preference for a particular form of government. It has concerned itself only with a *moral and rational community;* it has considered the demands of such a community as ones which must and can be realized under any form of government. Hence it has treated the monarchical principle not as a separate principle, but rather as the overall realization of the political principle. If this was an error, then it was not an error of underrating but of overrating.

The *Rheinische Zeitung,* moreover, has never tried to sow in public opinion malicious suspicion of the operations of the government. Instead, it has tried, out of good will, to sow suspicion only of measures repugnant to the spirit of the people. It has, furthermore, never contrasted the people with the government in an abstract way, but, rather, considered political weakness as much a weakness of the people as of the government.

In regard to the thoroughness and expertise, as well as the tone, of the *Rheinische Zeitung*, no other newspaper, at least in Germany, has developed more thoroughness and expertise. And the tone is truly serious, calm, and dignified, compared to the blustering tone of the servile (conservative) journals. In this respect, the reproach of unpopularity, of much too scholarly a form, which has been leveled against the *Rheinische Zeitung*, is not without justice and directly contradicts the reproach of the Ministry.

Just as little has the *Rheinische Zeitung* sought to incite individual classes of the nation against other individual classes; it has, rather, sought to incite each class against its own egoism and narrow-minded-ness; it has everywhere asserted civic reason against class unreason and human love against class hate. In this, furthermore, if it has sinned, it has committed a sin that is sanctioned by law and the morals of the Rhine Province.

The reproach of aiming to stir up "dissatisfaction with existing legal conditions" cannot be considered a reproach in this undefined version. Even the government has sought to stir up dissatisfaction with existing legal conditions, for example, the Old Prussian marriage regu-lations. Every form of law and revision, every progress, rests on such dissatisfaction.

Since a legal development is not possible without a development of laws, since a development of laws is impossible without a critique of the laws, since every critique of the laws estranges the citizen's mind, and hence his heart, from the existing laws, and since such es-trangement is felt as dissatisfaction, a loyal participation of the press in political development is impossible if it may not stir up discontent with existing legal conditions.

The reproach that the *Rheinische Zeitung* has pursued loyal organs with unworthy ridicule, if it refers to newspaper polemics, cannot provide the ground for suppression. The *Rheinische Zeitung* had been denounced from all sides, splattered with mud, attacked. It was its duty to defend itself. Furthermore, there is no *official* press.

The *Rheinische Zeitung* has not insulted foreign powers but has only censured their insults against Germany. In this it has merely pursued a *national* policy. As regards the German federated states, it has only expressed the views of the majority of the people's representa-tives in those states.

Finally, in regard to religion, it has acted pursuant to Article II of the Censorship Edict of 1819, namely, it has worked against the fanatical carrying over of religious truths into politics and the resulting confusing of ideas.[5]

II

If the *Rheinische Zeitung* had wanted to build a systematic oppo-sition against the government, it would have had to pursue a totally *opposite tactic*.

It would have flattered the prejudices of the Rhine Province instead of opposing them. It would above all have paid homage to *religious prejudices* and, in the manner of the ultramontanes, exploited the

---

5. The Censorship Edict of October 18, 1819, spoke of "fanatical carrying over" and "confusion of ideas."

antagonism between North and South German education, instead of supporting the importation of North German education into the Rhine Province.

It would have leaned on French, instead of German, theory.

It would have contraposed the political idea of unity with the provincial spirit of particularist limits, and thus, above all, like Görres, have taken the Provincial Diets under its protection.

It would have seen everything good on the side of the Estates and everything evil on the side of the government, as the usual liberalism does. It would not, in its criticism of the Rhenish Estates, in contrast to many Rhenish liberals, have pointed up the wisdom of the government as against the private egoism of the classes. Finally, it would have joined the other newspapers in the chorus that demanded enlarged rights for the Diet committees, instead of reporting such demands as politically unworthy.

III

Finally, it is an extraordinary exaggeration to speak of the *spitefulness* of the whole tendency, since according to this

(1) the struggle in defense of the Customs Union,
(2) in favor of Prussia in the Russian cartel affairs,[6]
(3) in favor of Prussian hegemony,
(4) the constant pointing to Prussia as the state of the future,
(5) the praise of Prussian national institutions, such as the army, administration, etc.,

would have been equally spiteful.

Similarly, the *Rheinische Zeitung* did not fight the bureaucracy one-sidedly. Instead, it asserted itself:

(1) against Bülow-Cummerow,
(2) against romantic tendencies.

It was, moreover, the only *liberal* newspaper that recognized its [Prussia's] good side, such as the good Old Prussian legislation.

Thus the *Rheinische Zeitung* alone defended the basic principle of the new divorce law, in contrast to virtually all other newspapers.

Thus, finally, it was the first and perhaps the only one to hail the rectifications of the Cabinet Orders[7] as a progressive step.

We bring up these examples only to prove that the *Rheinische Zeitung* did not carry out a *systematic*, abstract opposition, but always asserted what was rational according to its convictions, whether emanating from this side or that.

---

6. In March, 1830, Prussia and Russia had concluded a cartel-convention for the mutual extradition of deserters, criminals and defendants.

7. See "The Cabinet Order About the Daily Press," page 51.

Remarks on the Latest
Prussian Censorship Instruction*

WE ARE NOT among those malcontents who even before the appearance of the latest Prussian censorship edict[1] exclaim *"Timeo Danaos et dona ferentes."*[2] Rather, since an examination of laws already passed is permitted in the new instruction, even if it is not in accord with the government, we will begin with such a scrutiny. Censorship is *official criticism;* its norms are critical norms, which therefore must not be withheld from criticism, a field to which they belong.

Everybody will certainly be able to approve the *general tendency* expressed in the beginning of the Instruction: "In order to free the press even at this early date from the illegal limitations not intended by the Highest Authority, His Majesty the King, in an order addressed to the Royal State Ministry on the 10th of this month, disapproved any illegitimate censorship in the field of writing, and, recognizing the value of and need for frank and reasonable publications, empowered us again to remind the censors to pay proper attention to Article II of the Censorship Edict of October 18, 1819."

Of course! Once censorship is a necessity, frank and liberal censorship is even more so.

What must arouse a certain amount of surprise right away is the date of the law in question. How so? Is it perhaps a law which conditions of the time had to minimize? This does not seem to be the case, for the censors are reminded "anew" to pay attention to it. Until 1842, therefore, the law existed, but it was not observed; for in

---

* Written between January 15 and February 10, 1842. Published in *Anekdota zur neuesten deutschen Philosophie und Publicistik*, February, 1843.
1. The Censorship Instruction of December 24, 1841, disapproved of limitations on literary activity but in practice sharpened the existing censorship.
2. "I fear Greeks bearing gifts"—from Virgil, *Aeneid.*

order to free the press "even at this early date" from illegitimate limitations not intended by the Highest Authority, the law is resurrected.

The press—this is a direct consequence of these introductory remarks—has up to now been subject to illegal limitations *despite the law*.

Now does this speak against the law or against the censors?

We are hardly permitted to claim the latter. For twenty-two years illegal actions have been committed by an administration that controls the highest interest of the citizens, their minds, an administration that, even more than the Roman censors ever did, regulates not only the behavior of the individual citizen but also the behavior of the public mind. Should such unconscionable behavior and therefore disloyalty on the part of the highest civil servants be possible in the well-administered Prussian state which is so proud of its administration? Or has the state, constantly deluded, selected the most incompetent persons for the most difficult positions? Or is it perhaps that the subject of the Prussian state has no possibility of protesting against illegal measures? Are all Prussian writers so uneducated and stupid that they are unfamiliar with laws that affect their livelihood, or are they too cowardly to demand that the laws be observed?

If we blame the censors, we compromise not only their honor but also the honor of the Prussian state and of Prussian writers.

Furthermore, because of the lawless behavior of the censors for twenty years despite the laws, the *argumentum ad hominem* is offered that the press needs other guarantees against such irresponsible individuals besides these general regulations; it has been proved that in the nature of censorship there is a basic fault that no law can remedy.

But if the censors were able men, and the law was no good, why resurrect it anew to do away with the evil it has caused?

Or is it perhaps that the objective faults of an institution are to be ascribed to individuals, so that the semblance of improvement is achieved without a real improvement? This is the kind of pseudo-liberalism that is forced to make concessions and that sacrifices people to maintain the institution, the tools, and the object. The attention of a thoughtless public is thereby diverted. Objective embitterment is turned into a matter of personalities. With a change of persons one believes a change of things is achieved. Attention is deflected from censorship itself to the individual censors, and those little writers in the service of progress-by-command hurl trivial heroics against those who have been ungraciously treated, at the same time paying high homage to the government.

We encounter still another difficulty. Some newspaper correspondents consider the Censorship Instruction a new censorship edict. They are mistaken but their error is forgivable. The Censorship Edict of October 18, 1819, was to be in force only provisionally until the year 1824—and it would have remained a provisional law to this day, except that we now learn from the present Instruction that it was never enforced.

The Edict of 1819 was an *interim* measure, the difference being that the expectation of a definite five-year term was indicated, while in the new Instruction there is no time limit; then there was expectation of *laws on freedom of the press*, while now they are *laws of censorship*.

Other newspaper correspondents consider the Censorship Instruction a renewal of the old Censorship Edict. Their error will be demonstrated in the examination of the Instruction itself.

We consider the Censorship Instruction the *anticipated spirit* of a presumed censorship law. We deduce this precisely from the spirit of the Censorship Edict of 1819, in which state laws and ordinances are of equal importance for the press. (See the Edict, Article XVI, No. 2).

But let us return to the Instruction.

"According to this law," that is, Article II, "censorship shall not obstruct any serious and moderate pursuit of truth, nor put undue compulsion on writers, nor hinder the unrestricted sale of books."

The pursuit of truth, which is not to be impeded by censorship, is qualified as serious and moderate. Both qualifications point not to the content of the pursuit, but rather to something that lies outside the content. At the outset they divert from the pursuit of truth and bring into play an unknown third factor. If an investigation must constantly keep in mind this third factor, an exasperation supported by law, will it not lose sight of the truth? Is it not the first duty of the seeker after the truth to proceed directly at it, without glancing to the right or left? Do I not forget to speak about the substance if I must never forget to state it in a prescribed form?

Truth is as little moderate as light, and against what is it to be moderated? Against oneself? "*Verum index sui et falsi.*"[3] Hence, *against falsehood?*

When moderation shapes the character of the investigation, it is more a sign of shying away from the truth than from untruth. It is a drag on every step I take. *In an investigation, it is a prescription for fear of discovering the result,* a means of keeping one from the truth.

Furthermore, truth is universal. It does not belong to me, it belongs to all; it possesses me, I do not possess it. My *style* is my property; it is my spiritual individuality. *Le style c'est l'homme.* [The style is the man.] Indeed! The law permits me to write, only I am supposed to write in a style different from mine! I may show the profile of

---

3. "Truth is the test of itself and of falsehood"—Spinoza, *Ethics.*

my mind, but first I must present it in prescribed mien. What man of honor will not blush at this effrontery and prefer to hide his head under his toga? At least under the toga there may be a hint of a Jupiter head. The prescribed mien is nothing but *bonne mine à mauvais jeu* [putting on a good face at a bad play].

You admire the enchanting diversity, the inexhaustible wealth of nature. You do not demand that the rose smell like the violet. But the richest of all—the mind—is to exist only in *one* kind? I am humorous, but the law commands that I write seriously. I am daring, but the law commands that my style be modest. Gray on gray is to be the only permissible color of freedom. Every dewdrop that reflects the sun glitters in an inexhaustible play of colors, but the intellectual sun, in no matter on how many individuals it may be refracted, may produce only one, only the official color! The essential form of the mind is brightness and light, and you want to make the shadow its only appropriate manifestation; it is only to be clad in black, and yet among flowers there are no black ones. The essence of the mind is *always the truth itself*, and what do you make its essence? *Moderation*. Only a scamp is moderate, says Goethe, and you want to turn the mind into such a scamp? Or if moderation is to be that moderation of genius of which Schiller speaks, then you must first transform all citizens and especially all censors into geniuses. Yet the moderation of genius does not lie in the language of culture being without any accent or any dialect, but rather it speaks in the accent of the substance and in the dialect of its essence. Genius consists of forgetting moderation and immoderation, and of crystallizing the matter. The general moderation of the mind is reason, that universal liberality which is related to every nature according to its essential character.

Moreover, if seriousness is not to fit into Tristram Shandy's[4] definition, according to which it is a hypocritical behavior of the body to cover up the deficiencies of the soul—if it is, rather, substantive seriousness, then the entire [censorship] regulation cancels itself. For I treat the ridiculous seriously when I treat it with ridicule, and the most serious lack of intellectual moderation is to be moderate about a lack of moderation.

Serious and moderate! What wavering and relative concepts! Where does seriousness end and jest begin? Where does moderation cease and immoderation start? We are dependent upon the *moods* of the censor. To prescribe a temperament for the censor would be just as wrong as prescribing a style for the writer. If you wish to be logical in your aesthetic criticism, you must also prohibit a too serious and too moderate pursuit of the truth, for too great a seriousness is

---

4. Laurence Sterne's *The Life and Opinions of Tristram Shandy.*

most ridiculous, and too much moderation is the bitterest irony.

Finally, all this proceeds from a completely topsy-turvy and abstract view of *truth*. All objects of literary activity are subsumed under the one general concept of "truth." Even if we disregard the subjective aspect—namely, that one and the same object appears differently to different individuals and expresses its various sides in as many various intellects—shouldn't the character of the object exert some influence, even the slightest, on the investigation? Not only the result, but also the way to it belongs to truth. The pursuit of truth must itself be true; the true investigation is the unfolded truth whose scattered parts are encompassed in the result. And the nature of the investigation, should it change according to the object? If the object is humorous, the investigation is supposed to appear serious; if the object is embarrassing, the investigation is to be restrained. Thus you injure the rights of the object, just as you injure the rights of the subject. You conceive the truth abstractly and turn the mind into an inquisitor who drily records the proceedings.

Or is this metaphysical torment unnecessary? Is truth to be understood in such a way that it is what the government orders it to be, and that any investigation is a superfluous and obnoxious third element which, for reasons of etiquette, cannot be entirely rejected? It almost seems so. For investigation is understood as being *a priori* in *opposition* to truth, and therefore appears with that suspicious official accompaniment of seriousness and moderation which a layman is supposed to display before a priest. Governmental reason is the only political reason. Under certain circumstances concessions are to be made to other reasoning and its rigmarole; but at the same time this reasoning, conscious of the concession and its inherent illegality, presents itself moderate and subservient, serious and boring. When Voltaire says, "*Tous les genres sont bons, excepté le genre ennuyeux*" ["All species of people are good, except the bores"], the boring type here becomes the exclusive type, as is easily shown by the "Proceedings of the Rhineland Diets." Why not instead the good old German Curial [legal] style? You are to write freely, but every word is at the same time to be a curtsy to the liberal censorship, which lets your serious and moderate votes pass. But do not lose the consciousness of your devotion!

The legal emphasis is not put on truth, but on moderation and seriousness. Hence everything causes concern, seriousness, moderation, and above all a kind of truth under whose vague scope a very definite, very dubious truth seems to be concealed.

"Censorship," the Instruction continues, "is by no means to be carried out in a narrow-minded spirit that would go beyond this law."

By "this law" is meant, first of all, Article II of the Edict of 1819, but later the Instruction refers to the "spirit" of the Censorship Edict in general. Both regulations are easily combined. Article II is the concentrated spirit of the Censorship Edict, whose structure and specifications are found in the other articles. We believe we can do no better than characterize the above-mentioned spirit through the following statements of the same:

Article VII: "The freedom from censorship hitherto granted to the Academy of Sciences and the Universities is herewith suspended for five years."

Paragraph 10: "The present temporary regulation is to be effective for five years, starting today. Before the expiration date, the Federal Diet is to investigate thoroughly how the regulations on freedom of the press, under Article 18 of the Act, might be uniformly carried out; and then a definite decision on the legal limits of freedom of the press in Germany is to follow."

A law that suspends freedom of the press where it still exists, and that makes it superfluous through censorship in areas where it was to exist, cannot precisely be called a law favorable to the press. Section 10 also admits that a temporary censorship law is to be enacted in place of the freedom of the press perhaps promised in Article 18 of the Federal Act. This quid pro quo at least reveals that the character of the time calls for limitations on the press and that the Edict owes its origin to distrust of the press. This ill feeling is even excused, in that it is termed temporary, valid for only five years. Alas, it has lasted twenty-two years.

The very next line of the Instruction already contains the contradiction that, on the one hand, censorship is not to be applied so as to exceed the Edict, while, on the other hand, the procedure is prescribed as follows: "The censor may very well permit a frank discussion of domestic matters."

The censor *may;* he does not have to; it is not a necessity. But even this careful liberalism transgresses not only the spirit but also the definite limitations of the Censorship Edict, and in a very definite way. The old Censorship Edict, and particularly Article II cited in the Instruction, not only bans a frank discussion of Prussian affairs but also even Chinese ones.

"To this," states the commentary on violations of the security of the Prussian state and the German Federal States, "belong all attempts to present in a favorable light those parties which work toward an overthrow of the constitution in no matter what country."

Does this permit a frank discussion of Chinese or Turkish internal affairs? If such remote references might endanger the touchy security of the German Federation, how much more so might a disapproving word about domestic affairs?

If the Instruction thus departs on the liberal side from the spirit of Article II of the Censorship Edict, it likewise departs from the Edict on the illiberal side and adds *new press restrictions* to the old ones; the liberal departure, whose content will become evident later, is already formally suspect in consequence of Article II, only the first half of which has been cleverly cited in the Instruction, while the censor is referred to the Article itself.

Article II of the Edict reads: "Its" (the censorship's) "purpose is to control whatever opposes the fundamental principles of religion, without regard to the opinions and doctrines of particular religious groups and sects permitted in the state."

In the year 1819 rationalism still prevailed and generally viewed religion as religion according to reason. This rationalist viewpoint is also the viewpoint of the Censorship Edict, which, indeed, is so illogical as to take an irreligious point of view while aiming to protect religion. It contradicts the fundamental principles of religion in that it separates those principles from its positive content and specific quality, for every religion believes itself to be different from other, illusory religions by virtue of its particular nature, and conceives itself to be the true religion by virtue of its specific quality. The new Censorship Instruction, in its quotation of Article II, omits the limiting clause in which particular religious groups and sects are excluded from inviolability, but it goes on to offer the following commentary: "Nothing that opposes the Christian religion in general or a particular doctrine in a frivolous and hostile manner will be tolerated."

The old Censorship Edict does not mention the Christian religion at all. On the contrary, it distinguishes religion from any religious group or sect. The new Censorship Instruction not only changes religion into Christian religion, but it also adds its particular doctrine. A precious abortion of our science newly become Christian! Who can deny that it has forged new chains for the press? Religion is to be attacked neither in general nor in particular. Or do you perhaps believe that the words "frivolous" and "hostile" make these chains into a chain of roses? How cleverly put: *frivolous, hostile!* The adjective "frivolous" aims at the citizen's sense of propriety and is the exoteric term in the public mind, but the adjective "hostile" is whispered into the censor's ear, and is the legal interpretation of frivolity. We will find more examples of this finesse in the Instruction—here a subjective word that makes the public blush, and there an objective word for the censor that makes the writer pale. In this way one can set *lettres de cachet*[5] to music.

And what strange contradictions the Censorship Instruction en-

---

5. Royal orders for arbitrary arrest used in pre-Revolutionary France.

tangles itself in! Only that half of the attack which involves particular aspects without being profound and serious enough to go into the substance is frivolous—whereas the very move against *only a particular thing as such* is frivolous. An attack on the Christian religion in general is forbidden, and only a frivolous attack is permitted. Conversely, an attack on the general principles of religion, on its substance and upon particulars, insofar as they are manifestations of the substance, is a hostile attack. Religion can be attacked only in a hostile or frivolous way; there is no third way. This illogicality in which the Instruction is entangled is only a *semblance*, however, for it is based on the illusion that any kind of attack on religion is permitted; but it needs only a single objective glance to recognize this illusion. Religion is not to be attacked *at all*, neither in a hostile nor in a frivolous manner, neither in general nor in particular.

Still, since the Instruction, in open contradiction to the Censorship Edict of 1819, forges new chains on the philosophical press, it should at least be logical enough to free the religious press from the old chains put on it by that rationalistic Edict. The purpose of the new censorship is: "To oppose the fanatical injection of religious convictions into politics and the ensuing intellectual confusion."

To be sure, the new Instruction cleverly does not mention this provision in the commentary, but it does include it in the citation of Article II. What does fanatical injection of religious convictions into politics mean? It means that specific religious convictions can determine the state and that the particular nature of religion can become the criterion of the state. The old Censorship Edict could rightly oppose this confusion, for it left the particular religion and its specific content to criticism. Yet the old Edict was based on the shallow and superficial rationalism you despised. You, however, who base the state even in details on faith and on Christianity—since you want a *Christian state*, how can you expect censorship to prevent this intellectual confusion?

The confusion of political and Christian-religious principles has, indeed, become an *official sect*. Let us briefly clarify this confusion. To mention only the Christian religion as the recognized one, your state contains Catholics and Protestants. Both make the same demands on the state and have the same duties toward it. They disregard their religious differences and agree in demanding that the state be the actualization of political and legal rationality. You, however, want a Christian state. If your state is only Lutheran Christian, it becomes for the Catholic a church to which he does not belong, which he must reject as heretical, and whose innermost being he finds obnoxious. The reverse would be equally the case if the state were Catholic. Or if you make the general spirit of Christianity the particular spirit of your state, you nevertheless make your decision as to what the universal spirit of Christianity might be out of your Protestant background. You determine what the Christian state is, even though recent events have taught you that some government officials cannot draw the line between religion and secularism, between State and Church. Not the censors but the diplomats had to negotiate about this confusion. Finally, you put yourself into a heretical position when you reject a particular dogma as unessential. When you call your state universally Christian you are confessing with a diplomatic turn of phrase that it is un-Christian. Hence either you forbid religion in general to enter politics —but you do not want to do that because you wish to base the state not on free reason but on faith, with religion constituting the general *sanction of the positive*—or you permit the fanatical injection of religion into politics. Religion might be permitted to politicize in its own way, but you do not want that either; for religion is to support secularism without the latter being subordinated to it. Once religion is drawn into politics, it becomes an unbearable, indeed an irreligious, presumption to want to determine on secular grounds how it is to operate within politics. Whoever allies himself with religion out of religiosity must give it the decisive voice in all issues—or do you perhaps understand by religion the *cult of your own sovereignty and governmental wisdom?*

In another way, too, the orthodoxy of the new Censorship Instruction comes into conflict with the rationalism of the old Censorship Edict. The latter also subsumes under the purpose of censorship the suppression of "whatever offends morality and good conduct." The new Instruction quotes this from Article II. But although its commentary makes additions in regard to religion, it contains omissions in regard to morality. To offend morality and good conduct now becomes to injure "discipline, morals, and outward decency." One sees that morality as morality, as worldly principle, following its own laws, disappears; external manifestations, such as police-regulated respectability and conventional behavior, take its place. Credit where credit is due: this shows true consistency. The specifically Christian legislator cannot recognize morality as an independent sphere sanctified in itself, for he derives its inner universal essence from religion. Independent morality offends the basic principles of religion, and particular concepts of religion are contrary to morality. Morality recognizes only its own universal and rational religion, and religion only its own particular and positive morality. Under this Instruction, therefore, censorship will have to repudiate such intellectual heroes of morality as Kant, Fichte, Spinoza as being irreligious and threatening discipline, morals, and outward decency. All these moralists proceed from a principled opposition between morality and religion, for morality, they claim, is based on the autonomy, and religion on the heteronomy, of the human spirit.

From these undesirable innovations of the censorship—on the one hand, the relaxation of the moral conscience and, on the other hand, the rigorous sharpening of the religious conscience—we now turn to something more pleasant, to the *concessions*. It "follows particularly that writings which evaluate the whole administration or its individual branches, examine laws already enacted or yet to be enacted, expose mistakes and errors, indicate or propose improvements—are not to be censored on the ground that they conflict with the viewpoint of the government, so long as their form is decent and their tendency is well-intentioned."

Moderation and seriousness of investigation—both the Censorship Edict and the new Instruction contain this requirement; but the latter is as little satisfied with the "decent" form as it is with the content. The "tendency" has become the main criterion, indeed the pervading thought, whereas in the Edict not even the word "tendency" is to be found. Moreover, the new Instruction does not say what tendency consists of, but its significance can be seen from the following excerpt:

"It is an indispensable requirement that the tendency of the criticism of governmental measures be well intentioned and not hateful and malevolent; and it must be demanded from the censor that he have good will and insight, enabling him to distinguish one from the other. The censor has to pay special attention to the form and tone of the language used and must not permit publication of writings if their tendency is harmful because of passion, violence, and presumptuousness."

Hence the writer is subject to the most frightful terrorism, to jurisdiction based on suspicion. Tendentious laws, laws without objective norms, are laws of terrorism, such as those created by Robespierre because of a national emergency and by Roman emperors because of corruption of the state. Laws that make as their chief criteria not the *action as such* but the *sentiment* of the acting person are nothing but *positive sanctions of lawlessness*. It would be better to act like the Czar of Russia, who had everybody's beard cut off by official Cossacks, than to make the idea of wearing a beard the criterion for cutting it off.

Only insofar as I express myself and enter the sphere of actuality do I enter the legislator's sphere. As far as the law is concerned, I do not exist at all and am not subject to it, except in my action. It alone concerns the law; only because of it do I claim the right to exist, a right of actuality that makes me subject to actual law. But a tendentious law does not punish me for what I do, but for what I intend *apart* from any action. Hence it is an insult to the honor of the citizen, a hoax directed against my existence.

I can turn and twist as much as possible—action does not come into question. My existence is suspect; my innermost being, my individuality, is considered to be evil, and for this opinion I am to be punished. The law does not penalize me for wrongs I commit, but for wrongs that I do not commit. I am actually punished because my actions are *not illegal,* for in this way alone a mild and well-meaning judge is compelled to consider my evil sentiment, which I am clever enough not to bring out into the open.

This law about opinion is no law of the state for the citizens, but a law of one party against another party. The law of intentions abolishes the equality of citizens before the law. It is a law of division, not of unity, and all laws that divide are reactionary. It is not a law but a *privilege.* One person may do what another may not, not because the latter lacks the objective capability for action, as a child does in regard to writing contracts, but rather because his opinion and his intentions are suspect. The ethical state subordinates the view of the state to its members, even if they oppose an organ of the state or the government; but a society in which *one* organ thinks of itself as the only, exclusive possessor of political reason and political morality, a government that in principle opposes the people and assumes, therefore, their political opposition to be the universal, the normal opinion, the evil conscience of a faction—such a government invents laws of intention, *laws of vengeance,* against an opinion that exists only in the members of the government themselves. Laws of intention are based on disloyalty, and on an unethical, materialistic view of the state. They are an indiscreet outcry of a bad conscience. And how is such a law to be executed? Through means more outrageous than the law itself, through spies, or through *a priori* decisions to consider entire literary movements suspect, in which case one must discover to what movement an individual belongs. Just as in the law of intention, the *legal form contradicts the content,* and the government that promulgates it eagerly denounces the very thing it represents itself, namely, antistate opinion, so likewise it constitutes a topsy-turvy world of laws which measure with two yardsticks. What is law on the one side is lawlessness on the other. *Its laws become the opposite of what it proclaims to be law.*

The new Censorship Instruction is entangled in this dialectic. It is contradictory to make it the censors' duty to carry out the very thing that is condemned as being antistate when it takes place in the press.

Thus the Instruction forbids writers to suspect the attitude of individuals or whole classes, and in the same breath it orders the censor to divide all citizens into suspect and unsuspect, into well-meaning and ill-meaning. The criticism forbidden to the press becomes the daily duty of the governmental critic; but this inversion does not even end there. In the press, antistate opinion is viewed as something particular according to its content, and as something general according to its form; that is, it is left to a general judgment.

But now the matter is turned around. The particular now appears justified in regard to its content; the antistate opinion appears as the view of the state, as public law; as particular in regard to form, inaccessible to the light of day, banished from public view into the files of the governmental critic. Thus the Instruction aims to protect religion but violates the most universal principle of all religions, that of the sacredness and inviolability of subjective opinion. It makes the censor, in place of God, the judge of the heart. Thus it prohibits offensive utterances and defamatory judgments on individual persons, but every day it exposes you to the defamatory and offensive judgment of the censor. The Instruction aims to suppress the gossip of ill-intentioned or poorly informed individuals, and yet it forces the censor to rely on such gossip and spying by poorly informed and ill-intentioned individuals for its judgment, not in the sphere of objective content but in the sphere of subjective opinion or arbitrariness. Thus the intention of the state is not to be suspect, but the Instruction proceeds from the public's suspicion against the state. Thus a bad opinion is not to be concealed behind a good pretext, but the Instruction itself rests on a false pretext. Thus patriotism is to be promoted, but on the basis of a philosophy that degrades nationality. We are asked to behave lawfully and with respect for the law, but at the same time we are to honor institutions that make us lawless and replace law with arbitrariness. We are to acknowledge the principle of personality to such an extent that, despite the deficient institution of censorship, we trust the censor, and you violate the principle of personality so much that you judge, not the action but the opinion of the action. You demand modesty, and you proceed from the enormous arrogance of making the civil servant a spy of the heart, an all-knowing person, a philosopher, a theologian, a politician, a Delphic oracle. On the one hand you make it a duty to acknowledge arrogance, and on the other hand you forbid us arrogance. The essential arrogance consists in ascribing the perfection of a species to particular individuals. The censor is a particular individual but the press constitutes the species. You recommend trust to us, but you lend lawful force to mistrust. You place so much confidence in political institutions that you make the weak mortal, the official, into a saint so that the impossible becomes possible for him. But you distrust your political organism so much that you fear the isolated opinion of a private person; for you treat the press as a private person. You demand of the officials that they act impersonally, without anger, passion, narrow-mindedness, or human frailty. But the impersonal, the *idea*, you suspect to be full of personal intrigues and subjective vileness. The Instruction demands unlimited confidence in officialdom, but it proceeds from limitless distrust of nonofficials. Why shouldn't we repay with the same? Why shouldn't we be suspicious of officialdom? Likewise as regards character. From the outset, an unprejudiced person would have more respect for the character of a public critic than for that of a secret one.

What is generally bad remains bad, no matter whether the carrier of the evil is a private critic or one employed by the government, only that in the latter case the evil is authorized and regarded as a necessity by the higher-ups, in order to bring about goodness on a lower level.

The *censorship of intention* and the *intention of censorship* constitute a gift of the new liberal Instruction. Nobody will consider it amiss if we return with a certain mistrust to a further analysis of its regulations.

"Insulting utterances and defamatory judgments on individuals are not suitable for print."

Not suitable for print! Instead of this mild phrasing, it would have been desirable if what is considered insulting and defamatory had been given objective definitions.

"The same applies to casting suspicion on attitudes of individuals or" (a weighty "or") "entire classes, and to the use of names of political parties and other personalities."

Thus also the grouping under categories, the attack on entire classes, the use of party names—and man, like Adam, must give everything a name, so that it exists for him—and party names are necessary categories for the political press:

> Because every disease, as Doctor Sassafras believes,
> in order to be successfully cured,
> with a name must be secured.

All this refers to personalities. How does one begin? The personality of an individual must not be attacked, nor the class or general group, nor the moral man. The state—and here it is right—does not want to suffer injuries or be involved in personalities; but by the easy "or" the general is also subsumed under personalities. By the "or" the general is placed in the center, and by an insignificant "and" we finally learn that only persons were meant. The altogether easy conclusion is that the press is not permitted to check on officialdom where the latter is institutionalized as a class of individuals.

"If, according to these Instructions, censorship is exercised in the spirit of the Censorship Edict of October 18, 1819, decorous and frank journalism will have sufficient elbow room, and it is to be expected that thereby a greater participation in the interests of the fatherland will be aroused and that patriotism will be enhanced."

We admit that, according to these Instructions, more than sufficient elbow room is provided for decent journalism, decent in the meaning of the censorship; the very word "elbow room" is well chosen, for that room is intended to be one that is satisfactory for a playful, shadow-boxing press. Whether this applies to *frank* journalism, and where the frankness is to come from, that we leave to the sharp eye of the reader. In regard to the expectations expressed in the Instruction, patriotism may indeed be promoted in the same way that the sending of a hang-man's rope enhances Turkish nationalism; but whether the press, as moderate as it is serious, will awake some interest in the fatherland, that we leave to the press itself; a lean press cannot be fattened with stories about China. But perhaps we take the passage too seriously. Perhaps we will understand its meaning better when we regard it as merely the clasp in the chain of roses. Perhaps this liberal clasp contains a pearl of very dubious value. Let's look into it. Everything depends on the context. The enhancement of patriotism and the awakening of participation in the interests of the fatherland, which are expressed in the above passage as expectations, easily become transformed into an *order for a new restriction of the freedom* of our poor consumptive daily papers.

"In this way it is to be hoped that political literature and the daily press will recognize their tasks better than before, acquire richer material and a more dignified tone, and abstain in the future from playing on the curiosity of their readers by reporting meaningless items taken from foreign newspapers, gossip, and personalities written by malevolent or poorly informed correspondents—a tendency that it is the undoubted function of the censorship to combat."

In this indicated way, it is to be hoped that political literature and the daily press will recognize their task better, etc. However, better recognition cannot be commanded; it is a fruit still to be expected, and hope is hope. But the Instruction is much too practical to content itself with hopes and pious wishes. While the press is given hope for its future betterment *by this new comfort*, it is at the same time deprived by the benevolent Instruction of a right that it presently possesses. It loses what it still has, the hope of its betterment. The press fares like poor Sancho Panza, from whom the court physician withheld all food so that an upset stomach would not make him incapable of performing the duties required by the Duke.

At the same time we cannot let the opportunity pass without challenging the Prussian writer for his appropriation of this sort of decorous style. The preface [of the Instruction] reads: "In this way it is to be hoped that..." The "that" governs a whole series of regulations, that is, that political literature and the daily press recognize their tasks better than before, that they acquire a more dignified tone, etc., etc., that they abstain from printing meaningless reports from foreign newspapers, etc. All these regulations are still placed in the realm of hope; but the conclusion, connected to the preceding by a dash—"a tendency that it is the undoubted function of the censorship to combat"—saves the censor the tedious job of waiting for the hoped-for improvement of the daily press and empowers him, rather, to strike out anything disagreeable without further ado. The *internal cure* is replaced by an *amputation*.

"But to achieve this goal it is necessary that great caution be employed in the licensing of new journals and new editors, so that the daily press is entrusted into the hands of completely irreproachable men, whose scientific competence, rank, and character guarantee the seriousness of their endeavors and their loyalty."

Before we go into details, a general observation is in order. The licensing of new editors, that is, all future editors, is left entirely to the "great caution" exercised by government authorities—the censorship—whereas the old censorship, though under certain restrictions, left the choice of the editor *up to the publisher:*

"Article IX. The Superior Censorship Office is empowered to inform the publisher of a newspaper that the editor in question is not the type to inspire confidence, in which case the publisher is obliged either to appoint a new editor or, if he wishes to keep him, must set up bond for him, the amount to be determined by one of the State Ministers mentioned above at the recommendation of the said Superior Censorship Office."

In the new Censorship Instruction an entirely different depth, one might say a romanticism of the spirit, is expressed. While the old Censorship Edict prescribes external and prosaic bonds, which are therefore legally definable and by which even a displeasing editor could be licensed, the Instruction, on the contrary, deprives the publisher of a newspaper of any personal preference and leaves it to the preventive wisdom of the government, the great caution and the intellectual profundity of the authorities, to decide the internal, subjective criteria that cannot be defined from the outside. But when the imprecision, the sensitive inwardness, and the subjective extravagance of romanticism turn to the realm of the purely external—in the sense that the external fortuitousness no longer appears in its prosaic exactitude and limitation but in a wondrous glory and in illusory depth and splendor—the Instruction, too, will hardly escape this romantic fate.

The editors of the daily press, in which category all journalism falls, are to be completely irreproachable men. Scientific competence is stated to be the first guarantee of such complete irreproachableness. Not the slightest doubt is raised whether the censor possesses scientific competence to judge any sort of scientific competence. If it is true that Prussia has such a multitude of scientific geniuses who are known to the government—each city has at least one censor—why don't these encyclopedic brains show up as writers themselves? If these officials, overwhelming in number, mighty by virtue of their science and their genius, would rise for once and crush those wretched writers who are active in only one genre of writing, and even there without officially tested qualifications, the confusions of the press could be ended better than by censorship. Why do these clever men keep silent when, like the Roman geese, they could save the Capitol by their cackle? They must be men of too much modesty. The scientific public does not know them, but the government does.

And if those men are men such as no state could ever find, for never has a state known entire classes consisting of universal geniuses and polyhistorians, how much more gifted must be those who choose them! What secret science must the latter possess to be able to attest the scientific qualifications of officials who are otherwise unknown to the republic of science! The higher we climb in this *bureaucracy of intelligence*, the more wondrous are the minds we meet. Practically speaking, for a state possessing such pillars of a perfect press, is it worth the effort to appoint these men guardians of a deficient press, to use the perfect as a means for debasing the imperfect?

The more censors you employ, the more chances of improvement you take away from the realm of the press. You remove healthy people from your army to make them doctors for the sick.

Stamp the ground as Pompey did, and an armored Pallas Athena will spring out of every government building. The shallow daily press will collapse entirely before the official press. The existence of light suffices to refute darkness. Let your light shine and do not hide it under a bushel. Instead of the deficient censorship, whose sterling value is problematical even to you, give us a perfect press which is obedient to you, of which the Chinese state has been the model for centuries.

But is it not an intellectual criterion to make "scientific competence" the necessary requirement for the writers of the daily press, instead of the conventional requirement of privileged favoritism; isn't this a criterion of essence rather than of person?

Unfortunately, the Censorship Instruction interrupts our panegyric. Alongside the guarantee of scientific competence one finds requirements of rank and character. Rank and character!

Character, placed immediately after rank, seems to be almost a mere effluence of rank. Let us, above all, take a look at rank. It is so boxed in between scientific competence and character that one is almost tempted to doubt its good conscience.

The general requirement of scientific competence, how liberal! The special requirement of rank, how illiberal! Since scientific competence and character are very indefinite, while rank, on the contrary, is definite, why shouldn't we conclude that logically and necessarily the indefinite will lean on the definite and find support and content there? Would it be a great mistake of the censor to interpret the Instruction as saying that the external form of scientific competence and of character, as they appear in the world, constitute rank, the more since the censor's own rank assures him that this is the government's view? Without this interpretation it is, to say the least, completely incomprehensible why scientific competence and character are not sufficient guarantees in themselves, and why rank is made a necessary third requirement. Since these requirements are seldom if ever combined, the censor is in a dilemma over which to choose, for after all, somebody has to edit newspapers and periodicals. Scientific competence and character, in the absence of rank, because of their indefiniteness, can be a problem for the censor, since he must understandably wonder how such qualities can exist apart from rank. On the other hand, may the censor have doubts about character and science where rank is concerned? In such a case he would place less confidence in the judgment of the state than in himself, while in the opposite case he would place more confidence in the writer than in the state. Should a censor be so tactless and so wrong-headed? This should not be expected and it certainly was not expected. Rank, because it is the decisive criterion in case of doubt, is altogether the absolutely decisive one.

We have already seen that the Instruction conflicts with the Censorship Edict because of its orthodoxy, so now it does also because of its romanticism, which at the same time is always purposeful poetry. The money bond, which is a prosaic and real guarantee, becomes abstract, and this abstraction transforms itself into an entirely real and individual rank which acquires a magical, fictitious significance. The significance of the guarantee changes in the same way. No longer does the publisher select the editor, for whom he vouches to the authorities; the authorities select the editor, for whom they vouch to themselves. The old Edict expects the editor's work to be safeguarded by the bond the publisher puts up. The Instruction, on the other hand, does not concern itself with the editor's work, but with his person. It calls for a definite personal individuality which the publisher's money is to provide. The new Instruction is just as external as the old Edict; but where the latter expresses and delimits what is naturally prosaic and definite, the former lends an extremely fortuitous and imaginary spirit, and expresses what is merely individual in the poignancy of the universal.

But if the romantic Instruction in regard to the editor gives a tone of the most blithe indefiniteness to what is externally most definite, so it also gives the tone of legal definiteness to the most vague indefiniteness about the censor.

"Equal caution must be applied in appointing the censor, so that the office of censorship is put in the hands of men of proven character and ability, who are fully in accord with the honor of having confidence placed in them. Such men must be right-thinking and at the same time sharp-eyed, who understand how to separate form from substance, and overlook with sure tact minor objections that are not justified by the sense and tendency of the article as a whole."

What rank and character are for the writer, proven character is for the censor, since rank is assumed for him. More important is the fact that while scientific competence is required in the writer, only ability, without further modification, is required in the censor. The old Edict, which, politics apart, is rationalistic, requires in Article III "scientifically trained" and even "enlightened" censors. Both predicates are omitted in the Instruction; and in place of competence in the writer, which signifies a definite, trained, actual competence, in the censor only a predisposition to competence, a general ability, is expected. This means that a *predisposition to competence* is to *censor real competence*, despite the fact that in nature the situation is reversed. Finally, we note in passing that the competence of the censor is not defined in detail as to the actual content, hence, of course, its character becomes ambiguous.

Furthermore, the office of censorship is to be given to men "who fully deserve the honor of having confidence placed in them." No further discussion is needed for this pleonastic pseudo directive which says that only trustworthy men are to be appointed, that they will fully deserve the honored confidence, the honored trust placed in them, a very complete trust, of course, etc.

Finally, the censors are to be men who are "right-thinking and sharp-eyed, who understand how to separate form from substance and overlook with sure tact minor objections that are not justified by the sense and tendency of the article as a whole."

On the other hand, the Instruction further prescribes: "In regard to this" (that is, the investigation of the tendency) "the censors have to pay special attention to the form and the tone of the language used and must not permit publication of writings insofar as their tendency is harmful because of passion, violence, and presumptuousness."

On the one hand, then, the censor is to judge the *tendency from the form*, and on the other the *form from the tendency*. As previously the content had already entirely disappeared as a criterion for censorship, so now the form also disappears. If the tendency is good, then offenses against form are to be overlooked. Even if the article is not altogether very serious and moderate, even if it appears to be violent, passionate, and presumptuous, who would thereby be intimidated by the rough exterior? One must know how to separate the *form* from the *substance.* Any semblance of definiteness must be eliminated; the Instruction must end with a *complete contradiction of itself;* because anything that reveals tendency is actually first qualified by the tendency and can be recognized only by the tendency. The violence of the patriot is sacred zeal, his passion is the susceptibility of a lover, his presumptuousness is dedicated participation too boundless to be moderate.

All objective norms have been abandoned; the personal relationship is left, and the tact of the censor has to be called a guarantee. What, then, can the censor violate? Tact. And tactlessness is no crime. What is the writer threatened with? His existence. What state had ever made the existence of a whole class dependent on the tact of individual officials?

Let us say it again: *All objective norms have been abandoned.* For the writer, tendency is made the final content, ordered and prescribed, the object being a formless opinion. The tendency as subject, as opinion of the opinion, is at the discretion of, and is sole guide for, the censor.

Although the censor's arbitrariness—and the justification of mere opinion is justification of arbitrariness—is concealed behind the semblance of concrete directives, the Instruction, on the other hand, clearly asserts the arbitrariness of the Superior Censorship Office, which is given complete confidence. This confidence placed in the director is the ultimate guarantee of the press. Thus the essence of censorship in general is based on a police state's arrogant conceit about its officials. The public's sense and good will is not trusted with even the simplest thing; but for the officials even the impossible is to be possible.

This basic fault runs through all our institutions. Thus, for example, in criminal proceedings judge, plaintiff, and defendant are united in *one person.* This combination is contrary to all the laws of psychology. But the official is above the psychological laws to which the public is subject. Nevertheless, a deficient governmental principle may be excused; but it becomes inexcusable when it is not honest enough to be consistent. The difference between the *responsibility* of the officials and that of the public should correspond to the difference between officials and public; but it is precisely here, where only results could justify the principle and make it lawful within its own sphere, that it is abandoned and replaced with its opposite.

The censor, too, is plaintiff, defendant, and judge combined in one person; he is entrusted with the *administration of the mind*. The censor is *irresponsible*.

Censorship could acquire a provisional loyal character if it were subject to the regular courts, which, of course, is not possible so long as no objective censorship laws exist. But the worst possible way would be for the censorship also to be censored, by some director or a Superior Commission, for example.

Everything that was said about the relationship between the press and the censorship also applies to the relationship between the censorship and some superior censorship, and that of the writer and such superior censorship, even though an intermediary is shoved in between. It is the same relationship placed on a higher level, being the strange error of wanting to abandon the subject matter and give it another essence by replacing it with other persons. If the *dictatorial state* wanted to be loyal, it would dissolve itself. Every point would require the same compulsion and the same reaction. The superior censorship would again have to be censored in turn. To escape this vicious circle one decides to be disloyal; lawlessness then begins on the third or ninety-ninth level. Because officialdom is hazily aware of this it tries to raise the level of lawlessness to such a high sphere that it disappears from view, in the belief that it has vanished.

The real, *radical cure of the censorship* is its *abolition*. For it is a bad institution, and institutions are more powerful than men. Still, our opinion may be right or wrong. In any case, Prussian writers will gain something by this new Instruction, either a real freedom, or an ideal one: in *consciousness*.

"*Rara temporum felicitas, ubi quae velis sentire et quae sentias dicere licet.*"[6]

---

6. "Rare are the fortunate times in which you can think what you wish and say what you think"—from Tacitus.

THE *NEUE RHEINISCHE ZEITUNG* AND ITS SUPPRESSION

AFTER *a constant struggle with the Prussian censorship, Marx re-*
signed as editor in chief of the Rheinische Zeitung *on March 17, 1843.*
A few days later, on April 1, the government suppressed the newspa-
per. Marx left Prussia, moving first to Paris and then, in February of
1845, to Brussels, where he was active as a communist writer for about
three years.

When the 1848 revolutions broke out in Europe, including many
parts of Germany, Marx moved back to Cologne and reestablished his
old newspaper, this time calling it Neue Rheinische Zeitung, *with him-*
self as editor in chief. The first issue came out on June 1, 1848. In the
revolutionary turmoil of the period the Neue Rheinische Zeitung *be-*
came an increasingly sharp voice of radicalism. Once again, as in 1842–
43, Marx became embroiled in unceasing battle with the censorship.
For more than a week (September 26 to October 5) the Neue Rheinische Zeitung *was suspended under martial law. Marx, charged with*
lèse majesté and incitement to rebellion, was indicted and tried twice
in a Cologne court. He was finally acquitted, in February, 1849, but
the Prussian Government won the last battle. On April 16 Marx re-
ceived an order of expulsion from the country. On May 19 he pub-
lished the last issue of the Neue Rheinische Zeitung *and left Germany*
for good. He spent the rest of his life in London, where he was active
as a journalist—for ten years as the London correspondent of the New-
York Daily Tribune—*until 1862.*

Arrests*

Cologne, July 4

YESTERDAY we promised our readers we would return to the arrest of Herren Dr. Gottschalk and Anneke. Hitherto we have had details only about Anneke's arrest.

Between six and seven in the morning seven gendarmes entered Anneke's home, immediately manhandled the maid in the entrance hall, and sneaked silently up the stairs. Three remained in the vestibule, four broke into the bedroom, where Anneke and his pregnant wife were sleeping. Of these four pillars of justice, one was reeling,[1] at this early hour already more or less filled with "spirit," the water of true life, the firewater.[2]

Anneke asked what they wanted. He should go with them! was the laconic reply. Anneke begged them to spare his sick wife and wait in the vestibule. The gentlemen of the *Hermandad*[3] said they would not leave the bedroom, forced Anneke to dress hurriedly, and did not even allow him to speak to his wife. This to-do led to action in the vestibule, where one of the gendarmes smashed the glass door. Anneke was *pushed down* the stairs. Four gendarmes led him to the new prison, three remained with Frau Anneke, to keep an eye on her until the arrival of the Procurator.

According to the law, at least one official of the judicial police—

---

* *Neue Rheinische Zeitung*, July 5, 1848. It was for this article, by Marx and Engels, that Marx was indicted.
    1. The German word *wankte* can mean "reeling," "staggering," or "wavering." One may waver because of conscience or stagger because of liquor. The word was considered an "offense" to the police and figured in Marx's indictment.
    2. Marx used the literal German expressions for *eau de vie* and brandy.
    3. The Holy Brotherhood, an ironic reference to a sixteenth-century Spanish armed society, later meaning the police.

a police commissioner or his equivalent—must be present when an arrest is made. Why such formalities, when the people have two Assemblies, one in Berlin and one in Frankfurt, to represent their rights?

Half an hour later Herr State Procurator Hecker and Police Magistrate Geiger came to make a house search.

Frau Anneke complained that the Procurator left the arrest to the brutal gendarmes, without the presence of a magistrate to keep them in leash. Herr Hecker said he gave no *order for brutalities*. As if Herr Hecker could order brutalities?

Frau Anneke: It looks as if the gendarmes were sent alone so as not to have to account to anybody for brutalities. Moreover, the arrest did not take place with legal formality, since no gendarme showed any warrant for arrest, but only a scrap of paper, taken out of a pocket, which Anneke was not permitted to read.

Herr Hecker: "The gendarmes were *ordered by the court* to make the arrest." And the order of the judge, does it not stand under the command of the law? The State Procurator and the Police Magistrate confiscated a mass of papers and pamphlets, among them Frau Anneke's entire briefcase, etc. Police Magistrate Geiger, by the way, has been nominated to be Police Director.

In the evening Anneke was interrogated for half an hour. The reason for his arrest was an inflammatory speech he delivered at the last people's meeting in Gürzenich Hall.[4] Article 102 of the *Code Pénal*[5] deals with public speeches that *directly* incite plots against the Emperor and his family and aim to disturb the public peace through civil war, through illegal use of armed force, through public devastation and plundering. The Code does not know the Prussian "Incitement of Discontent." In default of Prussian *Landrecht* [national law][6] Article 102 is, for the time being, applied everywhere, even where its application is in the realm of legal absurdity.

For the arrest itself a big military force was deployed—beginning at four o'clock in the morning, a consignment of troops in the barracks. Bakers and artisans were let in but not let out again. About six o'clock hussars moved from Deutz to Cologne, traversing the whole city. The new prison was garrisoned by three hundred men. For today

---

4. At a meeting in Gürzenich Hall on June 25, 1848, members of three radical societies—the Democratic Association, the Workers' Union, and the Union of Workers and Employers—discussed the formation of a united organization.

5. The *Code Pénal*, introduced by Napoleon in 1810, also applied to the French-occupied Rhineland, where it continued in force even after the Prussians took over the area in 1815.

6. The *Allgemeine Landrecht für die Preussischen Staaten von 1794* (General National Law for the Prussian States of 1794) codified the laws that existed at the time, freezing them into a juridical jumble without coherence, consistency, or uniform philosophy.

four arrests—those of Jansen, Kalker, Esser, and a fourth—were announced. Jansen's wall poster, calling on the workers to remain peaceful, was torn down by the police last night, as eyewitnesses have assured us. Did this take place in the interest of order? Or did they seek an excuse to carry out long-cherished plans in the good city of Cologne?

Herr Chief Procurator Zweiffel is said to have asked the Superior Provincial Court in Arnsberg beforehand whether he should arrest Anneke in execution of a previous sentence and have him transported to Jülich. The royal amnesty seems to have stood in the way of this well-meaning intention. The matter went to the Ministry.

Herr Chief Procurator Zweiffel is said, furthermore, to have declared that within eight days he would put an end to the Nineteenth of March, the [political] clubs, freedom of the press, and other degeneracies of the bad year 1848 in Cologne on the Rhine. Herr Zweiffel does not belong among the skeptics.[7]

Does Herr Zweiffel perhaps combine the executive power with the legislative?[8] Should the laurels of the Chief Procurator cover the nakedness of the people's representative? We will once more carefully examine our much-beloved stenographic reports and give the public a faithful picture of the performance of Zweiffel the representative of the people, and Zweiffel the Chief Procurator.

These, then, are the acts of the Ministry of Action,[9] the Ministry of the Left-Center, the Ministry of Transition to an old-aristocratic, old-bureaucratic, Old-Prussian Ministry. As soon as Herr Hansemann has fulfilled his transitional mission he will be dismissed.

But members of the Left in Berlin[10] must see that the old power can safely leave them a few small parliamentary victories and great constitutional plans while it takes over all the really decisive positions in the meantime. It can confidently recognize the Revolution of March 19 in the Chamber, so long as it is disarmed outside the Chamber.

One fine morning the Left may discover that its parliamentary victories and its real defeat coincide. Perhaps German development needs such contrasts.

The Ministry of Action recognizes the Revolution in principle in order to carry out the counterrevolution in practice.

---

7. A pun: *Zweifel* (with one "f") means "doubt."

8. Zweiffel was also a delegate to the National Assembly.

9. The ministry in which David Justus Hansemann, a Rhineland capitalist, was Minister of Finance in Berlin from May to September, 1848, a period of revolutionary agitation.

10. In the National Assembly. The leaders of the Left (Waldeck, Jacoby, Jung, Berends, d'Ester) were often criticized in the *Neue Rheinische Zeitung* as not being radical enough.

Judicial Investigation of the
*NEUE RHEINISCHE ZEITUNG**

Cologne, July 6

WE HAVE just received the following reply to the article in the *Neue Rheinische Zeitung*, datelined Cologne, July 4, regarding the arrest of Herren Dr. Gottschalk and Anneke.

I declare it to be an untruth that, in connection with Frau Anneke's complaint about the arrest of her husband without the personal presence of a magistrate, I made certain statements:

"I gave *no order for brutalities.*" I stated, rather, that I must regret it if the gendarmes acted improperly.

Furthermore, I declare it as an untruth that I have made use of the following expressions:

"The gendarmes were *ordered by the court* to make the arrest." I said only that the arrest was made on a warrant issued by the Police Magistrate.

Under the law, warrants for arrest are served by the bailiff or armed agents of the court. The presence of an official of the judicial police is nowhere prescribed.

The slanders contained in the article, slanders against Herr Chief Procurator Zweiffel and the gendarmes respectively, which led to [Marx's] arrest, will find their assessment in the judicial investigation set up for this purpose.

Cologne,   *The State Procurator:*
July 5, 1848   HECKER

From the above our worthy readers will see that the *Neue Rheinische Zeitung* has acquired a new, promising collaborator—the *parquet.*[1]

---

* These two articles were published in the *Neue Rheinische Zeitung*, July 7, 11, 1848.

1. The office of the public prosecutor, or the body of magistrates.

We erred in *one* legal point. An arrest does not require the presence of an "official of the judicial police," but only an agent of the public authority. With what solicitous guarantees the Code surrounds the security of the person!

For the rest, it remains an illegality that the gendarmes did not show the order of arrest. It remains an illegality that, as we have been informed subsequently, letters were inspected before Herr Hecker and his companions made their appearance. But above all, the brutalities, which Herr Hecker "deplored," remain an illegality. We are astonished to see a judicial investigation, not of the gendarmes, but of the newspapers which denounced the impropriety of the gendarmes.

Our offense can apply only to one of the gendarmes, about whom it was asserted that at an early hour he "was reeling," either for spiritual or for spirituous reasons. But if the investigation should bring out the correctness of the fact—namely, the brutalities committed by agents of the public authority—which we do not doubt for a moment, then we believe that in carefully calling attention to this we brought out, with the full impartiality appropriate to the press, the only "mitigating circumstance," in our own interest as well as in that of the accused gentlemen; and yet the *parquet* transforms the philanthropic statement regarding the only mitigating circumstance into an "offense"!

And now the offense against Herr Chief Procurator Zweiffel!

As we indicated in the report itself, we simply reported *rumors*— rumors that came to us from a good source. The press not only has the right, it has the duty, to keep the strictest eye on the gentlemen representatives of the people. We indicated at that time that, in view of Herr Zweiffel's parliamentary performance, the statements inimical to the people that were ascribed to him were not improbable— and is the right of the press to judge the Parliamentary performance of a representative of the people to be curtailed? If so, why have a press?

Or doesn't the press have the right to find in People's Representative Zweiffel too much of the Chief Procurator and in the Chief Procurator too much of the People's Representative? Why, then, the debates over incompatibilities in Belgium, France, etc.?

In regard to constitutional usage one should read how *Le Constitutionnel*,[2] *Le Siècle*,[3] *La Presse*[4] under Louis-Philippe judged the parliamentary performance of Messrs. Hébert, Plougoulm, etc., when these gentlemen were both chiefs of the *parquet* and deputies. One should also read the Belgian papers, particularly the strictly constitu-

2. A Paris daily (1815–1870).
3. A Paris daily (1836–1939).
4. A Paris daily, which began to appear in 1836.

tional *L'Observateur Belge*,[5] *La Politique*,[6] *L'Émancipation*,[7] to see how they judged the parliamentary performance of M. Bavay hardly a year ago, when M. Bavay combined in his person the position of deputy and general procurator.

And what was always allowed under the Guizot Ministry and under the Rogier Ministry should not be allowed in the monarchy of the widest democratic foundation? A right which no ministry of the French Restoration contested—should it be regarded as wrong under the Ministry of Action, which the *Revolution* recognized *in principle?* ...

July 11, 1848

Yesterday eleven printers of our newspaper and Herr Clouth were summoned to appear before the Police Magistracy on Tuesday, July 11. It is still the question of discovering the author of the accused article. We recall that in the time of the old *Rheinische Zeitung*, in the time of censorship and the Arnim Ministry, when they wanted to discover who sent in a copy of the famous "Draft of the Marriage Law,"[8] neither a house search nor an interrogation of the printers was undertaken. Since that time we have, of course, experienced a revolution, which has had the misfortune of being recognized by Herr Hansemann.

We must once more return to Herr State Procurator's reply of July 5.

In this reply Herr Hecker charges us with *lying* about one or another of the utterances ascribed to him. Perhaps we now have the means at hand to correct the correction, but who will guarantee us that in this unequal battle we will not again be answered with Article 222 or 367 of the Penal Code?

The reply of Herr Hecker concludes with the following words:

"The slanders contained in the article, slanders against Herr Chief Procurator Zweiffel and the gendarmes respectively, which led to the arrest, will find their assessment in the judicial investigation set up for this purpose."

Their assessment! Did the black-red-gold colors of "judicial investigations" instituted by the Kamptz Ministry find their "assessment"?

Let us refer to the Penal Code. We read in Article 367: "He is

---

5. A Brussels daily (1835–1860).
6. A Brussels paper.
7. A Brussels paper.
8. On October 20, 1842, the *Rheinische Zeitung* published the secret draft of a pending divorce law; the Prussian Government demanded the name of the person who revealed it. The refusal to give the name was one of the reasons the newspaper was suppressed.

guilty of the offense of slander who accuses any person, in public places, or in an authentic and public document, or in printed or un-printed writings which are posted, sold or distributed, of facts which, if they were true, would expose that person to criminal or correc-tional police prosecution, or even only to the contempt and hatred of the citizens."

Article 370: "If the subject of the accusation should be legally proven true, the instigator of the accusation is free of all penalty. Legal proof is that which emanates from a judicial condemnation or some authentic document."

For elucidation of these paragraphs, Article 368 adds: "Pursuant to this, a petition of the instigator of the accusation to submit proof in his own defense will not be heard; just as little can he claim as a ground for excuse the notoriety of the document or of the facts, or that the accusations which led to the prosecution were copied or excerpted from foreign papers or similar printed materials."

The Imperial [Napoleonic] period, with all its artful despotism, shines out of these paragraphs.

In ordinary common sense a person is slandered when invented facts are ascribed to him; but in the extraordinary sense of the penal code he is slandered when accused of actual facts, which can be proved, but not in an exceptional way, not by a condemnation or by an official document. Wondrous powers of verdicts and docu-ments! Only condemned, only officially documented facts are *true*, are *real* facts. Did a legal code ever traduce ordinary common sense more scandalously? Did a bureaucracy ever throw up such a Chinese Wall between itself and the public? Covered by the shield of these paragraphs, the officials and deputies are as inviolable as constitutional kings. These gentlemen can commit as many acts as they please that would "expose" them "to the contempt and hatred of the citizen," but these facts must not be spoken about, written about, or printed, under penalty of loss of civil rights, in addition to obligatory prison sentences and fines. Long live the freedom of the press and speech as modified by Paragraphs 367, 368, and 370! You are imprisoned il-legally. The press denounces the illegality. Result: The denunciation finds its "assessment" in a "judicial investigation" of the "slandering" of the sacred officials who committed the illegality, unless by some miracle the illegality committed today was already sentenced yesterday.

No wonder the Rhineland jurists, among them Representative of the People Zweiffel, voted against a Committee on Poland[10] armed with plenary authority. From their standpoint the Poles, because of their "slandering" of Colomb, Steinäcker, Hirschfeld, Schleinitz, the

---

10. A National Assembly committee set up to investigate the atrocities com-mitted by Prussian troops during the Polish uprising in Posen.

Pomeranian militiamen and Old Prussian gendarmes, would have had to be condemned to a loss of their civil rights plus obligatory prison sentences and fines. In this the proper pacification of Posen would have been gloriously crowned.

And in the light of these paragraphs, what a contradiction it is to baptize as slander the rumor of a threat to do away with the "Nineteenth of March, the clubs, and freedom of the press"! As if the application of Articles 367, 368, and 370 of the Penal Code to political speeches and writings had not already thoroughly done away with the clubs and freedom of the press! What is a club without freedom of speech? And what is freedom of speech in the face of Articles 367, 368, and 370 of the Penal Code? And what is the Nineteenth of March without the clubs and freedom of speech? To suppress freedom of speech and the press through action, can there be a more striking proof that what is imagined here as slander is only intention? Beware of signing the address drawn up at the Gürzenich meeting yesterday.[11] The *parquet* will "assess" your address, in that it will institute a "judicial investigation" of the "slandering" of Hansemann-Auerswald —or may only ministers be slandered with impunity, slandered within the meaning of the French Penal Code, the Codex of political slavery chiseled out in lapidary style? Do we possess responsible ministers and irresponsible gendarmes?

Hence it is not the accused article that finds its "assessment" by the application of the paragraphs on "slander in the legal sense," slander in the sense of a despotic fiction that is outrageous to the sound human mind. What finds assessment in all this is solely and entirely the gains of the March Revolution. This is the apex that the counterrevolution has reached; it is the foolhardiness with which the bureaucracy takes up and applies the weapons still found in the arsenal of the old legal system against the new political life. This application of the articles on slander to attacks on the people's Representatives—what a splendid means this is of removing these gentlemen from the criticism and jury of the press!

Let us go from indictment for slander to indictment for insult. Here we encounter Paragraph 222, which reads: "If one or more governmental persons from the ranks of the administration or judiciary, in the performance of their official duties or in consequence of such performance, experience any insult by words which tend to impugn their honor or sense of delicacy, the person who has committed such an insult shall be punished with from one month to two years of imprisonment."

---

11. An address drafted at a meeting in Gürzenach Hall in Cologne, July 9, 1848, stating that the Auerswald-Hansemann Ministry "does not have the confidence of the country."

When the article in question appeared in the *Neue Rheinische Zeitung*, Herr Zweiffel was functioning as people's representative in Berlin, and in no way as a governmental person from the ranks of the judiciary in Cologne. Since he was not then performing any administrative duties, it was actually impossible to insult him in the performance of his duties or in consequence of such performance. But the honor and sense of delicacy of the gendarmes would come under the protection of the paragraph on insult, if they had been insulted *par parole* [by word]. But we *wrote* and did not *speak*, and *par écrit* is not *par parole* [by writing is not by speaking]. The moral is to speak with greater circumspection of the lowest gendarme than of the highest prince, and specifically not to have the presumption to touch the highly irritable gentlemen of the *parquet*. Once more we call the public's attention to the fact that in various places, in Cologne, Düsseldorf, Coblenz, the *same* persecutions have begun simultaneously. A singular coincidence!

The Prussian Press Bill*

Cologne, July 19

WE WANTED to cheer our readers again with the Unifier debates and report to them a brilliant speech by Deputy Baumstark, but events prevented us from doing it.

Everybody is closest to himself. When the existence of the press is threatened, one abandons even a deputy like Baumstark.

Herr Hansemann has proposed an interim press law to the Unifier Assembly. Herr Hansemann's paternal care for the press demands immediate consideration.

In the past the Code Napoléon was embellished with the edifying title of Civil Code. Now, after the Revolution, it has become different; now one enriches the general Civil Code with the most fragrant blossoms of the Code and of the September legislation. Duchâtel is of course no Bodelschwingh.

We reported the main points of this press law a few days ago. Hardly have we had the chance to prove, through the libel action, that Articles 367 and 369 of the *Code Pénal* are in the most glaring contradiction to press freedom, when Herr Hansemann moves not only to extend them to the entire monarchy but also to sharpen them three-fold. In the new bill we again find everything that has become so beloved and dear to us from practical experience:

We find the prohibition, punishable with a three-month to three-year penalty, against accusing anyone of things that are legally punishable or of "exposing him to public contempt"; we find the prohibition against stating the truth in any way other than by "valid documentary evidence"; in short, we again find the classic monuments of Napoleonic press despotism.

---

* *Neue Rheinische Zeitung*, July 20, 1848.

In reality Herr Hansemann is keeping his promise to make the old provinces share in the advantages of the Rhenish legislation!

Paragraph 10 crowns the bill with the following provisions: If government officials are libeled in connection with their duties, the ordinary penalty can be *raised by half*.

Article 222 of the Penal Code punishes with one to two months' imprisonment[1] anyone who *insults with words* (*outrage par parole*) any official in the course of carrying out his duties or on the occasion (*à l'occasion*) thereof. Despite the strenuous efforts of the Prosecutor's office, this article has so far not been applied, and with good reason. To correct his evil situation Herr Hansemann has transformed it into the above Article 10. First, "occasion" is changed to the more convenient "in connection with their duties"; second, the troublesome *par parole* is changed to *par écrit;* third, the penalty is tripled.

From the day this law goes into effect, the Prussian officials can sleep in peace. If Herr Pfuel burns the hands and ears of Poles in Höllenstein, and the press reports it—four and a half months to four and a half years in prison! If citizens are jailed by an oversight, although it is known that they are innocent, and the press reports it—four and a half months to four and a half years in prison! If district officers [*Landräte*] turn themselves into reactionary traveling salesmen and signature collectors for royalist addresses, and the press exposes this— four and a half months to four and a half years in prison!

From the day this law goes into effect, the officials can commit any despotism, any tyranny, any illegality, with impunity; they can coolly flog or order to be flogged, arrest and hold without a hearing; the only effective control, the press, has been made ineffective. The day this law goes into effect the bureaucracy can celebrate a festival of joy; it can become more mighty, more unrestrained, more strong than it was before March.

In fact, what remains of freedom of the press when what deserves public contempt can no longer be exposed to public contempt?

Under the hitherto existing laws the press could at least present the facts and proofs of its general assertions and complaints. This will now come to an end. The press will no longer *report*, but only be allowed to make general phrases, so that well-meaning people, from Herr Hansemann down to the beer-drinking citizen, can say with justice that the press only scolds but does not prove! This is precisely why it is forbidden to present proofs.

For the rest, we recommend to Herr Hansemann an addition to his benevolent bill. He should make it a punishable offense to expose the gentlemen bureaucrats not only to public contempt but also to

---

1. In the earlier article (see page 119) Marx quotes Paragraph 222 as providing "one month to two years of imprisonment."

public laughter. Otherwise they will find this gap in the law painful.

We are not going into great detail about the paragraphs on obscenity and the confiscation provisions. They outdo the *crème* of the press legislation under Louis Philippe and the Restoration. Here is one provision: Under Paragraph 21 the district attorney can order the seizure not only of already printed material but also the confiscation of the *manuscript prepared for print*, if he determines that the content might cause a crime or transgression! What a wide field for philanthropic prosecutors! What a pleasant distraction, to go to newspaper offices at any time one chooses and ask to see "the manuscript prepared for print," because, after all, it is possible that it could cause a crime or transgression!

How comical, next to all this, is the solemn earnestness of the paragraph in the draft of the Constitution[2] which, under the title, "Fundamental Rights of the German People," states: "Censorship can never be restored again"!

---

2. Draft of a Constitution for Prussia, May 20, 1848.

State Procurator "Hecker" and the

*Neue Rheinishche Zeitung**

Cologne, October 28

NUMBER 116[1] of the *Neue Rheinische Zeitung* published as a side issue, that is, outside the political section, "A Word to the German People," signed "Hecker."[2] This "historic document" had already been carried by German newspapers before it appeared in the *Neue Rheinische Zeitung*. Other German newspapers, not excepting those of Rhenish Prussia and Old Prussia, carried it later. Even the *Kölnische Zeitung*[3] had enough historic sense to publish Struve's Proclamation,[4] no less than that of Fuad Effendi.[5]

We do not know: Do the laurels of Hecker the republican prevent the sleep of Hecker the State Procurator? Should the astonished world have learned that the German Revolution has been doubly defeated, by the flight of Hecker the republican to New York and Hecker the State Procurator to Cologne? No one can deny it. Posterity will see in these two giant figures the dramatic contrasts of the modern movement. A future Goethe will tie them together in a new *Faust*. We leave it to him to decide which Hecker he will assign to the role of Faust and which to the role of Wagner.

---

* *Neue Rheinische Zeitung*, October 29, 1848.

1. No. 116 came out October 14, 1848.

2. Not the State Procurator, but Friedrich Franz Karl Hecker, a republican politician from Mannheim, who immigrated to the United States after participating in the Baden insurrection and became a Union colonel in the American Civil War.

3. A Catholic daily in Cologne.

4. Gustav von Struve was a leader in the Baden insurrection of September, 1848.

5. In September, 1848, after Turkish troops entered Wallachia (Rumania), Turkish commissioner Fuad Effendi issued a manifesto proclaiming the need for an orderly government "to eliminate the causes of the revolution" of July, 1848.

Enough. The fantastic parting words of Hecker the republican were followed by the no less fantastic *requisitorium* of Hecker the State Prosecutor.

Or do we deceive ourselves? Does Hecker the State Procurator believe that the "Word to the German People" was the fabrication of the *Neue Rheinische Zeitung*, and that in its inventive malice this paper signed its own proclamation with the name "Hecker," to make the German people believe that Hecker the State Procurator migrated to New York, Hecker the State Procurator proclaimed the German Republic, Hecker the State Procurator officially sanctioned pious revolutionary wishes?

Such a trick was credible, for the document printed in the supplement to No. 116 of the *Neue Rheinische Zeitung* was signed, not Friedrich Hecker, but *tout bonnement* [quite simply] "Hecker." Hecker without embellishment, simple Hecker! And does not Germany possess a double Hecker?

And which of the two is the "simple Hecker"? This simplicity remains ambiguous despite everything; we mean, incriminating for the *Neue Rheinische Zeitung*.

Be that as it may, Herr Hecker the State Procurator saw in the "Word to the German People" an obvious fabrication by the *Neue Rheinische Zeitung*. He saw in it a direct invitation to the overthrow of the government, high treason in its most perfected form, or at the very least participation in high treason, which, according to the Penal Code, is "simple" high treason.

Hence Herr Hecker charged the police magistrate to "designate" the editor in chief, Karl Marx, and not the manager of the paper,[6] as a person guilty of high treason. But to "designate" somebody as a person guilty of high treason means, in other words, putting him temporarily in jail and keeping him jailed pending further inquiry. What is involved here is the "designation" of the prison cell. The police magistrate refused. But once Herr Hecker has seized on an idea, he pursues it. To "designate" the editor in chief of the *Neue Rheinische Zeitung* became an *idée fixe*, just as the name "Hecker," signed under the "parting word," became a *fiction*. Hence he turned to the Council Chamber. The Council Chamber refused. From the Council Chamber he went to the Appellate Senate. The Appellate Senate refused. But Herr Hecker the State Procurator did not abandon his *idée fixe* of "designating" the editor in chief of the *Neue Rheinische Zeitung*, Karl Marx, in the above-mentioned sense. The ideas of the *parquet*, as can be seen, are not speculative ideas in the Hegelian sense. They are ideas in the Kantian sense. Notions of "practical" reason.

---

6. Hermann Korff.

Since Karl Marx could not be directly "designated" as a person guilty of high treason, the newspaper that printed facts or proclamations about revolution could be. Above all, it was a question of holding on to him who publishes the newspaper, especially in this case where the document in question was printed as a side issue. What remained? One idea leads to another. One could cite Karl Marx as an accomplice of the publisher for an alleged crime committed under Article 60 of the Penal Code. One could also cite him, if one wished, as an accomplice of that announcement, even if it were published in the *Kölnische Zeitung*. Hence Karl Marx received a summons to appear before the police magistrate, showed up in court, and was interrogated. The printers, so far as we know, were summoned as witnesses, the proofreader was summoned as a witness, the printing shop proprietor was summoned as a witness. But finally the manager was summoned as a witness. This last invitation we do not understand.

Is the alleged author to testify against his accomplices?

And to complete our story: A house search took place in the office of the *Neue Rheinische Zeitung*.

Hecker the State Procurator has surpassed Hecker the republican. The one creates facts about rebellion and publishes rebel proclamations. The other very reluctantly erases the facts from the memoirs of contemporary history, the newspapers. He makes what happened unhappen. If the "wicked press" reports facts and proclamations about revolution, it commits high treason doubly. It is a moral accomplice; it reports the facts about rebellion only because they titillate it. It is an accomplice in the ordinary legal sense in that it relates and spreads them, and in spreading them makes itself the instrument of revolt. Hence the press is "constituted" on both sides and enjoys the fruits of the "constitution." The "good press," on the other hand, will have a monopoly on reporting or not reporting, falsifying or not falsifying, revolutionary documents and facts. Radetzky applied this theory when he forbade the Milan newspapers to publish the Vienna facts and proclamations. In place of the great Vienna Revolution the *Mailänder Zeitung*[7] published an account of a little Vienna riot composed by Radetzky himself. Nonetheless, so it is rumored, a revolt did break out in Milan.

Herr Hecker the State Procurator is, as everybody knows, a contributor to the *Neue Rheinische Zeitung*.[8] Since he is a fellow contributor we forgive him much, but not the sins against the unholy "ghost" of our newspaper. And he commits such a sin when, with a

---

7. *Gazetta di Milano*, a pro-Austrian newspaper of North Italy.
8. See "Judicial Investigation of the *Neue Rheinische Zeitung*, page 115.

lack of critical sense unheard of in a contributor to the *Neue Rheinische Zeitung*, he transforms the proclamation of Hecker the refugee into a proclamation by the *Neue Rheinische Zeitung*. Friedrich Hecker comports himself *poignantly*, the *Neue Rheinische Zeitung critically*, toward the movement. Friedrich Hecker expects everything from the magic operations of individual *personalities*. We expect everything from the conflicts that emerge from economic *relationships*. Friedrich Hecker travels to the United States in order to study the "Republic." The *Neue Rheinische Zeitung* finds in the magnificent class struggles taking place inside the French Republic more interesting subjects for study than in a republic where class struggles do not yet exist in the western part and are developing in muted English form in the eastern section. For Friedrich Hecker social questions are the consequences of political struggles, for the *Neue Rheinische Zeitung* the political struggles are only the outward forms of social conflicts. Friedrich Hecker may be a good tricolor Republican. The real opposition of the *Neue Rheinische Zeitung* begins only with the tricolor Republic.

How, for example, could the *Neue Rheinische Zeitung*, without disavowing its past, call out to the German people: "Gather around the men who hold high the banners of popular sovereignty and who keep loyal guard over it, around the men of the extreme Left in Frankfurt am Main; join firmly in council and deed the brave leaders who raised the republican shield."

We have repeated frequently that we are not a "parliamentary" paper,[9] and hence that we do not hesitate from time to time to bring on our heads the wrath of the extreme Left in Berlin and Frankfurt. We have called on the gentlemen in Frankfurt to join the people, we have never called on the people to join the gentlemen in Frankfurt. And "the brave leaders who raised the republican shield"—where are they, and who are they? Hecker is, as we know, in America; Struve is in jail. Well, Herwegh?[10] In public mass meetings in Paris the editors of the *Neue Rheinische Zeitung*, particularly Karl Marx, came out decisively against the Herwegh undertaking without shunning the disfavor of the aroused masses. For this they became suspect to the utopians, who played revolutionists proper to the time (compare, among others, the *Deutsche Volkszeitung*).[11] And now that events

---

9. Marx in *Neue Rheinische Zeitung*, August 31, 1848: "We have never coveted the honor of being any kind of organ of the Parliamentary Left"; September 17, 1848: ". . . we speak for and support a party only insofar as it is *revolutionary*."

10. Georg Friedrich Herwegh, leader of the German Democratic Society in Paris, organized a volunteer force to fight in the German revolutions in 1848. His legion crossed into Germany in April, 1848, and was quickly defeated in Baden.

11. A Mannheim democratic daily.

have repeatedly confirmed our prognoses, are we to join the men of opposite opinions?

But we are just. Herr Hecker the State Procurator is still a young contributor to our paper. The beginner in politics, like the beginner in natural science, can be compared to the painter who knows only two colors, white and black, or if one prefers, black-white and red. The finer distinctions within each kind reveal themselves only to the trained and experienced eye. And furthermore, was not Herr Hecker obsessed with the fixed idea of "constituting" the editor in chief of the *Neue Rheinische Zeitung*, Karl Marx! It was a fixed idea that did not melt away in the purging fire of the police court, nor in the Council Chamber, nor in the Appellate Senate, hence it must be a fixed idea that is fireproof.

The greatest gain of the March Revolution is undoubtedly, to use Brutus Bassermann's words, the "rule of the noblest and best" and their rapid rise on the ladder of power. We hope, therefore, that the deserts of our honored contributor, Herr State Procurator Hecker, will also carry him, like the snow-white doves harnessed to Aphrodite's chariot flying like an arrow to Olympus, to the heights of the political Olympus. Our government is, as everybody knows, constitutional. Pfuel is enthusiastic about constitutionalism. In constitutional states it is customary to pay careful attention to the recommendations of the opposition papers. Hence we move on constitutional ground when we advise the government to bestow on our Hecker the vacated office of chief procurator in Düsseldorf. So far as we know, Herr Procurator Ammon of Düsseldorf, who has up to now not earned a medal for saving the Fatherland, will not hesitate for a moment to keep respectful silence about his own claims in the presence of higher deserts. However, should Herr Heimsoeth become Minister of Justice, which we hope, we recommend Herr Hecker for Attorney General. We expect even greater things for Herr Hecker. Herr Hecker is still young. And as the Russian said: The Czar is great, God is greater, but the *Czar is still young.*

The *Kölnische Zeitung*[*]

Cologne, November 16

THE EDITORS of the *Kölnische Zeitung*, in the November 16 issue, characterize themselves in the following ingenious way: "In our swinging back and forth between fear of anarchy today and fear of reaction tomorrow, we are strongly reminded of Luther's remark: 'Man is like a drunken peasant; if he mounts his horse on one side, he falls off on the other.'"

Fear is the poignancy of the *Kölnische Zeitung*.

---

[*] *Neue Rheinische Zeitung*, November 17, 1848.

The Chief Procurator and the
*Neue Rheinische Zeitung**

Cologne, November 21

WHO STANDS on legal ground, Oberpräsident Eichmann or the editors of the *Neue Rheinische Zeitung?* Who is to enter the prison ground, the editors of the *Neue Rheinische Zeitung* or Oberpräsident Eichmann? This question now lies before the official Zweiffel Ministry for decision. Will the official. Zweiffel Ministry take the side of the Brandenburg Ministry [in Berlin] or will Chief Procurator Zweiffel, as a former contributor to the *Neue Rheinische Zeitung*, take the side of his colleagues? This question now lies before the public for decision.

The *Neue Rheinische Zeitung* had urged the suspension of payment of taxes before the National Assembly resolved to do so;[1] this was made legal by the legislative authority. And if this anticipation of legality is an illegality, then the editors of the *Neue Rheinische Zeitung* stood on illegal ground for six full days. During those six days Herr Zweiffel should have made his inquiries but rested in his Inquisition zeal on the seventh.

---

* *Neue Rheinische Zeitung*, November 22, 1848.

1. On November 17, 1848, Marx printed an Extraordinary Supplement to the *Neue Rheinische Zeitung*, "No More Taxes!" It ended as follows (for complete text see *Karl Marx on Revolution*, page 455):

"The National Assembly was once again driven out of the Köllnische City Hall with armed force. It then moved to the Mielenz Hotel, where in the end, with 226 votes, it unanimously adopted the following resolution on *tax avoidance:*

" 'THE BRANDENBURG MINISTRY IS NOT AUTHORIZED TO DISPOSE OF GOVERNMENT MONEYS OR TO COLLECT TAXES, SO LONG AS THE NATIONAL ASSEMBLY IN BERLIN CANNOT CONTINUE ITS SESSIONS FREELY.

" 'THIS DECISION GOES INTO EFFECT ON NOVEMBER 17.

" 'THE NATIONAL ASSEMBLY OF NOVEMBER 15.' "

"FROM THIS DAY ON, ALL TAXES ARE THEREFORE SUSPENDED! ! ! TAXPAYING IS HIGH TREASON, TAX AVOIDANCE IS THE FIRST DUTY OF THE CITIZEN!"

But on the seventh day, after the work of creation was completed and Herr Zweiffel was celebrating the Sabbath and the National Assembly had made the refusal to pay taxes into law, Oberpräsident Eichmann turned to Herr Zweiffel and asked him to investigate those who had provoked the tax refusal. Who had provoked the tax refusal? The editors of the *Neue Rheinische Zeitung* or the National Assembly in Berlin? Whom should Herr Zweiffel arrest—his old colleagues, the deputies in Berlin, or his old collaborators, the editors of the *Neue Rheinische Zeitung*, or the prefect, Herr Eichmann? So far Herr Zweiffel has not arrested anybody.

Hence we propose that another Zweiffel should arrest Herr Zweiffel, because the latter did not arrest the editors of the *Neue Rheinische Zeitung* before the Sabbath and Herr Eichmann after the Sabbath.

Three Lawsuits Against the
*Neue Rheinische Zeitung**

Cologne, November 24

AT THE MOMENT three lawsuits are pending against the *Neue Rheinische Zeitung*—we do not include the indictments of Engels, Dronke, Wolff, and Marx for alleged "inopportune" offenses. We are assured by a well-informed source that at least another dozen investigations have been instituted against the "SCANDAL SHEET"—the official term of the *ci-devant* [former] Chief Procurator Hecker (*c'est du Hecker tout pur* [it is Hecker pure and simple]).

First Crime. Violent attack on the virginal "delicacy" of six Royal Prussian gendarmes and of the king of the Cologne Procurator's office, Herr Chief Procurator Zweiffel, the people's deputy in *partibus infidelium*,[1] who at the moment sits neither in Berlin nor in Brandenburg, but in Cologne on the Rhine. On the Rhine! On the Rhine! There grows our vine![2] We too prefer the Rhine to the Spree and the Hotel Disch to the Hotel Mielenz.[3]

Va pour la délicatesse des gens d'armes! [So much for the delicacy of the gendarmes!] In regard to the "delicacy" of Herr Zweiffel, for us it is *"noli me tangere"* [touch me not]! We were morally indignant at the indelicacy of the vote of no confidence with which the voters prevailed upon him to retire. As true guards of honor of the virginal delicacy of Herr Zweiffel, we beg him to *repudiate officially* the statement by Herr Weinhagen of Cleve. Herr Weinhagen declared in the *Neue Rheinische Zeitung*, under his own signature, that he possesses

---

* *Neue Rheinische Zeitung*, November 26, 1848 (second edition).
1. A Catholic expression meaning "in the land of the infidels."
2. *"Am Rhein! am Rhein! da wachsen unsre Reben"*—from Matthias Claudius' *"Rheinweinlied"* ("Song of the Rhine Wine").
3. Disch was a Cologne hotel; the Mielenz was in Berlin, where the Prussian National Assembly met on November 15, 1848.

facts injurious to the "honor and delicacy" of Herr Zweiffel. He could *prove* these facts himself, but must abstain from their publication so long as Herr Zweiffel takes refuge in the paragraph of the *Code Pénal* whereby even the most soundly established denunciation is prosecuted as *slander* so long as it cannot be proven by judicial decision or authentic documents. We therefore appeal to the "honor and delicacy" of Herr Zweiffel!

Second Crime. The simple Hecker or the divided Hecker.[4]

Third Crime. The crime, which took place in 1848, is prosecuted at the request of the National Ministry. The Crime Schnapphahnski! The *feuilleton* as criminal![5]

The National Ministry is said to have declared in its indictment that the *Neue Rheinische Zeitung* is the worst newspaper in a "bad press." We, for our part, declare the National Authority to be the most comical of all comical authorities.

---

4. See "State Procurator 'Hecker' and the *Neue Rheinische Zeitung*," page 124.
5. The reference is to a series of feuilletons, "*Leben und Taten des berühmten Ritters Schnapphahnski*" (Life and Deeds of the Famous Knight Schnapphahnski), by Georg Weerth, published anonymously in the *Neue Rheinische Zeitung*. They satirized Prince Felix Maria von Lichnowski, a reactionary Prussian general.

The Slanders of the *Neue Rheinische Zeitung**

Cologne, December 13

T HE JULY 4 article in the *Neue Rheinische Zeitung*,[1] for which its manager, Korff, its editor in chief, Marx, and the editor, Engels, are to appear before the Court of Assizes on the 20th of this month, concludes with the following words:

"These, then, are the acts of the Ministry of Action, the Ministry of the Left-Center, the Ministry of Transition to an old-aristocratic, old-bureaucratic, Old-Prussian Ministry. As soon as Herr Hansemann has fulfilled his transitional mission he will be dismissed.

"But members of the Left in Berlin must see that the old power can safely leave them a few small parliamentary victories and great constitutional plans while it takes over all the really decisive positions in the meantime. It can confidently recognize the revolution of March 19 in the Chamber, so long as it is disarmed outside the Chamber.

"One fine morning the Left may discover that its parliamentary victory and its real defeat coincide. Perhaps German development needs such contrasts.

"The Ministry of Action recognizes the Revolution in principle in order to carry out the counterrevolution in practice."

The facts have demonstrated how much the *Neue Rheinische Zeitung* has slandered the Prussian government and its henchmen.

---

* *Neue Rheinische Zeitung*, December 14, 1848.
1. See "Arrests," page 112.

The Role of the Press as Critic of Government Officials*

GENTLEMEN of the Jury! Today's proceedings have a certain importance because Articles 222 and 367 of the *Code Pénal*, referred to in the indictment of the *Neue Rheinische Zeitung*, are the only ones in Rhineland law available to the government in connection with direct incitement to revolt.

You all know with what special partiality the parquet pursues the *Neue Rheinische Zeitung*. Nevertheless, despite all its diligence, it has hitherto not succeeded in charging us with anything other than what is visualized in Articles 222 and 367. In the interest of the press, therefore, I consider it necessary to go into greater detail about those articles.

Before going into a legal analysis, allow me to make a personal remark. The public Ministry has labeled as a vulgarity the passage in the incriminating article which read: "Does Herr Zweiffel perhaps combine the executive power with the legislative? Should the laurels of the Chief Procurator cover the nakedness of the people's representatives?" Gentlemen! Anybody can be a very good Chief Procurator and at the same time a bad representative of the people. Perhaps he is a good Chief Procurator because he is a bad representative of the people. The public Ministry seems to have little familiarity with parliamentary history. The question of incompatibility, which occupies so

---

* This is Marx's defense speech at his trial.[1] It was published in *Neue Rheinische Zeitung* the following week, February 14, 1849. As editor in chief of the *Neue Rheinische Zeitung*, he was tried on February 7 in the Cologne Court of Assizes for having published derogatory remarks about government officials. He and his codefendants, co-editor Frederick Engels and manager Hermann Korff, were acquitted by the jury amid the jubilation of those present.

1. Marx had studied law at the University of Berlin, and his father had been a lawyer in the Rhineland.

much time in the proceedings of constitutional chambers—what does it rest on? On the distrust of executive officials, on the suspicion that an executive official easily sacrifices the interest of society to the interest of the existing government, and is therefore more suitable to be anything else than a representative of the people. And especially the position of being a state's attorney. In what country has that not been considered incompatible with the dignity of a representative of the people? I remind you of the attacks on Hébert, Plougoulm, and Bavay in the French and Belgian press and in the French and Belgian chambers, attacks aimed at the contradictory qualities of a Procurator General and a parliamentary deputy when combined in the same person. Never did those attacks result in a judicial investigation, not even under Guizot, and the France of Louise Philippe and the Belgium of Leopold were regarded as model parliamentary states. In England, of course, the situation is different in regard to the Attorney General and the Solicitor General. But their position is essentially different from that of a *procureur du roi* [public prosecutor]. They are more or less judicial officials. We, gentlemen, are not constitutionalists, but we put ourselves in the position of the gentlemen who indict us in order to beat them on their own ground with their own weapons. We therefore invoke constitutional usage.

The public Ministry wants to destroy a big slice of parliamentary history—with a moral platitude. I emphatically reject its accusation of vulgarity, which I explain on the ground of its ignorance.

I now take up the discussion of the legal question.

My defense attorney [Karl Schneider II] has already proved to you that without the Prussian law of July 5, 1819, the accusation of having offended Chief Procurator Zweiffel was untenable from the first. Article 222 of the *Code Pénal* speaks only of "*outrages par paroles*," of *oral* offenses, not of written or printed ones. Nevertheless, the Prussian law of 1819 meant to supplement Article 222, not abolish it. The Prussian law can apply the Article 222 penalty to written insults only when the Code misinterprets it as oral. Written insults must take place under the same conditions and circumstances that Article 222 presupposes for oral ones. It is therefore necessary to determine clearly the sense of Article 222.

The rationale that applies to Article 222 (*Exposé par M. le conseiller d'état Berlier, séance du février, 1810*[2]) state:

"*Il ne sera donc ici question que des seuls outrages qui compromettent la paix publique, c.a.d. de ceux dirigés contre les fonctionnaires ou agents publics dans l'exercice ou à l'occasion de l'exercice de leurs fonctions; et dans ce cas ce n'est plus un particulier, c'est l'ordre public qui est blessé ... La hiérarchie politique sera dans ce cas prise en con-*

---

2. Statement by Councillor of State Berlier, Session of February, 1810.

sidération: celui qui se permet des outrages ou violences envers un officier ministériel est coupable sans doute, mais il commet un moindre scandale que lorsqu'il outrage un magistrat."[3]

From these reasonings, gentlemen, you see what the legislature intended with Article 222. Article 222 is applicable "only" to insults that question the policy of public officials when they compromise the public order and peace. When is the public order, *la paix publique* [the public peace], compromised? Only when an incitement to the overthrow of the laws is undertaken or when the execution of the existing laws is interfered with; that is, when a revolt against an official who carries out the law takes place, when an *official action* of a functioning official is interrupted. The revolt can be confined to mere grumbling or insulting words; it can continue up to the point of action, of violent opposition. The outrage, the insult, is merely the lowest grade of violence, of opposition, of violent revolt. Hence the rationale speaks of insults *or* acts of violence. Both are identical in the concept; violence—the action—is only a graver form of outrage, of insult, against the functioning official.

Hence in these reasonings it is presupposed: (1) that the official is insulted when carrying out a public duty; (2) that he is insulted in his *personal presence*. In no other case does a real disturbance of the public peace take place.

You will find the same presupposition in the whole section that deals with "insults and acts of violence against the depositories of the public authority and power," that is, "insults and violence against those who are entrusted with the public authority and the public power." The various articles of that section posit the following series of insubordination: looks, words, threats, actions. Action itself is in turn differentiated according to the grade of seriousness. Finally, in all those articles penalties are augmented in accord with various forms of insubordination taking place in the hearings of a court of justice. Here is caused the greatest "scandal," and in the enforcement of the laws, the *paix publique* is most flagrantly disturbed.

As regards *written* insults against officials, Article 222 is therefore applicable only when they occur (1) in the personal presence of the official, and (2) during the carrying out of his duty. My defense attorney, gentlemen, has introduced such an example. He himself would fall foul of Article 222 if at this moment, during the court pro-

---

3. "Hence the question here is only of offenses that compromise the public peace, that is to say, those aimed against officials or public agents in the exercise, or on the occasion of the exercise, of their functions; in this case, it is no longer a particular person, but the public order that is injured . . . The political hierarchy will in this case be taken into consideration: Whoever permits himself offenses or acts of violence against ministerial agents is undoubtedly guilty, but he causes less of a scandal than when he insults a judge."

ceedings, he were to insult the president [of the court] in a written motion, etc. But on the other hand, this article of the *Code Pénal* can under no circumstances find an application to a newspaper article that "insulted" a functioning official in his absence, long after the event.

This interpretation of Article 222 explains to you an apparent gap, an apparent inconsistency in the *Code Pénal*. Why should I insult the King when I may not insult the Chief Procurator? Why does not the Code dictate a penalty for *lèse majesté*, as the Prussian law does?

Because the King himself never carries out an official act, but always does so only through others, because the King never confronts me personally, but only through representatives. The despotism of the *Code Pénal* that emerged from the French Revolution is worlds apart from the patriarchal-schoolmasterish despotism of the Prussian law. Napoleonic despotism struck me down the moment I really blocked the sovereign power, even if only through an insult to an official confronting me with that power while carrying out some public duty. But outside of his public duty he was an ordinary member of civil society, without privileges, without special protection. Prussian despotism, on the other hand, confronts me, in the person of the official, with a higher, a sanctified being. His character as an official is entwined in him just as consecration is in the Catholic priest. For the Prussian layman, that is, the nonofficial, the Prussian official always remains a priest. To insult such a priest, even one who is not functioning, who is absent, who has retired to private life, is a violation of religion, a desecration. The higher the official, the graver the violation of religion. The highest insult to the state-priest is therefore the insult to the King, the *lèse majesté*, which according to the *Code Pénal* belongs to a criminalistic impossibility.

But, it will be said, Article 222 of the *Code Pénal*, referring only to insults against officials "in the exercise of their functions," requires no proof that the *personal presence* of the official is assumed by the legislature and is the necessary condition of every presupposed insult under Article 222. Nevertheless, Article 222 adds to the words "*dans l'exercice de leurs fonctions*" ["in the exercise of their functions"]: the words "*à l'occasion de cet exercice*" [on the occasion of that exercise"].

The public Ministry has translated this, "in relation to its office." I will prove to you, gentlemen, that this translation is false and actually contradicts the intention of the legislature. Take a look at Article 228 in the same section. It says: Whoever physically attacks an official "in the exercise of his functions or on the occasion of that exercise" is to be punished with from two to five years' imprisonment. Can one then translate here, "in relation to their office"? Can one apportion *relative* beatings? Is the presumption of the personal presence of the official given up here? Can I physically attack somebody who is absent? Manifestly, it has to be translated: "Whoever beats up an official on the occasion of his performing his duties." But in Article 228 you find literally the same phrase as in Article 222. The expression "on the occasion of that exercise" has manifestly the same meaning in both articles. Hence this addition, far from excluding the condition of the *personal presence* of the official, actually presupposes it.

The history of French legislation offers you a further striking proof. You will recall that during the early period of the French Restoration the parties fought each other pitilessly, in the chambers, in the courts of justice, and with daggers in the south of France. In those days the juries were nothing but martial-law tribunals of the victorious party against the defeated one. The opposition press lashed the jury decisions unsparingly. The government found no weapon against this displeasing polemic in Article 222, because the latter was only applicable to insults against the jurors while sitting, in their personal presence. Hence in 1819 they produced a new law punishing any attack on the *chose jugée*, the verdict passed. The *Code Pénal* does not recognize the impunity of a judicial decision. If Article 222 had dealt with insults "in relation" to the function of the office, would it have been supplemented by a new law?

But what is the purpose of the addition, "on the occasion of that exercise"? Its aim is nothing else than the protection of the official from attacks shortly *before* or *after* the performance of his duty. If Article 222 had stated "insult and action" against an official during the performance of his duty, I could, for example, throw a bailiff down the stairs after he has executed his warrant, and then maintain that I have insulted him only after he has ceased to confront me in his capacity as bailiff. I could attack and beat up a justice of the peace while he is on the way to my house to execute a judicial warrant against me, and then escape punishment under Article 228 by maintaining that I maltreated him, not during, but before the execution of his duty.

The addition, "on the occasion of that exercise," is thus designed to protect the official in his functioning capacity. It relates to insults or actions which, although they do not occur immediately during the execution of his duty, do so shortly before or after it, and, what is the essential thing, stands in living relationships with the performance of the duty, and hence presuppose the *personal presence* of the maltreated officials in all circumstances.

Does it require more exposition to explain that Article 222 is not applicable to our newspaper article regarding the insult to Herr Zweiffel? When that article was written Herr Zweiffel was *absent*; he did not live in Cologne then, but in Berlin. When that article was written,

Herr Zweiffel did not function as Chief Procurator, but as a Unifier [in the Prussian National Assembly of 1848]. Hence he could not be insulted, or abused, as a functioning Chief Procurator.

Apart from my whole exposition up to this point, there is another way of showing that Article 222 is not applicable to the incriminating article in the *Neue Rheinische Zeitung*.

This follows from the distinction that the *Code Pénal* draws between *insult* and *slander*. You will find this distinction clearly stated in Article 375. . . .[4]

What, therefore, constitutes calumny? Aspersions blaming the aspersed person for a *specific act*. What constitutes insult? The accusation of a specific error and, in general, insulting expressions. When I say: You have stolen a silver spoon, I slander you in the sense of the *Code Pénal*. If, on the other hand, I say: You are a thief, you have thievish appetites, I insult you.

The article in the *Neue Rheinische Zeitung* in no way reproaches Herr Zweiffel: Herr Zweiffel is a traitor to the people, Herr Zweiffel has made infamous assertions. Rather, the article says specifically: "Herr Zweiffel is said, furthermore, to have declared that within eight days he would put an end to the Nineteenth of March, the clubs, freedom of the press, and other degeneracies of the bad year 1848 in Cologne."

Thus Herr Zweiffel is charged with a very specific utterance. Hence if one of the two Articles, 222 and 367, were applicable, it could not be Article 222, dealing with insult, but only Article 367, dealing with calumny.

Why did the public Ministry apply to us Article 222 instead of Article 367?

Because Article 222 is much more vague and can be used much more easily to sneak in a condemnation, if such is decided upon. Injury to "*délicatesse et honneur*" ["sensitivity and honor"] is not in any way measurable. What is honor, what is sensitivity? What is injury in regard to them? This depends entirely on the individual with whom I have to deal, on the level of his education, on his prejudices, on his conceit. There is no other yardstick to measure the *noli me tangere* [touch me not], the pompous vanity of an official who deems himself incomparable.

But even the calumny article, 367, is not applicable to the piece in the *Neue Rheinische Zeitung*.

Article 367 requires a "*fait précis*" ["definite fact"], "*un fait, qui peut exister*" ["a fact that can be real"]. But Herr Zweiffel was not charged with abolishing the freedom of the press, of closing the clubs,

---

4. The quoted paragraph, in French, is omitted.

of destroying the achievements of March in this or that place. He is charged with a mere utterance. Article 367, however, requires an accusation of specific facts "which, if they were true, would expose that person to criminal or correctional prosecution by the police, or even only to the contempt and hatred of the citizens."

But mere *utterance* about doing this or that does not expose me either to criminal or correctional prosecution. It could not even be claimed that the utterance necessarily exposes one to the hatred or contempt of the citizens. An utterance, to be sure, may be of a very vile, hateful, and contemptible nature. Nevertheless, may I not in a moment of excitement burst out with an utterance that threatens action of which I am incapable? Only action could prove that I meant the utterance to be *serious*.

And the *Neue Rheinische Zeitung* says: "Herr Zweiffel is *said* to have declared." In order to slander anyone, I myself must not question my own assertion, as is done here with "is *said* to have," but I must state it apodictically.

Finally, Gentlemen of the Jury, the *citoyens*, the citizens, to whose hatred and contempt I am being exposed as *slander* under Article 367— I say that such citizens do not in fact exist any more in political matters. Only partisans remain. What exposes me to hatred and contempt from the members of one party exposes me to the love and respect of the members of the other party. The organ of the present ministry, the *Neue Preussische Zeitung*,[5] has chastised Herr Zweiffel for being a kind of Robespierre. In their eyes, in the eyes of their party, our article has not exposed Herr Zweiffel to hatred and contempt, but rather has rid him of the hatred and contempt weighing upon him.

It is of the highest interest to emphasize this remark, not for the pending case but for all cases in which the public Ministry will try to apply Article 367 to political polemics.

In general, Gentlemen of the Jury, if you apply the calumny article, 367, to the press in the sense of the public Ministry, you abolish freedom of the press through the penal law, whereas you have given recognition to that freedom in a constitution and have fought for it in a revolution. You would sanction every caprice of officialdom. You would permit every official vileness. Then why the hypocrisy of a free press? When existing laws get into open collision with a newly achieved stage of social development, then, gentlemen, it is up to you to step between the dead commandments of the law and the living demands of society. It is up to you to anticipate legislation until the latter understands how to meet the needs of society. This is the noblest attribute of the jury courts. In the pending case, gentlemen, this task

---

5. A royalist daily founded in Berlin in 1848.

is eased for you by the literal meaning of the law itself. You have only to interpret it in the sense of our time, our political rights, and our social needs.

Article 367 concludes with the following words: "*La présente disposition n'es point applicable aux faits dont la loi autorise la publicité, ni à ceux que l'auteur de l'imputation était, par la nature de ses fonctions ou de ses devoirs, obligé de révéler ou de réprimer.*"[6]

There is no doubt, gentlemen, that the legislature did not think of a free press when it spoke of the duty of denunciation. But likewise it did not think this article would ever find application to a free press. As is known, there was no freedom of the press under Napoleon. Hence if you want to apply the law to a political and social stage of development for which it was not designed at all, then apply it in its *entirety*, interpret it in the spirit of our time, use the last sentence of Article 367 for the benefit of the press.

Article 367, viewed in the narrow sense of the public Ministry, excludes the need for proof of the truth and permits denunciation only if it is supported by official documents or already available judicial decisions. Why should the press do any denouncing at all *post festum*, after a decision has been passed? It is the function of the press to be the public watchdog, the tireless denouncer of the rulers, the omnipresent eye, the omnipresent mouth of the spirit of the people that jealously guards its freedom. If you interpret Article 367 in this sense—and you must so interpret it, unless you wish to confiscate the freedom of the press in the interest of the authorities—the Code at the same time offers you a handle against the encroachment of the press. According to Article 357, in a denunciation action and decision in regard to the slander are postponed during the investigation of the facts. According to Article 373, the denunciation is punished if the facts prove it to have been slanderous.

Gentlemen! It needs only a single glance at the incriminating newspaper article to prove to you that the *Neue Rheinische Zeitung*, far from having had any *intention* to insult or slander, only fulfilled its duty to denounce, when it attacked the local court and the gendarmes. The examination of the witnesses has proved to you that in regard to the gendarmes, we reported only the actual facts.

But the point of the whole article is the prediction of the counter-revolution that took place subsequently, an attack on the Hansemann Ministry which made its debut with the strange assertion that the more police there are, the more free the state is. The Ministry had the delusion that the aristocracy was defeated; that it had only a single task

---

6. "The present disposition is not applicable to facts which the law permits to be made public nor to those which the author, by the nature of his functions or his duties, is obliged to reveal or suppress."

left, to rob the people of its revolutionary achievements in the interest of one class, the bourgeoisie. Thus it paved the way for the feudal counterrevolution. What we denounced in the incriminating article was nothing more and nothing less than the palpable appearance, torn from our immediate environment, of a systematic counterrevolutionary activity on the part of the Hansemann Ministry and the German governments in general.

It is impossible to view the arrests in Cologne as an isolated fact. To be convinced of the contrary, one has only to cast a quick glance at the conditions of the time. Shortly before the arrests there were the press persecutions in Berlin, based on the paragraphs of the old common law. A few days later, on July 8, J. Wulff, president of the Düsseldorf People's Club, was arrested and many house searches of the members of that club took place. The jurors later acquitted Wulff and not a single political persecution of that time received their sanction. On the same July 8, Falkenhain, president of the Society "Germania" in Breslau, was arrested. On July 15 Chief Procurator Schnaase, speaking before the Citizens' Society in Düsseldorf, made a formal attack on the People's Club, whose president was arrested on the eighth at his instigation. Here you have an example of the lofty impartiality of the court, an example in which the Chief Procurator appeared as a party partisan and a Chief Procurator at the same time. Undeterred by our persecution because of our attack on Zweiffel, we then denounced Schnaase.[7] He was careful not to reply. On the same day Chief Procurator Schnaase delivered his philippic against the Düsseldorf People's Club, the Democratic District Society in Stuttgart was suppressed by royal order. On July 19 the Democratic Student Society in Heidelberg was dissolved and on July 27 the same happened to various democratic societies in Baden, and shortly thereafter in Württemberg and Bavaria. And should we have kept silent in the face of this palpably treasonable conspiracy of the various German governments? The Prussian Government did not then dare to do what Baden, Württemberg and Bavaria did. It did not dare because the Prussian National Assembly had just begun to suspect the counterrevolutionary conspiracy and to rise up on its hind legs against the Hansemann Ministry. But, Gentlemen of the Jury, I say this frankly, with the most certain conviction: If the Prussian counterrevolution is not soon frustrated by a Prussian people's revolution, freedom of association and of the press will be completely destroyed. It has already been partly killed under martial law. They have even dared to reintroduce censorship in Düsseldorf and in a few Silesian districts.

Not only the general German conditions, but that of Prussia, ob-

---

7. A report from Düsseldorf in *Neue Rheinische Zeitung*, July 18, 1848, criticized Schnaase's activities there.

ligate us to watch every movement of the government with the most extreme distrust, and to denounce to the people the slightest symptoms of the scheme. The local Cologne court gave us a special occasion to expose it to public opinion as a counterrevolutionary tool. In the month of July alone we denounced three illegal arrests. In the first two cases State's Attorney Hecker kept silent; the third time he sought to justify himself, but remained mute at our reply, for the simple reason that there was nothing to say.[8]

And under these conditions how does the public Ministry dare maintain that what is involved here is not a denunciation but a petty-malevolent aspersion? This view rests on an inherent misunderstanding. I, for my part, assure you, gentlemen, I prefer to follow the great world events, to analyze the course of history, rather than tussle with local idols, with gendarmes and courts. No matter how great these gentlemen may consider themselves in their own imaginations, they are *nothing*, altogether *nothing* in the titanic struggles of the present time. I regard it as a real sacrifice when we decide to break a lance with *these* opponents. But once and for all it is the duty of the press to speak up for the oppressed in its immediate vicinity. And also, gentlemen, the house of servitude has its own proper support in the subordinate political and social authorities that directly confront the private life of the person, the living individual. It does not suffice to fight general conditions and the higher authorities. The press must decide to enter the lists against *this* particular gendarme, *this* procurator, *this* district administrator. On what was the March Revolution shattered? It reformed only the highest political summit, it left the foundations of that summit untouched—the old bureaucracy, the old army, the old courts, the old judges who were born, trained, and grew gray in the service of absolutism. The first duty of the press, therefore, is *to undermine all the foundations of the existing political system.* (Applause in court.)

---

8. *Neue Rheinische Zeitung* exposed the arrest of J. Wulff on July 10, 1848, that of Falkenhain on July 13, and of Joseph Wolff on August 1. State Attorney Hecker's "reply" was printed on August 3, and the newspaper's counter reply on August 4.

Drafts of Three New Laws*

Cologne, March 12

THE PRUSSIAN KINGDOM considers it time to develop its full glory. Today the "undebilitated" Crown[1] by the Grace of God has dictated to us three drafts of new laws, on clubs and associations, on posters, and on the press, for which the legislative chambers are ordered to confront us with a closed phalanx reminiscent of the amiable September laws.[2]

Tomorrow we will report the texts of the drafts, with their reasonings, so far as they are known to us. We will return—more than once —to these splendid Prussian products. For now, merely a brief résumé:

I. The *Club Law*. "All meetings must be announced twenty-four hours in advance." Quickly assembled meetings for sudden events that are important are hereby suppressed, and yet such meetings are after all the most important ones. Everyone should be allowed to enter, hence it is forbidden to charge admission, which defrays the cost of the meeting. In case of meetings organized by associations, one-fourth of the hall must be left for nonmembers, so that the associations will be obliged to secure larger and more expensive halls, thereby enabling paid police agents to disturb all deliberations and to make all sessions impossible by uproars, rantings, and blusterings. And if all this doesn't work, then the "representatives of the police authority" are free at the first pretext "to dissolve immediately" any meeting in the same

---

* *Neue Rheinische Zeitung*, March 13, 1849.
 1. At the opening of the United Diet, on April 11, 1847, King Frederick Wilhelm IV declared from the throne: "As heir to an *undebilitated* Crown, which I must and will preserve undebilitatedly for my successors . . . I know myself to be completely free from all obligations to what has not been carried out . . . by my exalted predecessors. . . ."
 2. The reactionary laws of September, 1835, by which French King Louis Philippe restricted freedom of the press and other civil rights.

way the highest peak of "police authority," His Majesty, our All-Gracious King himself, "immediately dissolved" the United Diet. And as soon as the police have declared the meeting dissolved, everybody must leave, if he does not want what happened to the Berlin United Diet to happen to him, that is, if he does not want to be removed from the hall with bayonets.

The clubs, to be sure, are not required to have a "prior license," but they have to fill out such a mass of prior notices and formalities with the authorities that this alone makes it almost impossible for them to function. Public meetings under the open sky, processions, etc., etc., on the other hand, require, of course, prior police permission. And finally, to put an end to the red armbands, cockades, and caps, a renewal of the old hunting-down ordinances against the black-red-gold insignia has been ordered.

This is the "right of association and meeting" that the truth-loving and promise-keeping Hohenzollern guaranteed us with trembling lips a year ago.

II. The *Poster Law*. All posters with political content, except invitations to lawful, *permitted* meetings (all meetings are thus once more graciously "permitted" ones!), are forbidden. Hence the club committees are not allowed to use posters to call upon the people to be calm even in agitated times, so that not a single victim will escape the heroic soldiery! Furthermore: The sale or distribution of printed matter on public streets is equally forbidden, which makes it a concession that is revocable at any time! In other words: The Prussian kingdom is seeking to bless us with an *improved version* of the law on *crieurs publics* [town criers] that was extorted from the frightened Chambers in France in the worst period of the Louis Phillippe bourgeois despotism.

And the reasons for this law? Because the posters and their hawkers block traffic in the streets and the posters disfigure some public buildings.

III. The *Press Law*. But all this is nothing compared to the charming proposals for muzzling the press. We know that since 1830 the main Hohenzollernish blessing for the people consisted merely of ennobling Prussian paternal patriarchalism by coupling it with the modern cunning servitude of Louis Philippe. They retained the cudgel and added the convict-prison to it; they let the censorship stand and at the same time blessed us with the blossom of the September legislation; in a word, they left us the advantages of feudalistic servitude, bureaucratic police administration, and modern bourgeois *lawful* brutality at the same time. This is what they called "the world-famous liberality of Frederick William IV."

The new Hohenzollern draft of the press law, after a long series of burdensome formal provisions, blesses us with an unsurpassable fusion of (1) Code Napoléon, (2) the French September laws, and mainly (3) the laudable *Prussian common law!*

Paragraph 9 replaces the Code: In the provinces where the common law prevails the invitation to commit a crime was punished less severely, even if it was crowned with success, than the crime itself. In those provinces the provision in the Code is now changed so that the invitation to a successful crime is punishable like the crime itself.

Paragraph 10, the French September-legislation: Whoever attacks the *property* or the *family* foundations of bourgeois society, or incites citizens to *hatred or contempt for each other*, is subject to up to two years' imprisonment.

Compare the Law of September 9, 1835, Article 8: "*Toute attaque contre la propriété . . . , toute provocation à la haine entre les diverses classes de la société, sera punie*" ["All attacks against property . . . all provocation to hate among the various classes of society, shall be punished."], etc. But the Prussian translation: to incite *citizens* in general against each other, etc., is ten times more incalculable.

All the following paragraphs of the draft are designed only to bless the Rhineland province once more with those common law splendors that were taken from us soon after March 18, after we had enjoyed them in fullest measure for thirty-three years. They want to impose on us, among other things, new crimes totally unknown to Rhineland legislation:

1. *Hatred and contempt for the institutions of the state or its government* by means of factual untruths or legally unprovable facts.

2. "Excluding" *legally existing* religious societies (according to the proclaimed constitution, even Turks and heathen are after all legally existing religious societies) in a way that is bound (!) to spread hatred and contempt for them.

These two new crimes introduce among us (a) the Old Prussian "incitement of discontent" and (b) the Old Prussian concept of insult to religion, and are to be punished with up to two years' imprisonment.

3. *Lèse majesté*, and particularly the *injury to the respect* (!!) due to:

   (a) The King (!),
   (b) the Queen (!),
   (c) the Heir to the Throne (!!!),
   (d) any other member of the royal house (!!!!),
   (e) the head of the German State (!!!!!),

all of which is to be punishable with from one month to up to five years' imprisonment.

4. The edifying provision that an assertion even of provable facts is to be punished as an insult, if an *insult was intended* thereby!

5. Insulting

(a) *either of the two Chambers,*

(b) any of its members,

(c) any government *department* (the Code does not recognize insult to corporations as such)

(d) an official or a member of the armed forces.

All of this "in connection with their office." Imprisonment up to nine months.

6. *Insult and slander in Private Life.* The Code Napoléon recognizes only *publicly uttered* or spread insults or slanders. The new draft of the law, on the other hand, declares as punishable all private conversations made in one's house and in the bosom of one's family, as well as utterances in private letters, and these are to be made subject to control by the police and the public authority, that is, those who organize the most vile and common spying. The military despotism of the all-powerful French Empire at least respected the freedom of private conversation; it stopped—at least in legislation—at the threshold of the home. But the Prussian paternal-constitutional surveillance and correction extends into the innermost center of the private home, into the most intimate asylum of family life that even barbarians consider inviolate. And this same law, in the preceding three articles, punishes all attacks on the family with two years' imprisonment!

These are the new "gains" they want to offer us. Supplementing the three most brutal laws with one another, to achieve a pinnacle of brutality and perfidy hitherto unheard of—this is the price the undebilitated Crown wants the chambers to barter in exchange for the suspension of the state of siege in Berlin!

Whatever one desires lies at hand. On the old provinces at least, the press law draft does not impose very much that is new. The common law was already bad enough. The main animus of the Incorporated Grace of God is directed against us Rhinelanders. They want to inflict on us the same infamous common law of which we had barely rid ourselves, and since the removal of which, so long as we were chained to Prussia, we could at last breathe somewhat freely again.

What the Crown by the Grace of God wants is clearly expressed in the reasoning of the charming official document spoken through the mouth of its vassal Manteuffel: *the restoration of a possibly uniform legal system*—that is, the removal of the hated French law and the general introduction of the disgraceful common law. It wants, furthermore, to "fill the gaps" that have developed "in the greatest part of the Rhine province" (listen to this!) "by the suspension of the penal laws regarding *lèse majesté* as a result of the ordinance of April 15, 1848"!

That is, the new penal law is taking from us Rhinelanders the only thing we still possess as a consequence of the so-called Revolution of 1848: *our own laws remaining in inviolable effect.*

We are to become Prussians at any price, Prussians after the heart of the All-Gracious, with common law, aristocratic insolence, bureaucratic tyranny, saber rule, cudgelings, censorship, and obedience. These drafts of the law are only the beginning. The plan of the counter-revolution lies before us, and our readers will wonder what plans are in mind for the future. We do not doubt that the gentlemen in Berlin will once more remarkably deceive themselves in the Rhinelanders.

But we will again return to these disgraceful proposed laws, for which alone *the Ministers must be indicted.* This, however, we should already say today: Should anything even remotely resembling these drafts pass the Chamber, *it is the duty of the Rhineland representatives immediately to leave a Chamber that by such decisions wants to hurl its constituents back into the patriarchal barbarism of Old-Prussian legislation.*

Censorship*

Cologne, March 14

THE GERMAN DAILY PRESS is truly the most flaccid, the most indolent, and the most cowardly institution under the sun! The greatest infamies can be perpetrated before its own eyes, even against itself, and it keeps silent and conceals it all; if one does not discover by accident what splendid March violets have cropped up in certain places through the grace of God, one will surely never find out about it from the press.

In Düsseldorf last autumn citizen and communist Drigalski tried to reintroduce censorship under the pretext of the state of siege. It succeeded for two days; then the storm of public opinion forced the gentlemen saber-draggers to drop their censorship lust immediately.

And what is the situation in the old provinces?

In two different districts censorship in its full glory has prevailed for three months now, and the entire Old Prussian press lets this unheard-of attack on its rights continue unchallenged!

One hears: Rosenberg, in Silesia, March 7. The *Rosenberg-Kreuzburger Telegraph* features the following in its issue No. 19:

> We beg the honored readers of our paper not to blame us for the belated and incomplete edition of this issue, but to keep in mind that we still find ourselves in a state of siege, and that the *Telegraph*—which has been censored recently by the Royal *Landrat,* Herr Sack, who was elected Deputy to the Second Chamber—has now been placed under direct military censorship after his departure for Berlin.
>
> *The Editors.*

Furthermore: In Erfurt, censorship has existed since November 25,

---

* *Neue Rheinische Zeitung*, March 15, 1849.

equally unchallenged. The press there has been censored first by Herr F .W. Huthsteiner, present police inspector, ex-editor of the *Barmer Zeitung* when it was allegedly liberal and so to speak democratic under censorship, but later under Duncker and continuous Prussian police-men. Although this gentleman has deleted articles even in the unhappy Berlin *National-Zeitung*(!), still his censorial work was found not Prussian enough and he was replaced by an army officer. Thus in Erfurt, too, *military censorship* prevails.

As if this were not enough, censorship is applied abroad, that is, to the papers and writings printed outside the siege radius. . . .

The reintroduction of censorship, the tightening of the usual kind by military censorship—these are surely matters that touch the press intimately. And the press of the neighboring places—that of Breslau, of Berlin, of Leipzig—takes it as if it were a matter of course! In truth, the German press is still the old "good press."

But we ask our indolent deputies in Berlin if they are still not ready to propose the indictment of ministers immediately.

The Suppression of the *Neue Rheinische Zeitung* under Martial Law[*]

Cologne, May 18

SOME TIME AGO Berlin put a demand to the local authorities that they declare a state of siege in Cologne again. The aim was the elimination of the *Neue Rheinische Zeitung* by martial law, but unexpected difficulties were encountered. Later the Cologne government turned to the local *parquet*, to effect the same aim by arbitrary arrests. This was frustrated by the legal doubts of the *parquet*, which had already lost twice to the sound common sense of the Rhineland Assizes.[1] Hence there was nothing left but to take recourse to a police trick, by which the object was achieved for the moment. The *Neue Rheinische Zeitung ceases to appear for the time being.* On May 16 its editor in chief, Karl Marx, received the following piece of paper from the government:

> In its latest pieces [!] the *Neue Rheinische Zeitung* has come out ever more decisively with incitements for contempt of the existing government, for its violent overthrow, and for the establishment of a social Republic. Hence the right of hospitality [!], which he has so disgracefully abused, is to be taken away from its editor in chief, Dr. Karl Marx, and since he has not obtained permission for a further residence in these states, he is to leave same within twenty-four hours. Should he not voluntarily comply with this request, he is to be taken to the frontier by force.
> *Cologne, May 11, 1849*   *H. M. Government*
>   MOELLER
>
> *To H. M.'s Police Director, Herr Geiger, here*

Why these silly phrases, these official lies?
In their tendency and language the latest pieces in the *Neue Rhein-*

---

[*] *Neue Rheinische Zeitung*, May 19, 1849.
1. See "Acquittal of the *Neue Rheinische Zeitung*," page 193.

ische Zeitung do not differ one iota from its first "specimen." That first specimen said, among other things, "Herr Hüser's project" (in Mainz) "is only a part of the great plan of reactionary Berlin, which strives... to deliver us defenselessly... into the hands of the Army."

Eh bien, messieurs, qu'en dites vous maintenant? [Well, gentlemen, what do you say now?]

As regards our tendency, was it really unknown to the government? Did we not state before the jury that "the *first duty of the press is therefore to undermine all the foundations of the existing political system*"?[2] In regard to the Hohenzollern Underlord especially, read the issue of October 19, 1848, which says:

"The King is consistent. He would have continued to be consistent if during the March days, alas, that fatal piece of paper [the Constitution] had not been shoved in between His Majesty and the people. At this moment His Majesty seems again, as before the March days, to believe in the 'iron heel' of Slavdom, and perhaps the people in Vienna are the magicians who will change the iron into clay."

Est-ce clair, messieurs? [Is it clear, gentlemen?]

And as for the "social Republic," did we proclaim it in only the "most recent pieces" in the *Neue Rheinische Zeitung?*

As for the weak-minded, whom the "red" thread of our opinions and presentation of the whole European movement did not tangle up, did we not speak of them openly and unmistakably?

"Suppose it to be true," we wrote in the *Neue Rheinische Zeitung* on November 7,[3] "that the counterrevolution lives in all of Europe through *arms*, it will die in all of Europe through *money*. The fate that will clinch the victory will be European bankruptcy, the bankruptcy of the state. On the 'economic' points, the tips of the bayonets will shatter like tinder.

"But development does not wait for the due date of the promissory note which the European states have drawn on European society. In Paris the devastating counter stroke of the June revolution will be defeated. With the victory of the 'red Republic' in Paris, armies from the countryside will pour over the frontiers, and the real power of the contending parties will emerge clearly. Then we will remember June and October, and we too will cry out: *Vae victis!* [Woe to the vanquished!]

"The fruitless butcheries since the days of June and October, the tedious invocations of the martyrs since February and March, the can-

---

2. See the last paragraph of Marx's defense speech in court, February 7, 1849; in *Neue Rheinische Zeitung*, February 14, 1849.

3. Marx, "Victory of the Counterrevolution in Vienna," *Neue Rheinische Zeitung*, November 7, 1848; see *Karl Marx on Revolution*, Vol. I of this series, pp. 40–42.

nibalism of the counterrevolution itself, will convince the nations that there is only one way to shorten, to simplify, to concentrate, the murderous death pains of the old society and the bloody birth pains of the new society: only one way—*revolutionary terrorism.*"

Est-ce clair, messieurs?

From the beginning, we considered it superfluous to hide our opinions. In a polemic with the local *parquet* we exclaimed to you: "The real opposition of the *Neue Rheinische Zeitung* begins only with the tricolor Republic."[4]

And we then spoke to the *parquet.* We summed up the old year 1848 (on December 31) in these words: "The history of the Prussian bourgeoisie, as well as the history from March to December of the German bourgeoisie in general, proves that in Germany a purely bourgeois revolution and the establishment of bourgeois rule in the form of a constitutional monarchy is impossible, and that the only possibility is a feudal absolutist counterrevolution or a *social-republican revolution.*"[5]

Did we then come out unmistakably with social-republican tendencies only in the "latest pieces" in the *Neue Rheinische Zeitung?* Did you not read our articles on the June Revolution,[6] and was not the June Revolution the soul of our newspaper?

Then why these hypocritical phrases, snatching at an impossible pretext?

We are ruthless, we demand no consideration from you. When our turn comes, we will not gloss over our terrorism. But the *royalist terrorists*, the terrorists by the Grace-of-God-and-of-Right, are brutal, contemptible, and vulgar in practice, cowardly, covert, and deceitful in theory, and *dishonorable* in both.

The Prussian government's piece of paper is silly enough to speak of a certain editor in chief Karl Marx as having "disgracefully abused the right of hospitality."

The right of hospitality, which the insolent intruders, the Borussians,[7] have imposed on us Rhinelanders on our own soil, has been, of course, "disgracefully" abused by the *Neue Rheinische Zeitung.* For this we believe we have earned the thanks of the Rhine Province. We have saved the revolutionary honor of the soil of our homeland. In

---

4. See "State Procurator 'Hecker' and the *Neue Rheinische Zeitung*," page 124.

5. "The Bourgeoisie and the Counterrevolution," in *Neue Rheinische Zeitung,* December 31, 1848; see *Karl Marx on Revolution,* page 476.

6. For Marx's articles on the June Revolution see *Karl Marx on Revolution,* pages 430–438.

7. Prussians. The word "Prussia" derives from the Slavic "Borussia," suggesting that Prussians are of Russian origin, which presumably makes them an inferior breed in the eyes of Rhinelanders and other Western-oriented Germans.

the future only the *Neue Preussische Zeitung*[8] will enjoy full citizenship rights in the Rhine Province.

At parting, we recall to our readers the words of our article of January 1:

"REVOLUTIONARY UPRISING OF THE FRENCH WORKING CLASS, AND WORLD WAR—these are the auguries of the year 1849."[9]

And already a mixed revolutionary army, made up of fighters from all nations, confronts the coalition troops of old Europe in the Russian army in the East, already the "red Republic" threatens from Paris!

---

8. A Berlin daily, organ of the Prussian Junkers.
9. "The Revolutionary Movement," in *Karl Marx on Revolution*, pages 43-44.

LETTERS

From letter to Arnold Ruge (*in Dresden*)
TRIER, JULY 9, 1842

Dear Friend:

If circumstances did not excuse me, I would give up every attempt at an excuse. It goes without saying that I consider it an honor to contribute to *Anecdotis*[1] and only unpleasant outside matters have kept me from sending in my articles.

Since the month of April I have not been able to work more than four weeks, and even then not without interruptions. I had to spend six weeks in Trier because of another death,[2] and the rest of the time was fragmented and discordant with the most disagreeable family controversies. Despite their easy circumstances, my family put obstacles in my way which put me momentarily in the most pressing situation. I can hardly burden you with the tale of these private rascalities; it is truly lucky that the public rascalities make every possible irritation with the private ones impossible for a man of character. During this period I wrote only for the *Rheinische Zeitung*, to which I had already owed articles for some time. I would have informed you of these intermezzos long ago if I had not hoped from moment to moment to finish my work. In a few days I leave for Bonn and will touch nothing until I have finished the articles for the *Anekdota*. Naturally, under these circumstances I will not be able to make the article "on art and religion" as thorough as the subject requires.

For the rest, don't you believe that we in the Rhineland live in a political Eldorado. It takes the most steadfast tenacity for a paper like

---

1. Ruge's publication, *Anekdota*, which published Marx's "Remarks on the Latest Prussian Censorship Instruction," (see page 89) and "Luther as Arbiter Between Strauss and Feuerbach."

2. Ludwig von Westphalen, to whose daughter, Jenny, Marx was then engaged, died on March 3, 1842, at the age of seventy-two.

the *Rheinische* to fight its way through. My second article on the Diet, dealing with the church troubles, has been stricken out.[3] In it I demonstrated how the defenders of the state took a clerical position and the defenders of the church a political one. This incident is the more unpleasant for the *Rheinische* in that the stupid Cologne Catholics fell into the trap and the subscribers were decoyed into a defense of the Archbishop. For the rest, you can hardly imagine how vilely and at the same time how stupidly the men of power leaped around the orthodox blockhead. But the work was crowned with success; Prussia has kissed the Pope's slipper before the whole world, and our governmental automata walk the streets without blushing. The *Rheinische Zeitung* now shies back from the article, whose battle is just beginning. In the *Kölnische Zeitung* the man who wrote the leading article, Hermes, ex-editor of the late *Hannoversche Zeitung*, took the Christian party's side against the philosophical newspapers in Königsberg and Cologne. If the censor doesn't play another trick, the next supplement [of the *Rheinische Zeitung*] will carry a reply by me.[4] The religious party is the most dangerous in the Rhineland. The opposition has become too accustomed to doing its opposing in church. . . .

Yours,

K.M.

Rutenberg weighs heavily on my conscience. I got him in as editor of the *Rheinische*, and he is totally impotent. Sooner or later he will be removed.

In case the archiepiscopal article does not receive the imprimatur of the higher censorship police, what do you advise? It must be printed, because of (1) our Diets, (2) the government, and (3) the Christian state. . . .

From letter to Arnold Ruge (in Dresden)
COLOGNE, NOVEMBER 30, 1842

Dear Friend!
My letter today will confine itself to "confusion" and to the "*Freien.*"[1]

---

3. This article has been lost.
4. See "The Leading Article in No. 179 of the *Kölnische Zeitung*," page 48.

---

1. The *Freien*—the Free—were a group of Berlin littérateurs, among them the Young Hegelians Bruno Bauer, Edgar Bauer, Eduard Meyen, Ludwig Buhl, and Max Stirner.

You already know that the censorship is mutilating us pitilessly every day, so that the paper can hardly appear. In this way a mass of articles by the "Freien" was eliminated. As much as the censorship itself, I myself took the liberty of canceling them, since Meyen and Company sent in heaps of scribblings pregnant with world revolution, written in a slovenly style, permeated with atheism and communism (which the gentlemen have never studied). Because of Rutenberg's total lack of critical sense, independence, and talent, they had become accustomed to look upon the *Rheinische Zeitung* as *their* will-less organ, but I no longer considered myself obliged to allow this urine as before. This omission of a few unreliable productions of "freedom," a freedom which by preference strives "to be free from all thought," was thus the first ground for a darkening of the Berlin sky.

Rutenberg ..., through the immense stupidity of our Providential government, had the good fortune to be considered dangerous, although he was dangerous to nobody except the *Rheinische Zeitung* and himself. Rutenberg's removal was forcibly demanded. The Prussian Providence, this *despotisme prussien, le plus hypocrite, le plus fourbe* [Prussian despotism, the most hypocritical, the most deceitful], spared the editor an unpleasant scene, and as a new martyr, who by his face, manner, and speech already knew how to strike the martyr's attitude with some virtuosity, Rutenberg exploited this opportunity to write to everybody, to write to Berlin, that he was the *exiled principle* of the *Rheinische Zeitung*, which had now taken a *different position* toward the government. It goes without saying that thereupon came demonstrations by the freedom heroes on the Spree, "the dirty water, which washes souls and dilutes tea."[2]

Finally your and Herwegh's relations to the *"Freien"* came out, and the angry Olympians' cup spilled over.[3]

A few days ago I received a letter from little Meyen, whose favorite category is, righteously, the *should*, questioning my relationship (1) to you and Herwegh, (2) to the *"Freien,"* (3) to the new editorial position and my own stand vis-à-vis the government. I answered immediately and frankly expressed my views about the deficiencies in their work, which finds freedom more in a licentious, sans-culottish, and lazy form than in a *free* one, that is, independent and profound content. I demanded less vague rationalization, fewer high-sounding phrases and self-complacent preening, and more precision, more pene-

---

2. From a poem by Heine, in *Die Nordsee*, Cycle *"Frieden."*
3. On November 29, 1842, the *Rheinische Zeitung* published the statement that "Herwegh and Ruge have found that the 'Freien,' by their political romanticism, mania for genius, and bragging are compromising the cause of the party of freedom."

tration into concrete conditions, more expertise in their analysis. I said that smuggling communist and socialist dogmas—that is, a new *Weltanschauung* [philosophy of life]—into incidental theater criticisms, etc., was improper, indeed, unethical, and asked for a quite different and more thorough discussion of communism, if it was to be discussed at all. I demanded that religion be criticized in the critique of political conditions rather than political conditions in religion, as such a direction is more in conformity with the essence of a newspaper and the enlightenment of the public, since religion, in itself empty, lives not from heaven but from earth, and with the dissolution of the reverse reality, whose theory it is, it collapses of itself. Finally, I demanded that if philosophy is to be discussed at all, there should be less dallying with the *Firma* [business] of "atheism" (which is being like children who tell everybody who will listen that they are not afraid of the bogeyman), and more content for the people. *Voilà tout.*

Yesterday I got an insolent letter from Meyen, who had not yet received my own, asking me about all kinds of things: (1) I should declare my position in regard to their quarrel with [Bruno] Bauer, about which I know nothing; (2) why I did not accept this and that article, accusing me of conservatism; (3) the newspaper must not soften but must do the *utmost*—that is, quietly give way to the police and the censorship, instead of maintaining its position in a struggle invisible to the public but none the less a stubborn duty. Finally, it reported insultingly about Herwegh's betrothal, etc.

Out of all this shines a frightful dose of vanity which does not comprehend how, to save a political organ, one can sacrifice a few Berlin windbags who generally think of nothing but their own cliquish stories. Added to that, the little man strutted like a peacock, beat his breast protestingly, waved his sword, hinted something about "his" party, threatened displeasure, declaimed à la Marquis Posa but somewhat worse, etc.

Since we are burdened from morning to night with the most frightful censorship harassments, ministerial scribblings, gubernatorial complaints, Landtag accusations, stockholders' screamings, etc., etc., and I remain in the job only because I consider it a duty to frustrate the intentions of the authorities as much as I am able, you can imagine that I am somewhat irritable and that I gave Meyen a pretty rough reply. It is therefore probable that the *"Freien"* will withdraw for a moment. Hence I appeal to you urgently not only to support us with your articles but also to ask your friends to do the same.

Yours,

MARX

Letter to Arnold Ruge (in Dresden)
COLOGNE, JANUARY 25, 1843

Dear . . .[1]

You probably know that the *Rheinische Zeitung* has been suppressed, prohibited, received a death sentence. It has been given its termination at the end of March. During this gallows reprieve it has a double censorship. Our censor [Wiethaus], an honorable man, has been put under the censorship of Regierungspräsident [Governor] von Gerlach, a passively obedient blockhead, and specifically, our entire paper must be presented to the police nose for sniffing, and when the latter smells something un-Christian, un-Prussian, the paper must not appear.

Several special causes combine in this prohibition: our circulation;[2] my defense of the Mosel correspondent;[3] in which the highest statesmen are brought into disrepute; our stubborn refusal to name the informant of the marriage law;[4] the convocation of the Provincial Estates, in which we could agitate; finally, our criticisms of the prohibition of the *Leipziger Allgemeine Zeitung*[5] and the *Deutsche Jahrbücher.*

The Ministerial Rescript, which is to appear in the newspapers presently, is if possible even weaker than the previous ones. As explanations, the following are given:

1. The *lie* that we had no license, as if in Prussia, where not even a dog can live without a police permit, the *Rheinische Zeitung* could appear even for a day without meeting official conditions essential to life.

2. The Censorship Instruction of December 24 aimed at a *tendency* censorship. Tendency was understood to mean the *fancy*, the romantic belief, of possessing freedom, which in reality one would not be permitted to possess. Where the intelligent Jesuitism which dominated the previous government had a stern intellectual visage, the romantic Jesuitism has the power of imagination as its main requisite. The censored press has to know how to live with imaginary freedom and with that gorgeous man [the King] who graciously permits this imagination. But

1. The name is unclear in the original.
2. The *Rheinische Zeitung*, which started with 400 subscribers, ended with 3,400.
3. "Defense of the Mosel Correspondent," page 69. January 15, 17, 18, 19, 1843.
4. "The Draft of the Marriage Law," *Rheinische Zeitung*, December 19, 1842.
5. "The Suppression of the *Leipziger Allgemeine Zeitung*," page 53.

while the Censorship Instruction demanded a tendency censorship, the present Ministerial Rescript declares: *Prohibition, suppression,* was invented in Frankfurt for thoroughly bad tendency. Censorship exists only for censoring the excrescences of good tendencies, even though the Instruction had said the opposite, namely, excrescences were permitted in good tendencies.

3. The old fiddle-faddle of bad intentions, hollow theory, tweedledum, etc.

I was not surprised at anything. You know what I thought of the Censorship Instruction.[6] Here I see only a consequence, I see in the suppression of the *Rheinische Zeitung* a *progress* in political consciousness, and am therefore resigning. Furthermore, the atmosphere had become very oppressive for me. It is bad to perform menial services even for freedom, and to fight with needles instead of clubs. I became tired of hypocrisy, stupidity, raw authority, and our cringing, bowing, back turning, and word picking. Thus the government has given me my freedom again.

I have, as I already wrote you, fallen out with my family and, so long as my mother is alive, I have no right to my property. Moreover, I am betrothed and neither can, should, nor will leave Germany without my fiancée.[7] If it were possible for me to co-edit the *Deutsche Boten* in Zurich with Herwegh I would be pleased. In Germany I can no longer begin anything. One falsifies oneself here. Should you therefore give me advice and information in this matter, I would be very grateful.

I am working on a number of things, which could find neither censor nor publisher nor any possible existence at all here in Germany. I await your prompt reply.

Yours,
MARX

From postscript to letter to Arnold Ruge (in Dresden)
COLOGNE, MARCH 13, 1843

In regard to the *Rheinische Zeitung,* I will not remain here *under any conditions;* it is impossible for me to write under Prussian censorship or live in the Prussian atmosphere.

---

6. "Remarks on the Latest Prussian Censorship Instruction," page 89.
7. Jenny von Westphalen, whom Marx married on June 19, 1843.

From letter to Ludwig Feuerbach (*in Bruckberg*)
KREUZNACH, OCTOBER 3, 1843

Highly Esteemed Sir!
... Schelling, as you know, is the thirty-eighth member of the Diet. The whole German police is at his disposal, as I have learned from my experience as editor of the *Rheinische Zeitung.* The censorship regulation cannot permit anything against ... the holy Schelling. Thus in Germany it is practically impossible to attack Schelling in anything except volumes of more than twenty-one printer's sheets, but such are not the books of the people. Kapp's work is very noteworthy, but it is too detailed and is clumsy in its separation of judgment from facts. Furthermore, our governments have found means to make such works ineffectual. One is not permitted to discuss them. They are either ignored or dismissed in a few contemptuous words by the licensed review institutions. ...

Sincerely yours,
DR. MARX

From draft of letter to Karl Wilhelm Leske (*in Darmstadt*)
BRUSSELS, AUGUST 1, 1846

Dear Sir:
This is an *immediate* reply to your letter expressing doubts about the publication.[1] In regard to your question about its "scientific character," I reply to you: The book is to be scientific, but not scientific by the definition of the Prussian Government, etc. If you will recall your first letter, you had written with anxiety about the Prussian warning and police investigation, the latter of which had just happened to you. I then wrote to you immediately that I would look around for another publisher. ...

Respectfully yours,
DR. MARX

1. On July 29, 1846, Leske, a Darmstadt publisher, expressed doubts about publishing Marx's planned work, *Critique of Politics and National Economy,* for which the two men had signed a contract in Paris on February 1, 1845. This work was never published.

From letter to Georg Herwegh (in Paris)
BRUSSELS, AUGUST 8, 1847

Dear Herwegh:
... The police magistrate himself stated that these lawsuits[1] are *pour le roi de Prusse* [to no purpose]. On the other hand, the *Deutsche-Brüsseler Zeitung*—which despite its many weaknesses has always had something meritorious about it, and could be improved, especially now, when Bornstedt has declared himself ready to be on our side in all possible ways—is threatened with sudden financial ruin. And how did the noble Germans behave in this matter? The bookdealers *betrayed* Bornstedt because he cannot prosecute them legally. Instead of doing the slightest thing, either literarily or financially, all shadings of the opposition found it more comfortable to find offense in the name Bornstedt. And would these people ever lack excuses for doing nothing? One time the man is no good, another time it is the wife, a third time it is the tendency, still another time it is the style, and once again it is the format, or the distribution is fraught with more or less danger, etc., etc. The roast pigeons are to fly straight into the mouth of the gentleman. When there is only one censorship-free opposition paper, at which the government takes great offense; whose editor as a result of the enterprise itself, shows himself to be sympathetic to all progressives—shouldn't such an opportunity be used and, if insufficient, be made sufficient? But no! Our Germans always have a thousand philosophical proverbs *in petto* [in reserve] to show why they must let the opportunity pass unused. An opportunity to do something only embarrasses them.

My manuscripts are in more or less the same state as the *Deutsche-Brüsseler Zeitung*, and withal jackasses write day after day asking why I am not publishing anything, and even reproach me with preferring to write in French or not at all. One will have to atone a long time for having been born a Teuton. ...

MARX

---

1. Three lawsuits had been instigated by the Prussian Embassy in Brussels, against Adalbert von Bornstedt, a former Prussian officer who was editor and publisher of the *Deutsche-Brüsseler-Zeitung*, a twice-weekly German-language refugee paper in Brussels, to which Marx occasionally contributed articles.

From letter to Georg Herwegh (in Paris)
BRUSSELS, OCTOBER 26, 1847

Dear Herwegh:

... When you come here again you will find that more can be done by way of direct propaganda in this little Belgium than in big France. Hence I believe that public activity here, no matter how small, has an endlessly refreshing effect on everybody.

It is possible that now, with a *liberal* ministry at the helm, police chicanery is in store for us, for liberals don't change their ways. But we will deal with them. This is not like Paris, where foreigners stand isolated in the presence of the government.

Since it is impossible under present conditions in Germany to use any publisher there, I have undertaken, in agreement with Germans from Germany, to found a review—a monthly—supported by shareholders. In the Rhine Province and Baden a number of shares have already been sold. We will start as soon as we have raised enough money for three months.

If the income permits, we will establish our own composing room here, to print other independent writings. . . .

Yours,
MARX

From letter to Frederick Engels (in Geneva)
COLOGNE, OCTOBER 26, 1848

Dear Engels:

... The newspaper has been appearing since October 11, *tale quale* [unchanged].[1] This is not the moment to write in greater detail, as haste is necessary. As soon as you can at all, write news reports and lengthier articles. Since everybody except Weerth and Freiligrath, who joined only a few days ago, is away, I am in it up to my ears, never manage to do any extensive writing, and, in addition, the public prosecutor does everything to steal my time. . . .

Yours,
K. M.

1. The *Neue Rheinische Zeitung* was suspended temporarily on September 27, 1848.

From letter to Frederick Engels (in Lausanne)
COLOGNE, MID NOVEMBER, 1848

Dear Engels:

I am truly surprised that you have not yet received the money from me. A long time ago *I* (not the mailing department) sent to you in Geneva, at the given address, 61 Taler, 11 of them in banknotes, 50 in money orders. Do inquire about it and write me immediately. I have a postal receipt and can reclaim the money.

In addition, I sent 20 Taler to Gigot and 50 Taler to Dronke for you, always out of my own pocket—a total of about 130 Taler.

Tomorrow I will send a little bit more again. But do inquire about the money. In the money order there was a recommendation of you to a Lausanne money philistine.

I am limited in money. I brought back 1,850 Taler from the trip; I received 1,950 Taler from the Poles.[1] I used up 100 Taler on the trip. I advanced 1,000 Taler to the newspaper (to include you and other refugees). Five hundred Taler are still to be paid this week for the machine.[2] Three-fifty remains. And with this I have not yet received one penny from the paper.

In regard to your editorship, I indicated in the first issue (1) that the committee remains the same, (2) explained to the idiotic, reactionary shareholders that they were at liberty to consider you people as no longer belonging to the staff, but that I was also at liberty to pay *as high honorariums as I wish*, and that therefore they would gain nothing financially thereby.

Rationally speaking, I should not have advanced so large a sum to the newspaper, as I have three or four press indictments on my neck, am in danger of prison any day, and will then have to cry for money like a deer for fresh water. But one must hold this *fortress* at all hazards and not give up the political position.

The best thing—after you have arranged the financial matter in Lausanne—would be to go to Bern to carry out the plan you proposed. You can, moreover, write as you wish. Your letters always arrive in good time.

That I could have left you in the lurch even for a moment is pure

---

1. In August–September, 1848, Marx went to Berlin and Vienna to raise money for the *Neue Rheinische Zeitung*. After negotiating with Polish refugee democrats he received the above-mentioned sum from Wladislaw Koscielski.
2. A steam printing press.

fantasy. You always remain my *intimus* [intimate friend] as I hopefully am yours.

K. MARX

Your old man is a *Schweinhund* [scoundrel, swine]; we'll write him a rude letter.

From letter to Frederick Engels (in Bern)
COLOGNE, NOVEMBER 29, 1848

Dear Engels:

... Our paper constantly operates in a state of *émeute* [commotion], but despite all governmental orders about its publication, circumnavigates the Penal Code. It is now very much in vogue. We also put out daily posters. *La révolution marche.* [The revolution advances.] Write diligently.

I have drawn up a sure plan for squeezing money out of your old man, since we have none now. Write a money-letter (if possible, crassly) to me telling your troubles up to now, but in such a way that I can report it to your mother. The old man will then begin to be afraid.

I hope to see you soon.

Yours,
MOHR

From letter to Eduard Müller-Tellering (in Vienna)
COLOGNE, DECEMBER 5, 1848

My dear Tellering:

... Our paper is momentarily *sans sou* [penniless]. But the subscribers....[1] The idiots at last sense what we always correctly predicted; if the government does not suppress us we will be on top of things early in January, and I will do everything to reward your performance appropriately. Your correspondence is indubitably the best we get, entirely in conformity with our tendency, and since it is picked up from our paper by the French, Italian, and English journals,

---

1. Indecipherable word.

you have contributed greatly to the enlightenment of the European public.

I cannot begin to tell you what sacrifices of money and patience I have to make in order to maintain the paper. The Germans are crackbrained asses. . . .

Draft of letter to Police Councilor Wilhelm Stieber (in Berlin)
COLOGNE, DECEMBER 29, 1848

The editorship has received your letter[1] and takes notice of the correction sent from Frankfurt. In regard to your threat of suing for slander, it only shows your ignorance of the *Code pénal*, whose calumny does not apply to the correspondence published in No. 177. For the rest, to ease your mind, this correspondence was sent to us by a Frankfurt deputy[2] before the *Neue Preussische Zeitung* reported the same news. Your previous Silesian operations did not seem to contradict the content of said correspondence, although we, on our part, found it extraordinary that you should want to exchange your lucrative and honorable Berlin position for a precarious and ambiguous, though always *legal* one.

As to your protestations about your Silesian operations, we shall try to put at your disposal materials, public or private, as you wish.

The lesson on democracy and democratic organs contained in your letter we excuse on account of its novelty.

Draft of letter to Colonel Engels[1] (in Cologne)
COLOGNE, MARCH 3, 1849

To Colonel and Second Commandant Engels
Sir:
The day before yesterday two noncommissioned officers of Company 8, Sixteenth Infantry Regiment, came to my residence to speak

---

1. On December 26, 1848, Wilhelm Stieber wrote a letter of protest against the *Neue Rheinische Zeitung,* which in a dispatch from Frankfurt on December 24, had charged that Stieber was known as a Prussian police spy.
2. Probably Friedrich Wilhelm Schlöffel.

---

1. Colonel Engels—no relation to Frederick Engels—was Cologne city commandant in 1848–49 and became a general in 1851.

to me privately. I was away in Düsseldorf. They were therefore sent away. Yesterday afternoon these two gentlemen came again and demanded a private talk.

I had them enter a room, where I soon followed them. I asked the gentlemen to sit down and inquired what they wanted. They said they wanted the name of the author of the article (No. 233 of *Neue Rheinische Zeitung*, dated February 28) against Captain von Uttenhoven.[2] I told the gentlemen: (1) that the article in question does not concern me, since it was not editorial matter but only an advertisement; (2) that they are at liberty to send in a denial gratis; (3) that they are at liberty to sue the paper. To the remark by the gentlemen that the whole Company 8 [of which Uttenhoven was Captain] felt itself insulted by that advertisement I replied that only the signatures of all the members of Company 8 would convince me of the correctness of this assertion, which, moreover, was irrelevant.

The noncommissioned gentlemen then told me that if I did not name the "man," "deliver" him, they could "no longer restrain our people," and something "bad would happen."

I replied to the gentlemen that threats and intimidations had not the least effect on me. They then left, muttering between their teeth.

All discipline must have gone far toward dissolution, all sense of legal order must have ceased, when military companies, like robber bands, send agents to individual citizens to bully them into confessions of this or that through threats. Specifically, I do not understand the sense of the sentence: "We can no longer restrain our people." Do these "people" have the authority to exercise their own jurisdiction, do these "people" have at their disposal still other illegal means of recourse?

I must ask you, Colonel, to institute an investigation of this incident and to explain to me that strange presumption. I would regret having to take recourse to publicity.

Draft of letter to Colonel Engels (in Cologne)
COLOGNE, MARCH 5, 1849

To Colonel and Commandant Engels
Sir:

In the conviction that Royal Prussian noncommissioned officers would not deny words uttered in private, I did *not* bring in any *witnesses* to the conversation in question. As for my alleged statement that

---

2. The article mentioned that Captain von Uttenhoven had been publicly accused of selling government-owned firewood illegally.

"the courts, as one has seen recently, could do nothing to me," even my political enemies would admit that, even if I thought of such an absurdity, I would not express it to third persons. And do not the noncommissioned gentlemen themselves admit that I explained to them that matters *hinter dem Striche* [in a *feuilleton*] are entirely outside my jurisdiction, I being responsible for only that part of the newspaper which I sign myself? Hence there was no cause at all for me to speak of *my* position vis-à-vis the courts.

I renounce the offer of further investigation, the more so as I was concerned, not to have the noncommissioned gentlemen punished, but to have their superiors call their attention to the limits of their powers.

As for your kind final observation, the *Neue Rheinische Zeitung*, by its silence on the recent frictions in the military itself, has shown that it knows very well how to make allowance for the prevailing public agitation.

Letter written in French to the editor of La Presse
PARIS, JULY, 1849*

Your notice published in *La Presse*[1] July 26 regarding my stay in Paris, which other papers reprinted literally, contains such erroneous statements that I am compelled to reply to them in a few words.

To begin with, the *Neue Rheinische Zeitung*, of which I was proprietor and editor in chief, has never been suppressed. It was prohibited for only five days because of the state of siege.[2] After the siege was lifted the paper appeared again, and did so for the next seven months. Since the Prussian Government saw no possibility of suppressing the paper in a legal way, it utilized a remarkable means: It got rid of the proprietor; that is, it forbade my residence in Prussia. As for the legality of this measure, the Prussian Chamber of Deputies, which is to meet shortly, will decide that.

After my residence in Prussia was forbidden I first went to the Grand Duchy of Hesse, where, as also in other parts of Germany, my residence was not prohibited. I did not come to Paris as a refugee, as your paper asserts, but freely, with a regular passport and with the sole aim of completing my work on the history of political economy, begun almost five years ago.

---

* Published July 30, 1849.
1. A Paris republican daily.
2. Cologne was put under a state of siege on September 26, 1848, and the *Neue Rheinische Zeitung* was suspended temporarily on the following day.

Just as little did I receive an order to leave Paris *immediately;* I was given time to address a complaint to the Interior Ministry. I did send in this complaint and am now awaiting the result.[3]

Accept my, etc.

DR. K. MARX

Letter to Joseph Weydemeyer (in Frankfurt)
LONDON, JUNE 8, 1850

Dear Weydemeyer:

How goes it with our Revue?[1] Especially with the money? The question is the more urgent because over here the Prussian Government is taking all possible steps to have the English Government exile me from England. If I were not sitting here *sans le sous* [without a penny] I would already have moved to the interior of England and the government would have lost sight of me.

How goes it with the "red issue"?[2] Orders for it have come from America. How many copies have been sold? How many pieces do you still have?

Your newspaper[3] seems to combine with others in a *conspiration du silence* [conspiracy of silence] in regard to our *Revue*. Of course I understand that for the readers of the *Neue Deutsche Zeitung*, Raveaux is more interesting.

Regards for Dronke and your wife.

Yours,
K. M.

---

3. The Interior Ministry did not rescind Marx's order of expulsion from Paris, which was issued on July 19, 1849. On August 24 Marx left Paris for London.

---

1. *Neue Rheinische Zeitung. Politisch-Ökonomische Revue*, a journal Marx and Engels prepared in London and had printed in Hamburg in 1850; for dates of the *Revue*, see Chronology.

2. The last issue of the *Neue Rheinische Zeitung*, May 19, 1849, came out in red ink.

3. *Neue Deutsche Zeitung*, a Darmstadt daily of which Weydemeyer was one of three editors.

Letter written in English to the London Daily News
LONDON, JANUARY 16, 1871*

To the Editor of the Daily News:
Sir,
In accusing the French Government of "having rendered impossible the free expression of opinion in France through the medium of the press and members of parliament," Bismarck evidently only intended to crack a Berlin joke. If you wish to become acquainted with "true" French opinion, please apply to Herr Stieber, the editor of the Versailles *Moniteur* and the notorious Prussian police spy! . . .

At Bismarck's express command, Herr Bebel and Liebknecht have been arrested, on a charge of high treason, simply because they dared to do their duty as German members of parliament, i.e., to protest in the Reichstag against the annexation of Alsace and Lorraine, vote against new war credits, express their sympathics with the French Republic, and denounce the attempt to convert Germany into a Prussian barracks. For expressing similar opinions the members of the Brunswick Committee of the Social Democratic party have, since the beginning of last September, been treated like galley slaves, and are still undergoing a ludicrous prosecution for high treason. The same fate has befallen numerous workmen who circulated the Brunswick Manifesto. On similar pretexts, Herr Hepner, subeditor of the Leipzig *Volksstaat*, had been charged with high treason. The few independent German journals existing outside Prussia are prohibited in the Hohenzollern domains. German workmen's meetings in favor of an honorable peace with France are daily dispersed by the police. According to the official Prussian doctrine, as naïvely laid down by General Vogel von Falkenstein, every German attempting to counteract the aims of the Prussian military command in France is guilty of high treason. If M. Gambetta and his confrères were, like the Hohenzollerns, compelled to suppress public opinion by force, they would only have to apply the Prussian method and on the plea of war, proclaim throughout France a state of siege. The only French soldiers on German soil rot in Prussian jails. Nevertheless, the Prussian government feels itself bound rigorously to maintain the state of siege, that is to say, the crudest and most revolting form of military despotism, the suspension of all law. The soil of France is infested by almost a million German invaders. Yet the French Government can safely dispense with the Prussian methods of "rendering possible the free expression of opinion." Compare the

---

* Published January 19, 1871.

one picture with the other! Germany, however, has proved too narrow a field for Bismarck's all-absorbing passion for the free expression of opinion. When the Luxemburgers gave vent to their sympathies with France, Bismarck made this expression of sentiment one of his pretexts for renouncing the London neutrality treaty. When the Belgian press committed a similar sin, the Prussian ambassador at Brussels, Herr von Balan, invited the Belgian Ministry to put down not only all anti-Prussian newspaper articles, but even the printing of reports calculated to encourage the French in their war of liberty. A very modest request this, indeed, to suspend the Belgian constitution *"pour le roi de Prusse"* [in vain]. No sooner had some Stockholm papers indulged in some mild jokes at the notorious "piety" of Wilhelm *Annexander,*[1] than Bismarck came down on the Swedish cabinet with grim missives. Even under the meridian of St. Petersburg he contrived to espy too licentious a press. At his humble supplication the editors of the principal Petersburg papers were summoned before the Censor-in-Chief, who bade them refrain from all critical observations concerning the faithful Borussian vassal of the tsar. One of these editors, M. Zagulyaev, was imprudent enough to publish the secret of this warning through the columns of the *Golos.* He was at once pounced upon by the Russian police and bundled off to some remote province. It would be a mistake to believe that these gendarme proceedings are only due to the paroxysms of the war fever. They are, on the contrary, the truly methodical application of the spirit of Prussian law. There exists in point of fact a curious proviso in the Prussian criminal code, by virtue of which any foreigner, domiciled in his own or another foreign country, may be prosecuted for "insult to the Prussian king" and "high treason to Prussia"! France—and her cause is fortunately far from desperate—fights at this moment not only for her own national independence, but for the liberty of Germany and Europe.

I am, sir, yours respectfully,

KARL MARX

---

1. A pun combining "annexes" and Alexander, King Wilhelm I.

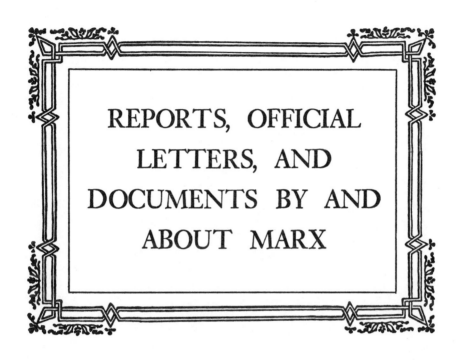

REPORTS, OFFICIAL
LETTERS, AND
DOCUMENTS BY AND
ABOUT MARX

Letter for Joseph Engelbert Renard, Publisher of the *Rheinische Zeitung**

Highly Esteemed Herr Oberpräsident!
Sir!

On the twelfth of this month Your Honor presented me, through Regierungspräsident Herr von Gerlach in Cologne, with a rescript from the Censorship Ministry, plus two additional orders, and summoned me to make a verbal deposition about them. In view of the importance of the explanations requested of me, I preferred to express them to Your Honor in writing, instead of a verbal protocol.

1. In regard to the rescript of the Ministry of Censorship and particularly the request that the *Rheinische Zeitung* change its direction in favor of one pleasing to the government, I can interpret this only as regards *form*, in the moderation of which, insofar as the content allows it, one can acquiesce. The direction of a newspaper which, like the *Rheinische*, is not merely a mindless amalgam of dry reporting and base flattery, but one that, conscious of its noble purpose, critically illuminates the political conditions and institutions of the Fatherland, seems to us, according to the latest Censorship Instruction and other expressed views of His Majesty, to be a tendency with which the government could only agree. Moreover, disapproval of this tendency has, until now, never been conveyed to the responsible editor. Since the *Rheinische Zeitung* is subject to the most rigorous censorship, how can its suppression be justified after a *first warning?*

This I can assure Your Honor: The *Rheinische Zeitung*, insofar as it can, will also in the future help lead in the progress in which Prussia leads the rest of Germany. For precisely this reason, therefore, I

---

* Marx wrote this letter November 17, 1842, to protest demands made by Cologne Governor von Gerlach. Renard signed it and sent it to von Schaper, *Oberpräsident* (governor) of the Rhine Province.

must reject the reproach made in the rescript that the *Rheinische Zeitung* has sought to propagate French sympathies and ideas in the Rhineland. Instead, the main objective of the *Rheinische Zeitung* has been to direct the many [Germans], whose viewpoints are still focused on France, toward Germany, and to bring forth a German, instead of a French, liberalism, which surely cannot be disagreeable to the government of Friedrich Wilhelm IV. In this the *Rheinische Zeitung* has always pointed to Prussia, whose development that of the rest of Germany depends upon. Proof of this is found in the polemic, "Prussian Hegemony,"[1] against anti-Prussian efforts in the *Augsburger Zeitung* articles on the subject. Proof is found in all the articles on the Prussian Customs Union, articles which opposed those in the Hamburg *Correspondent* and other newspapers, in which the *Rheinische Zeitung* presented in the greatest detail the adherence of Hanover, Mecklenburg, and the Hanseatic Cities [to the Customs Union] as uniquely beneficial. Proof, above all, is found in the constant pointing out of North German science in contrast to the superficiality not only of that of the French but also of South German theories. The *Rheinische Zeitung* was the first Rhenish, and for that matter South German, paper to introduce the North German *Geist*[2] into the Rhineland and South Germany; and in what better way could one inseparably knit the severed [German] tribes together again than through intellectual [*geistig*] unity, which is the soul as well as the only guarantee of political unity against all external storms!

In regard to the alleged *irreligious* tendency of the *Rheinische Zeitung*, it cannot be unknown to the highest authorities that all of Germany, and especially Prussia, is split into two warring camps over the substance of a certain positive faith—and this is the only subject under consideration; not religion itself, which we have never touched and will never touch—and that each of the camps counts among its champions eminent men of science and politics. Should a newspaper not deal with, or discuss only in an officially prescribed way, an undecided contemporary struggle? Moreover, we have never overstepped the proper terrain of a newspaper, but have touched on dogmas and church doctrines and conditions only insofar as other newspapers have made religion into a constitutional law and wanted to shift from their own sphere into the sphere of politics. It would, in fact, be easy for us to cover all our pronouncements with similar and stronger ones by a Prussian king, Frederick the Great, and we consider him an authority on which Prussian journalists can well rely.

---

1. Articles discussing Prussian hegemony were published in the *Rheinische Zeitung*, May 15, 26, June 21, and July 14, 1842.

2. *Geist* has numerous meanings, among them "spirit," "mind," "soul," and "intellect."

Hence the *Rheinische Zeitung* is justified in believing that it has chiefly realized His Majesty's wish for an independent and enlightened press, as laid down in the Censorship Instruction, and has thereby contributed not a little to the blessings which currently follow the upward-striving course of His Majesty our King in all of Germany.

Your Honor, the *Rheinische Zeitung* has not been established for a publisher's speculation, nor with any expectation of profit. A large number of the most eminent men of Cologne and the Rhine Province, justly indignant over the lamentable state of the German press, thought that they could not better honor the will of His Majesty the King than by establishing, in the *Rheinische Zeitung*, a national monument, a newspaper that would characteristically express the fearless speech of free men and—a rare phenomenon, of course—cause His Majesty to hear the true voice of the people. The unprecedently rapid growth of this newspaper proves how well it has understood the desires of the people. For this purpose those men contributed their capital; for this purpose they have shied away from no sacrifice; and now Your Honor may decide for yourself whether I, as the voice of these men, could or should state: The *Rheinische Zeitung* will change its direction; whether or not its suppression would do violence to one single person rather than to the Rhine Province and the German *Geist* in general.

For the rest, to prove to the government how very much I am prepared to fulfill its wishes, insofar as they are compatible with the work of an independent newspaper, I will, as has already been done for some time, abstain from all possible churchly and religious subjects, unless other papers and political conditions themselves make such a reference necessary.

2. Second, in regard to Your Honor's demand that Dr. Rutenberg be immediately dismissed, I had already informed *Regierungspräsident* [Governor] von Gerlach on February 14 that he [Rutenberg] was in no way the editor of the *Rheinische Zeitung* but functioned merely as a translator on its staff. As for the threat conveyed to me by the *Präsident* Herr von Gerlach to suppress the paper immediately if Rutenberg was not dismissed, I, submitting to force, have temporarily removed him from all participation in the newspaper. But since no judicial determination that could justify this point in the rescript is known to me, I request Your Honor to make public such a determination and if possible a speedy decision whether the order remains in force or not, so that I may, by appeal to a higher court, claim my legal right.

3. As for the third point, the presentation of an editor [for approval], according to the censorship law of October 18, 1819, Paragraph IX, only the higher censorship authorities are empowered

to demand the presentation of an editor. I know of no legal decision that transfers this prerogative to the Governor. I therefore beg you to mention, if possible, such a decree by the Censorship Ministry. Then, but only then, will I gladly consent to the presentation of an editor for approval.

Prussian Police Orders

ORDER BY VON ARNIM, PRUSSIAN MINISTER OF INTERIOR,
BERLIN, APRIL 16, 1844

THE FIRST and second issues of the *Deutsch-Französische Jahrbücher*, as well as the whole tone of that journal, published in Paris by Arnold Ruge and Carl Marx, contain numerous criminal passages, in effect constituting attempted high treason and *lèse majesté*. The publisher and the authors of the individual articles are to be held responsible.

I ... hereby respectfully enjoin the respective police authorities[1] to arrest, and seize the papers of, Dr. Arnold Ruge, Carl Marx, Heinrich Heine, and Ferdinand Coelestin Bernays as soon as they cross our side of the frontier, without attracting undue attention. . . .

ORDER BY VON ARNIM,
BERLIN, DECEMBER 21, 1844

... The descriptions of Dr. Ruge, Bernays and Marx are so far not yet available. In any case, these individuals, should they be apprehended, are to be transported and delivered, under secure guard, to the Royal Police Headquarters here. . . .

---

1. The order was sent to all Prussian provincial governors, who in turn informed their police chiefs.

DESCRIPTION OF MARX, WRITTEN IN FRENCH BY VON
ARNIM, BERLIN, FEBRUARY 13, 1845

DESCRIPTION OF DR. MARX (CHARLES)

BORN	Trier
AGE	27 years
HEIGHT	5 feet, 5 inches
HAIR	Black
EYEBROWS	
FOREHEAD	Straight
EYES	Brown
NOSE	Thick
MOUTH	Medium
BEARD	——
CHIN	Round
FACE	Oval
COMPLEXION	Clear
PROFESSION	Doctor of Philosophy

Judicial Investigation and Prosecution
of the *Neue Rheinische Zeitung**

Cologne, July 7

THE MANAGER of the *Neue Rheinische Zeitung*, Korff, and its editor in chief, Karl Marx, were examined yesterday in the Police Magistrate's office, both of them being accused of offenses against the gendarmes and Herr Chief Procurator Zweiffel in connection with the arrest of Anneke. The examination began at four o'clock. At the end of it, about six o'clock, the Police Magistrate and Procurator Hecker accompanied the defendants to the newspaper office, where, with the assistance of a police commissioner, a search took place for the manuscript and, hence, the author of the accused article. They found a note in an unknown handwriting, which, however, was not the copy of the guilty article. This note was put in the dossier of indictments against Marx and colleagues. From the latter expression it appears that they want to take legal proceedings against the editorial staff *en masse*, even though manager Korff alone underwrites the paper and, of course, assumes legal responsibility for it.

Cologne, July 22

This morning Karl Marx, editor in chief of the *Neue Rheinische Zeitung*, was again summoned before the Police Magistrate to be examined about the guilty article in connection with Herr Anneke's arrest. The manager, H. Korff, was not summoned this time.

---

* Published in the *Neue Rheinische Zeitung*, July 8, 23, August 5, 13, September 6, 1848.
1. See "Arrests," page 112.

Cologne, August 4

Our involvements with the public Ministry pursue their course. Last Monday Manager Korff was again summoned before the Police Magistrate, and yesterday two of our editors, Dronke and Engels, were cited as witnesses. Dronke has been absent for a time. Engels showed up, but was not examined under oath, as it is assumed that the note recently confiscated in our office was in his handwriting, and hence it is possible that he, too, will be involved in the indictment.

One sees that the public Ministry is not satisfied with the fact that the manager functions as the sole responsible director. They want to implicate the editor in chief, they want to discover the author of the article in question, they want to have the editors, each one of whom could be the author of that article, bear witness *against one another*, yea, if possible, *against themselves*.

Cologne, August 12

The interesting relations of our newspapers with the public Ministry still pursue their course. Yesterday one of our editors, Ernst Dronke, was again summoned as a witness before the Police Magistrate. There was no examination under oath, as on the table before him there lay a denunciation that on the evening after Anneke's arrest, Dronke visited the latter's wife and took notes about it. To the question of the witness as to whom the indictment was directed against, the answer was "Marx and colleagues," with the explanation that it was hoped to indict the responsible manager Korff as the eventual, but the editor in chief Karl Marx as the probable, author of the guilty article.

For the rest, Dronke stated that he did not consider himself obliged to make admissions, since as an editor he might possibly be implicated in the authorship of the article and could not bear witness against himself.

Cologne, September 5

Yesterday Frederick Engels, one of our editors, was again summoned before the Police Magistrate for the investigation of Marx and colleagues, but this time not as witness, but as codefendant. The preliminary examination is over, and if the public Ministry makes no further motions, then within a short time the Council Chamber will have to decide if Marx, Engels, and Korff are to appear before the Assizes for the offense against Herr Chief Procurator Zweiffel and the six gendarmes.

Marx Protests His Loss of Citizenship*

Herr Minister!

I TAKE the liberty of appealing to you against the local royal government in a matter of personal concern to me.

In 1843 I left my Rhenish-Prussian homeland to settle temporarily in Paris. In 1844 I learned that the royal governor in Coblenz had sent out to the frontier police an order for my arrest because of my writings. This news was also published in the censored press of Berlin. From that moment on I considered myself a political refugee. Later—in January, 1845—I was expelled from France at the direct instigation of the Prussian Government, and settled in Belgium. Since here too the Prussian Government tried to have the Belgian Ministry expel me, I finally found it necessary to be released from Prussian citizenship. I had to use that means in order to escape further such persecutions. The best proof that I did so only out of necessity is that I have not sought citizenship in any other country, although it was offered to me in France by members of the Provisional Government after the February Revolution.

After the March Revolution I returned to my homeland and in the month of April, in Cologne, I applied for citizenship, which was granted by the local city council without delay. Pursuant to the law of December 31, 1842, the matter went to the Royal Government for confirmation. I received from the local police director, Herr Geiger, the following communication [August 3, 1848]: "... the royal government ... does not act favorably on your application ... for the privileges of a Prussian subject ... You are, therefore, to be regarded as a foreigner as hitherto."

---

* Marx wrote this letter to Friedrich Christian Hubert von Kuehlwetter, Prussian Minister of Interior, August 22, 1848. It was printed in the *Neue Rheinische Zeitung* on September 5, 1848.

I consider the decision of the royal government illegal, for the following reasons. . . .

For all these reasons I request that you, Herr Minister, instruct the royal district government to confirm the [Cologne] city council's approval of my right to residence and confirm thereby my renaturalization as a Prussian.[1]

---

1. On September 12 Kuehlwetter rejected Marx's appeal.

Report of the Management of the *Neue Rheinische Zeitung* on the Suppression of the Paper*

To Our Honorable Subscribers!

In the state of siege that has begun in Cologne, where the pen must be subordinated to the sword, the

Neue Rheinische Zeitung

is forbidden to appear and cannot meet its obligations to the honorable subscribers for the time being.

In the meantime, we may hope that the exceptional condition will last only a few days, and that in the course of the month of October our paper, in *enlarged format* and supported by *vigorous new means*, will reach our subscribers the more punctually in that we will shortly be printing with a new steam printing press.

THE MANAGEMENT

---

* Published as an extra, a special edition of the *Neue Rheinische Zeitung*, September 28, 1848.

Invitation for Subscriptions to the
*Neue Rheinische Zeitung**

THE *Neue Rheinische Zeitung*, which during the state of siege in the city of Cologne has been suppressed in the most irresponsible way for several days by armed reaction, now that the siege has been lifted today, will *again represent the democratic interests of all the people with energy and thoughtfulness. This is the more necessary now that we have all seen with what impudent ruthlessness the armed reaction has recently confronted the rightly won freedoms of the people.* In making this report to the followers of democracy, we appeal for numerous subscriptions for the fourth quarter now beginning, since the democratic papers now, moreover, hated from many sides, *especially need the vigorous participation of their followers.*

Subscription price for Cologne, per quarter: 1 Taler, 15 Silver Groschen. Outside Cologne, in Prussia: 1 Taler, 24 silver Groschen, 6 Pfennig. Outside Prussia: the extra charge of foreign newspaper postage.

Advertisements: the four-column rows, 1 silver Groschen, 6 Pfennig per space.

H. KORFF
Manager of the *Neue Rheinische Zeitung*

---

* From a special edition of the *Neue Rheinische Zeitung*, October 3, 1848.

The Reappearance of the
*Neue Rheinische Zeitung**

WITH the support given in Cologne for the maintenance of the *Neue Rheinische Zeitung*, it has been possible to overcome the financial difficulties caused by the state of siege and to publish the paper again. The editorial committee remains the same. Ferdinand Freiligrath has recently joined it.

KARL MARX
Editor in Chief of the *Neue Rheinische Zeitung*

---

* Published in the *Neue Rheinische Zeitung*, October 12, 1848.

The Cases Against the
*Neue Rheinische Zeitung**

Cologne, December 5

A FEW days ago the editor in chief of the *Neue Rheinische Zeitung*, Karl Marx, was again summoned before the Police Magistrate. Four articles have moved the authorities to make the accusation of slander: (1) Schnapphahnski; (2) an article from Breslau on Lichnowski; (3) an article mentioning a "falsified" report by a certain "comical Stedtmann"; (4) a reprint of the "declaration of treason against the people," passed in Eiser Hall, against the Frankfurt Assembly majority, in connection with Schleswig-Holstein affairs.

Now the *Neue Rheinische Zeitung* longingly awaits further accusations of slander from Berlin, Petersburg, Vienna, Brussels, and Naples.

On December 20 the first proceedings of the *Neue Rheinische Zeitung* versus the *parquet* and gendarmes will take place.[1]

Up to now we have not heard that any Rhineland *parquet* has ever succeeded in applying any article of the Penal Code in support of the crude and palpable violations of the law by the Rhenish authorities.

"*Distinguendum est!*" "*Il faut distinguer*" ["One must distinguish!"] is the motto of the brave Rhenish *parquet*.

Cologne, December 20

The case against the *Neue Rheinische Zeitung* came up before the Assizes today. Herr Dr. Marx, editor in chief, Herr Korff, manager of the *Neue Rheinische Zeitung*, and Herr Engels were the defendants. The latter was absent. The complaint dealt with an insult to Chief Procurator Zweiffel and slander of the gendarmes. The case was postponed for lack of evidence.

---

* Published in the *Neue Rheinische Zeitung*, December 6, 21, 1848.
1. The trial was postponed to February 7, 1849.

Acquittal of the *Neue Rheinische Zeitung**

Cologne, February 8

As WE reported in a few issues of our paper yesterday, yesterday's session of the Assizes took up the indictment of editor in chief Marx, editor Engels, and the manager of the *Neue Rheinische Zeitung*, for the article that appeared in the issue of July 5, 1848. The article dealt with the arrest of Herr Anneke, and led to the indictment for slandering the gendarmes who carried out the arrest (Article 367 of the Penal Code), as well as for insulting Chief Procurator Zweiffel (Article 222 of the Penal Code). The defendants were *acquitted* by the jury after a brief deliberation.

This case, the first of the many press cases against the *Neue Rheinische Zeitung*, is therefore of importance, because this time the jurors in their decision interpreted and applied the above-mentioned Articles 222 and 367 (in connection with Article 37) differently from what used to be the case in previous Rhenish police courts. But Articles 222 and 367, apart from those dealing with direct incitement to civil war and rebellion, are the only ones that the ingenious Rhenish *parquets* have hitherto succeeded in applying to the press. Hence the jury's verdict of acquittal is a new guarantee of freedom of the press in Rhenish Prussia.

We will report extracts of the proceedings as soon as possible.

Today Marx stands once more before the jury, together with Schneider, the deputy from Cologne, and Schapper, because of the call for TAX REFUSAL, which they issued as members of the democratic district committee.

---

* Published in the *Neue Rheinische Zeitung*, February 9, 1849.

Two Lawsuits Against the
*Neue Rheinische Zeitung**

Cologne, February 8

YESTERDAY and today two more press cases were dealt with by our Assizes involving Marx, editor in chief of the *Neue Rheinische Zeitung*, Engels and Schapper, collaborators on the paper; and today the case against Marx, Schapper, and Schneider, indicted for having stirred up the people against the government in connection with tax avoidance. The size of the crowd was extraordinary. In both cases the defendants acted as their own counsel and sought to show the groundlessness of the indictment, succeeding so well that in both cases the jurors declared them *Not Guilty*. Again the government has had no luck at all with its political cases before jurors. Things may go worse for a couple of officers of the local garrison who participated in the popular movements of September last year, and when the matter went awry made it across the frontier into Belgium, but they have now returned for trial, which has already begun.[1]

---

* Published in the *Deutsche Londoner Zeitung*, February 16, 1849.
1. Lieutenants Adamski and Niethake, after fleeing to Belgium and being deported to France, returned to Germany and were tried before a military court on December 14. On May 29, 1849, Adamski was sentenced to a loss of his military rank and to nine months' imprisonment.

Press Comment on the End
of the *Neue Rheinische Zeitung*

Deutsche Zeitung, May 22, 1849

Cologne, May 19

THE FOLLOWING has happened to the individual editors of the *Neue Rheinische Zeitung:* Fr. Engels is being criminally prosecuted for his speech at Elberfeld; Marx, Dronke, and Weerth had to leave, because of their being non-Prussians. F. Wolff, because of avoidance of military service, and W. Wolff, because of offenses said to have been committed earlier in Old Prussia, are under investigation. Korff's release on bail was denied today by the Council Chamber.

Neue Kölnische Zeitung, May 22, 1849

Cologne

Yesterday morning the former editor in chief of the *Neue Rheinische Zeitung*, Herr Karl Marx, in the company of a few other editors, left Cologne and went to the Upper Rhine; there his work will be as successful as it has been here.

Neue Deutsche Zeitung, June 1, 1849

Cologne, May 29

Today the Correctional Police Court took cognizance of the slander of the Frankfurt National Assembly deputies, pending since last September. Summoned were K. Marx, E. Dronke, G. Weerth, H. Becker, H. Korff, and the printers Dietz and Bechthold. The first three did not appear. With the exception of Korff, all were acquitted; Korff (as former manager of the *Neue Rheinische Zeitung*) was sentenced to one month's imprisonment and one-seventh of costs for insult to the "comical Stedtmann." The court sharply rejected the indictment against Weerth for the Schnapphahnski-Lichnowski articles.

Biographical Index

Adam, 44, 101

Alexander II (1818–1881), Czar of Russia, 1855–1881, 175 & n

Anneke, Friedrich (c.1817–c.1872), Cologne communist, publisher of *Neue Kölnische Zeitung*, xxix, 112–114, 115, 185–186, 193

Annenkov, Pavel V. (1812–1887), liberal Russian writer and landowner, xxii

Arnim, Karl Eduard, Prussian ambassador to France, xxv

Arnim-Boytzenburg, Adolf Heinrich von (1803–1868), Prussian statesman, Minister of Interior, 1842–1845, xxiv, 117, 183

Auerswald, Rudolf von (1795–1866), Prussian liberal statesman, 119 & n

Bakunin, Michael Alexandrovich (1814–1876), Russian revolutionist and Anarchist leader, xxii, xxv

Balan, Hermann Ludwig von (1812–1874), German diplomat, ambassador in Brussels, 1865–1874, 175

Balzac, Honoré de (1799–1850), French novelist, xxiii

Bassermann, Friedrich Daniel (1811–1855), German Centrist member of the Frankfurt National Assembly, 128

Bauer, Bruno (1809–1882), German philosopher, Young Hegelian, ix, 160n, 162

Bauer, Edgar (1820–1886), German writer, Young Hegelian, brother of Bruno, 160n

Baumstark, Eduard (1807–1889), professor in Greifswald, liberal member of Prussian National Assembly, 121

Bavay, Charles-Victor (1801–1875), Belgian jurist, 117, 136

Bebel, August (1840–1913), leading founder of German Social Democratic Party, Reichstag deputy, 174

Bechthold, Arnold, typesetter of the *Neue Rheinische Zeitung*, 195

Becker, Hermann Heinrich (1820–1885), Cologne communist journalist, 195

Béranger, Pierre-Jean de (1780–1857), French poet, satirist, 41 & n

Berends, Julius (b.1817), Berlin printer, left-wing member of National Assembly, 114n

Berlier, Théophile, Comte de (1761–1844), French jurist, collaborator in the *Code civil*, 136

Bernard of Clairvaux (c.1091–1153), French theologian, 41–42

Bernays, Karl Ludwig (1815–1879), German refugee journalist in Paris, emigrated later to U.S., xxiv–v, 183

Bismarck, Otto von (1815–1898), Prussian Prime Minister, 1862–1871, German Imperial Chancellor, 1871–1890, 174–175

Böhme, Jakob (1575–1624), German shoemaker, mystical philosopher, 42

Bornstedt, Adalbert von (1808–1851), ex-Prussian officer, publisher of *Deutsche-Brüsseler-Zeitung* in Brussels, 166 & n

Brandenburg, Friedrich Wilhelm von (1792–1850), Prussian general, Prime Minister, 1848–1850, 130

Bürgers, Heinrich (1820–1878), Cologne communist journalist, 160n

Buhl, Ludwig Heinrich Franz (1814–c.1882), Young Hegelian journalist, 160n

Bülow-Cummerow, Ernst Gottfried Georg von (1775–1851), conservative Prussian journalist and politician, 61, 88

Cabet, Étienne (1788–1856), French utopian, author of *Voyage en Icarie* (1840), xviii

Caesar, Julius (102? B.C.–44 B.C.), Roman general and statesman, 3

Subject Index